The Long Journey Home

THE
LONG JOURNEY
HOME

by Carol Ferland

ALFRED A. KNOPF　　*New York*　　1980

THIS IS A BORZOI BOOK
PUBLISHED BY ALFRED A. KNOPF, INC.

Copyright © 1980 by Carol Ferland

All rights reserved under International and Pan-American Copyright
Conventions. Published in the United States by Alfred A. Knopf, Inc.,
New York, and simultaneously in Canada by Random House of
Canada Limited, Toronto. Distributed by Random House, Inc.,
New York.

Library of Congress Cataloging in Publication Data

Ferland, Carol.   The long journey home.

1. Psychotherapy patients—United States—Biography. I. Title.
RC464.F47A33   1980   616.89'09   79-3478
ISBN 0-394-50801-7

Manufactured in the United States of America

FIRST EDITION

In memory of
    Don
and to our children
Dave, Ki, Jim, Tom, and Peter
    and
to all of us sorrowful ones who must climb that mountain to
survive. We don't climb the mountain alone. I dedicate this to
the ones who hold our hands, those noble ones who help us
finally to laugh and be happy.
    and to
Judy, Ralph, Jane, Sylvia, Pat and Joe, Marge and Bud,
Michael, and Wayne

Preface

I have always been a compulsive reader. Throughout my therapy I read hundreds of books, many of them suggesting plausible-sounding shortcuts. I think I was looking for an easy way out. I wanted to do the whole thing in one weekend, or at most in one month. But it just doesn't work that way. It angered me after a while, because I couldn't seem to pull it off in a short time. As one consequence of this anger I wrote things down. This turned out to ease some of the tremendous tensions within and to be a positive way for me to communicate to my therapist things which seemed unspeakable. My illness involved a physical expression. I choked on my thoughts. I couldn't speak them, but I could write them down. At the time I never intended for these notes to be read. They were angry, extremely personal, extremely subjective, gut notes.

Before any significant and positive therapeutic change can occur, dramatic and painful upheaval must, in some cases, take place. For four years I worked with a doctor to excise, almost in the sense of cutting out a malignant growth, my crippling mental problems. Deep down I knew I needed to do so in order to survive. At times my journal entries were, quite simply, my lifeline. Later, as the writing gained in momentum and scope, its therapeutic value and my self-esteem increased tremendously. My husband and my therapist realised before I did that this wealth of material—written in times of deep thought, of despair, and sometimes of elation—might be the basis for a book. I discovered, however, that it was something that I wanted to do. When my husband died suddenly in 1976, I had to put the work down. I groped around in exile, until, after six months, I could begin to write again.

This was not an easy period. Fears, doubts, depression, sometimes relapses—all had to be faced. But the raw, searing pain was gone; the basic treatment had been completed. The sense of what had been accomplished could be recaptured, and this time more easily. Every victory encouraged the next. I look at my writing. I hold it to me. Knowing myself has brought me untold freedom—freedom that makes me realise I am one of the privileged people who has had the opportunity to find those elusive truths necessary for survival and for happiness. The treatment has worked.

I have come out of a forbidden land.

Carol Ferland
1979

Author's Note

In the following narrative, all but seven names have been changed. The exceptions are my own name and the names of my husband and my five children. Dates and locations have also been altered in order to avoid causing anyone hurt or embarrassment.

Part One

THE OFFICE

Wednesday, February 26, 1969

Sweet Jesus help me, I'm dying. What the hell is happening to me? I can't breathe. I can't breathe right. Oh my God, the kids are going to see me die and I don't even know what I'm dying of. Race upstairs now, into the bathroom. I see myself in the mirror. I pull out my tongue with my fingers and see if I can see the growth. My God, it must be there. It's shutting off my air. It's making me breathe so fast now, I'm getting dizzy. Oh Christ, why couldn't Nick see it? He had me all checked over. He even sent me to Springfield to the allergy man. How the hell can it be an allergy? It's a growth and it's choking me to death. Why can't I see it? Why couldn't they believe me? My heart's beating too fast and I'm too dizzy. My poor little babies. They're going to see me die. Race downstairs. How could it come on like this? All of a sudden? I did so many things today. I got the ceiling all painted—I'm ready to wallpaper. How can I die when I have to wallpaper? Get myself a drink—gin, a double martini. Don will look at me funny like he does—but it won't matter much. I'll be dead. Maybe I can hold on until he comes home—oh, Jesus, Jesus help me. The kids are watching *Gilligan's Island*—do people really die during *Gilligan's Island*? How awful. Can't breathe, can't breathe—skin feels funny—have to get out of the house so kids don't see me. Run to the front door—Don. Don's home.

"Please help me, Don, quick—oh please, please, get me to the hospital. Can't breathe. The growth is choking me. Please hurry."

I'm in the car—holding on to the dash. Oh God, please hurry, Don. He's on the phone. He's getting George to look after the kids. He's called Herbie to cancel the tennis game in Springfield. Doesn't he know it'll be too late if he does all that? I put my head back with my chin jutting forward. It seems I can get a little more air that way. Why isn't he hurrying more? Oh my God, Don is somehow mad at me for dying like this. He isn't saying much. Is it my fault? Somehow it is. I'm to blame. Sorry—so sorry.

Race into the emergency room—where's Dr. Stebbins? Where's Nick? I yell at the nurse that I'm choking to death—she stares at me. Don is talking to her. She says for me to calm down. Fat chance, lady, fat chance. I'm dying. Dr. Stebbins is on his way. Oh Nick, please get here on time. She says lie down on the table. My God, I can't lie down, I choke all the more—get your hands off me—get a doctor. No one is moving, no one is doing anything. They are looking at me—Christ, they are looking at me funny. I leap toward the door and I'm out in the corridor. I'm going to find a doctor. They won't and it'll be too late—don't they understand? I see this guy here by the corner—he's got a suit on—God, maybe he's a doctor.

"Who are you? Can you save my life? Are you a doctor?"

I put my hands on his shoulders and I shout at him.

"Are you a doctor?"

He looks at me strange and says real quiet, "I'm the Reverend Floyd Perkins."

Oh my God, a reverend.

"A reverend, Reverend?"

I push him away. I need a doctor, not a reverend. Then people come up to me and take me back into the room.

Nick comes in then. Oh, thank God. Now I can die with a doctor here. Nick gives me a shot—he says if it's an allergy, then I'll feel better. He still thinks it's an allergy.

"What about my throat, Nick? I can't breathe right."

Nick tells me to calm down now. They take my blood pressure. I keep my head way back, with my chin up, so I can breathe better. After a while Nick says we can go to another room. The nurses are relieved to have me go. I'm still breathing pretty hard but more calmed down. I'm so scared. Oh wow, I'm so scared. I had such a close call and I don't even know the disease. Nick will fix me up though. I know that. He's really nice. We walk down the corridor and things seem pretty strange. I have to keep my head tilted back like that and I'm slightly dizzy. Also my heart's pounding way too fast.

Nick is talking to me very calmly, so I try to listen to what he's saying. He says he's going to keep me in the hospital overnight but that he really isn't sure what the trouble is. He tells Don to go along home, that he'll call him later. So Don leaves and Nick asks me to sit down. But I can't sit down.

"Have a seat, Carol."

"Can't. I don't know why."

So I start walking around the room very fast. Nick starts walking around the room with me. He wants to talk. We keep going around and around. He gives up. He says I can keep doing that, that it's making him tired. He flops down in a chair and sprawls his legs over the other chair and lights a cigarette. He gives me one. Things will be all right I think, now that Nick's here. It's freezing outside. Nick has on a red sweater. I wish I had my sweater. I keep walking fast. Nick wants to know if Don and I are having problems. What? What the hell does he want to know that for? But if I don't talk to him he'll send me home to die in front of my kids.

"Yes, Nick, Don and I are having problems. Everybody has problems. He doesn't love me anymore. No, I don't know why. I don't think anybody loves me. Maybe it's because I'm fat—think so, Nick? Don't know anything, Nick, anything—what does this have to do with my throat? my growth?"

No answer. No answer. Nick takes me back now, through the corridor to a room. They get a history. But I keep walking. I can't sit down. I'm not so afraid now. They are going to take care of me and fix this growth in my throat. It's so funny. I always thought when people died they got weak and had no strength and felt sick and died. And here I am, with all this energy. I almost feel like breaking into a run but the room is too small. This makes it hard to talk to me because I am moving around so fast. I probably have some choking disease that makes people race around. Oh hell. So I keep on like that throughout the night. Head tilted back, walking, walking, walking. Nick will see me in the morning and we'll get this cleared up. He'll give me some kind of pill and I'll be all better.

Thursday, February 27, 1969

Choking again, in the hospital. Choking all the time. Oh Nick, why don't you help me? Nick always asking about our problems. Oh, why waste time, give me some pills so I can stop choking and walking. The whole next day and night. I don't understand. Don has brought me some clothes. I am ashamed. I don't want to see him. He hates me for doing this. Whatever this is I am doing. Confused all the time. Too scared to make any decisions about going home. Just keep walking. Nick says he's talked to another doctor about me. A doctor I don't know. Oh good—good, Nick. Now maybe he'll know what's the matter with me. It's nighttime. I'm still walking. Nick says he's a nice man, that he lives in Chester. I don't care, Nick, I don't care, just get me fixed up, okay?

"He's a psychiatrist."

"What? What?"

"He's a psychiatrist."

"A psychiatrist? What for? What in God's name for? I'm dying. I'm choking—I want a doctor."

"He is a doctor, Carol. He's very nice. I don't think I can help you anymore."

"Oh Nick, what are you talking about? I've told you our troubles. I can't possibly tell them again—to an outsider. My God—what for?"

"He'll be able to help you more than I can. I can't find anything physically wrong with you."

"What do you mean, nothing physical? It's all physical. This whole thing is physical. It's my body not behaving, Nick, my body. I don't need a psychiatrist."

"Then maybe you're ready to go home?"

"Go home! I'll die there. Die. I can't go home."

Why is Nick doing this to me? He knows I'm scared of going home. And if I don't see this psychiatrist, then I have to go home to die. What a bad decision.

"I don't understand, Nick. I don't know anything. I guess if that's what I have to do. . . . Oh my God, I can't stop walking."

"This doctor will prescribe something that will help you to slow down. Also, something to help you sleep."

"Why can't you do it? You could."

"No, I can't. That's his field."

"Shit."

"Will you see him?"

"Yes—but shit."

"That sounds more like you again, Carol."

Afraid, afraid of something and I don't know what. Thinking about law school. Don and I were in Oxford and he was working all the time. He came home from classes. It was a Friday night. He only had two hours for us. Me and the kids. Then he had to work at the liquor store. I had everything all organized for a nice supper. We had beef birds. But I was feeling uptight. I had that scared feeling that always came back. So I said to Don maybe it was because Milton Ludwin, down cellar, was picked up by the police. A rapist-strangler was on the loose. So Don gets some big nails out of his toolbox and nails the windows. Crash. Bang, bang. Every single window, he nailed shut. Don always knew when I was getting this feeling. We never knew what to do. I told him I'd watch *Wagon Train* or something on TV when he was gone. That I'd be all right. Before he left, a lady came to the door to see about the apartment upstairs. I could get five dollars from the land-lord if I rented it again. But it was a God-awful mess up there. I dreaded showing it. It crumpled me somehow. I couldn't talk to this lady. I ran into the bedroom. It was too late. No backing out. The lady had on white socks. Awful white socks with one of those awful quilted coats. And her hair was pulled back in an awful pony tail. And she was fat. And after Don showed her the rooms she said, "Them don't look too good." That's when I left. She pushed me over into that feeling. I picked up the flashlight next to the bed and started hitting myself. Over and over. Harder and harder. Had to keep doing that until I could cry. When Don came in I stopped. Had to stop until he left. He tried to hold me but I was hard inside. After he left I started again. But it didn't work. I didn't feel anything. I couldn't make myself cry. So I got under the bed. I took some blankets and covered myself up. I went close to the wall and hid there, tight like that—a long time. Don found me when he got home from work. He got me out by moving the whole bed over. We just didn't know what to do. He held me. We didn't talk about it, never mentioned it. In the middle times it was forgotten—and it didn't come very often.

Don and I always lived for the middle times and we could almost always forget. And now here in the hospital I have the fear again. That feeling creeping up. Psychiatrist. One part of my life —never talk about, never think of—or I would be lost forever. My pacing got faster and faster—before I even met the man. Here in the hospital, I have the fear again. An executioner coming, to hack me to pieces.

Friday, February 28, 1969

Okay, tiles down to the end. Take one step for two tiles. Smile nice at everybody—anything to get rid of the choking. For God's sake, try to act normal, whatever that is. I can't believe I'm acting like this. I have no control over myself. My stupid body won't be still. I was in the room pacing around when the psychiatrist came. I was caught unprepared. "Hi, I'm Dr. Ashley," and he shook my hand. So I'm not scared at all because he took me by surprise. Okay, Carol, so you were afraid of nothing, right? He looks like a nice man and he says he'll get some pills to quiet everything down. Good, oh good. No sweat. Looks nice—acts nice. Okay. Things will be okay. The pills will take away the choking and I can go home and wallpaper.

"How old are you?"

"Thirty-two."

"Do you have children?"

"Yes, five."

All things like that. This is a snap. He's really nice, he looks nice. Never, never any reason at all to ever think about—or ever talk about—the other.

Pills, pills. That's the answer. Got Nick, got new doctor. Everything's okay.

Saturday, March 1, 1969

I try to explain to the new doctor about my physical problem of choking. He listens. He sits in the chair by my bed and he writes down things that I say. It's a physical problem, you see. I'm going to choke to death. He doesn't understand because I have to tell him over and over. It's physical. He says maybe this choking is caused by my being uptight. Okay, new doctor. I don't believe you, not at all. But I will talk to you, all right? I will play by the rules.

"No, things aren't perfect. Don and I are having problems. I drink too much. I race around too much. I'm too fat. Love Don, yes. We love each other. We've been under a lot of pressure, of course. A new law practice with all our kids. No, never got along with my mother. I mean who really does these days, you know? Why? Oh, don't know, just a personality difference, that's all. No problem."

Oh, God, can't stop my arms from moving, and that choking feeling again—oh, new doctor, can't you please just help me with that?

"Maybe if you talk about things, the choking feeling will go away. What do you think?"

"Maybe, okay." But I don't believe him. How could that make the choking go away? What about me dying in the meantime? What about that?

"Were you happy as a kid?"

"Yes, of course, my goodness. Very happy, had lots of fun all the time, never cried. Christmas and all that. And of course I always had my father."

"How about your father now? Could you tell me about him?"

"Oh, well, we got along. See, he's nice, I mean he was nice, he's dead. But no problem. Good nice handsome man."

Can't talk now because my eye is funny. I mean my right eye keeps blinking. God, my body is acting strange. So new doctor comes over to the bed. He is coming to look at my eye and he brings his hands toward my face and I gasp and pull back on the bed away from him. Don't want him near me. Don't want him near me. Don't want to talk to him. Don't like him anymore. Am confused now—body acting up. Eye twitching, hands going all over. Don't like him anymore.

Says he'll come back tomorrow. Have to get hold of Don and tell Don. He'll help me. Don will save me somehow from this fear.

"Dr. Ashley is scaring me somehow, Don, and he made my eye twitch funny. Oh, my dear Don. I'm really sorry about me. But I know that if I keep talking to this man I'll end up hating my father. Please can't you get me out of here? Oh God, I'm still choking."

"You have to talk to him, Carol, he won't hurt you. He's very understanding. We can't go on like we have been. Just stay put for a while. The kids are fine and I'm okay. Just get better, okay?"

Don goes out the door and writes on a piece of paper what Carol has said to him. He tells the nurse to give it to Dr. Ashley. Carol is there by the door, open just a crack. She thinks maybe she is betrayed. What has he written down? What do they say about me? Do they think I'm crazy?

Don't want to see Don now—or tell him these things anymore. He's on their side. The doctors' side. Hate them. Hate them all. Those men.

I'll always hate men. Won't tell them anything. Any man. Ever.

Sunday, March 2, 1969

Have to hold on, get hold of myself, or I'll be lost. Dr. Ashley asks questions that bother me. Past was good, good. Don't want him sitting there waiting for me to talk. He's quiet, waiting. Reading my mind. He feels evil to me. Somehow got to think this out. Mixing me up. He's nice. I like him. And I like his pills—they help me. So really I need him. I need him more now than Nick. But it's awful because he scares me.

"Tell me more about your father?"

"Sure, well, he was the kind of nice person everybody loved. He was tall and handsome and all my girlfriends loved him too. One time it was a fall day and we were all playing out in the back yard. The leaves were blowing and we were maybe six years old. My Dad comes to the back steps and says that the maple tree, not the big one, but the smaller one there, is a candy tree. None of us believe him but he keeps on telling us that if we shake it real hard candy will come out. We talk to him for about ten minutes about this. Finally, we go over and shake and shake. And this candy comes falling out of the tree—it was hard candy wrapped in cellophane. It was so neat. After that, we could always see some neighborhood kid stroll by the tree and give it a shake. I was his favorite—we had an understanding—like we knew that each was special. . . . I don't want to talk anymore—don't want to—so goodbye—go."

"Is there any reason you feel uncomfortable about talking further?"

"No—just can't anymore. I'm sorry. I keep choking so it's hard to think."

Dr. Ashley made me feel funny. I was confused.

Don brought me some knitting. When I could stop pacing, I knit. Fast. Knit, knit, knit, knit. That was good.

Monday, March 3, 1969

Go to the main desk and ask a nurse if I can have a razor to shave my legs. Get my soap, towel, powder and head for the shower. Stopped in the hall by another nurse. Two nurses together. They ask me for the razor I'd just been given. I'm dumbfounded, and give it to them. They mumble something. I go back to the room. What was that all about? What the hell was that? Oh, the psychiatrist, you fool. You're talking to a psychiatrist, therefore you're probably going to slash your wrists. Oh shit. So that's how it is. Must be very careful how I act from now on. They're watching me. Will they take away the knitting needles too?

Well, I'll take a bath though, show them I'm 100 percent okay, all right, fine. I'll smile and laugh and joke and worm my loving self into their hearts. But I'm so scared. This choking has an awful hold on me. I don't want to die. What can I do? I have to fool them, outwit them. I go to the bathroom and I run the water. I smile. My heart is pounding, I am choking and I am shaking like a leaf. See, I am going to die in the tub and all they'll find will be my fat, naked body—awful to be drowned. But I have to do this so they'll know I'm a normal, mentally healthy lady.

I suffer. I have fooled them.

Tuesday, March 4, 1969

Don and Nick and Dr. Ashley—I can hear them in the hall, whispering about me. Oh God, why don't they like me? This place is making me feel funny. Polly and George Sloan came to see me and I gripped the side of the couch, containing myself, pretending I was normal. I was afraid I might start screaming—that feeling coming more and more over me. Oh God, I really have cracked up, haven't I? I've lost all power. Have to get some power back. I have a plan. Dr. Ashley comes in every day at the same time, right? He always sits in the big chair there and I always jump in bed and cover up. So now tonight before he comes, I'll put the chair here, nearer the knitting basket. I'll stick out the loose needles like this and time him. If he does it inside of three minutes after sitting down, then I've won. Three minutes is cutting it pretty close. But that makes it more fair. If it's after three minutes, that means I've lost. If he does it at all, but not until after three minutes, I have won, but only conditionally. If he doesn't do it at all, then I've lost.

It's time now and I'm already in bed and covered up. I want him to come. I'm looking forward to talking to him. I'm almost excited.

"Hi, Dr. Ashley. How are you? Today was a little upsetting. They wouldn't [he sits down—okay now, TIME, TIME] let me shave my legs. And I was upset and choking a lot. And I felt funny when I had visitors, like I would fall apart."

"Maybe if you did let go more, it would be better, Carol. You're all clenched up and your muscles get . . ."

TIME—he did it, he did it! I won. It was two minutes and forty-five seconds. He did it before three minutes. Oh, I feel good —he picked up the knitting needle. So I won. I have power over him. I willed him to do it. He's playing with it now—neat. I'm going to do this every day.

". . . tense. Try not to clench all up that way and the anxiety will decrease. What do you think about going home?"

"NO—can't go home. No, never. I'll die there. I'll choke to death."

He doesn't understand this choking at all. How can he scare me like that—sending me home. Have to think a long time about this.

Thursday, March 6, 1969

Wake up early, go out and talk to the night nurses. They give me coffee. Start my pacing. The snow is blowing outside, nearly a blizzard. The safe feeling about the hospital is disappearing because three days in a row now Dr. Ashley has mentioned going home. Tense feelings come back. If I do sit down, then my hands go up, down; up, down. I'm in the room and it's a little after lunch. That's when it hits me the hardest. I am fighting off the choking all morning and then it hits. Cannot breathe.

"Help me, help me, help me, please someone help me!"

I can't stop myself. And I get louder and louder and I keep on. Two nurses come in and they tell me please don't make so much noise. But you see, I don't really mean to, I don't want to—but I can't stop myself. And I'm too scared to be embarrassed. I'm screaming, and these screams seem to come from someone else. Someone is now holding my back and my hands, but it doesn't work. I keep on screaming. I am dying. People run around and get mad at me, but I still keep on. It seems like a long time. Then a nurse comes in. She looks different to me. She doesn't look mad at me or scared of me. She looks nice, she comes right up to me and puts her arms around me and says I am okay, that it is okay for me to do this. It doesn't matter. She doesn't blame me. As soon as she does this my screaming stops. Right then. And the screams turn to sobs. Me, I am crying. I cry and cry. I am very amazed at this. I never cry.

This nurse is Mrs. Lunen. She said if she ever had problems, she certainly would talk to Dr. Ashley, that I'm smart to talk to him. She makes me feel smart and okay too. A regular person. I'm not jumpy after that for a while. I sleep a long time.

Dr. Ashley comes in when I wake up and we talk about me crying. I am very very ashamed by then. I don't want to come out from under the covers. I hate myself. He says my crying was a very good thing. He says the other nurses might not understand, but that Mrs. Lunen does.

"You must try to cry more often. It's all right to cry."

"But I never cry. I can't. I'm surprised it happened and I don't understand."

"Do you see what the crying did for you? You are nowhere near as tense. There's nothing wrong with crying."

"I was brought up not to cry, so I can't now and I think it's wrong—I mean I feel inside it's wrong, so I can't."

"You were brought up that it was wrong?"

"Oh, I don't know, I don't know. We never showed emotions too much and crying made me feel . . . I just never dared."

"Never showed emotions?"

"Well, when I was about eleven or so our dog Dandy was killed by a car and my mother told me. It was an awful pain—he was my dog and my real friend. But nobody cried or swore or showed anything, any kind of sadness. They all just went along. I couldn't stand it. I ran upstairs and started hitting, I didn't know what to do with myself. Nobody helped me, nobody ever helped me. I almost cried then. But I felt guilty, ashamed, as if somehow it was my fault. I can't say what I mean the right way—never mind. Forget all this. I don't know. Crying is wrong for me. I don't dare. A feeling I have. That something will happen."

"Is it that if maybe you start, you'll never be able to stop?"

"Yes. Something like that. So you see how I can't do it?"

"You really can though, Carol, nothing bad will happen if you cry. Why do you feel you would never stop crying?"

"I have no idea. Never mind. It doesn't matter. I'll be all right."

"Have you given any more thought to going home?"

"No, no—not yet because my choking will kill me. Maybe that's why I cried. You think so?"

"No."

"I do. I do. . . ."

Now Dr. Ashley frightens me again. This is a close call. He gets me talking like that and I forget who he is and I slip up and tell him things no one must know. Things I don't even know. This is a scary thing. Scary things make me choke. Maybe it isn't a growth. I wonder.

Saturday, March 8, 1969

"Evelyn, oh I'm glad to see you. You can't believe the mess I'm into here. I've flipped, Evelyn. Flipped."

"You haven't flipped, Carol. You're just tensed up. Have them give you some Librium."

"They've given me lots of shots and pills. Don't know what they are."

"You mean they never told you what pills you are on?"

"Well, as a matter of fact I never asked."

"Carol, are you seeing a psychiatrist?"

"Yes—Dr. William Covelle Ashley."

"Oh, I've heard of him. . . ."

"He's really nice. Sort of."

"What's it like? Does he ask all sexual things?"

"Well, no, I haven't talked about anything sexual. I mean, I shouldn't?"

"Hell, be careful. Don't tell him anything. Do you say anything that comes to mind?"

"No, not me. I mean. No way. Why?"

"Well, that means he's not a psychoanalyst. Did you check his credentials?"

"Of course he's a psychoanalyst. I mean, I think he is."

"If I were you, I'd check on him. And remember. Don't tell him anything I wouldn't. Heh, heh. If you know what I mean. If he's a psychoanalyst you know you have to lie on a couch. If you get the picture? Does he have a couch in his office? Will you go see him when you get out of here? If he's only a psychotherapist, chances are he's not a doctor and you won't have to tell everything."

"Gee, I just don't know. A couch? No way."

"Dr. William Covelle Ashley . . . hmm. What do you call him? Let's think of a good one. Billy? Billy is a dilly who does it with a dip stick in his old fur hat. Ha!"

"I call him Cove. He really is rather nice, you know. I like talking to him sometimes."

"Be very careful, Carol, with this kind of thing. Don't want to lose you."

"What do you mean? Lose me where?"

"In the wrong hands, psychology can be very, very dangerous. But don't worry. They'll never change the ole Carol. You and I are alike. They'll never change us. . . .

"We don't know this guy. Don't worry, I'll check it out. Just tell me everything. Hope you get Valium—they're great. I could use a few antidepressants at the moment, myself."

"I don't take antidepressants. I'm not depressed."

"Of course you are. If you're not, then you're crazy."

"Oh Evelyn, now we're really silly. It feels good to laugh."

"How long do you have to stay in here? They can't keep you, you know."

"Well, to tell the truth Dr. Ashley, I mean Cove . . ."

"Cove-babe."

"Cove-babe wants me to go home as soon as I can. But I'm sort of scared, you know. With the choking feeling and all."

"He'll pump you full of pills and you can go on your merry way. We're incorrigible neurotics. Believe me, Carol, we're two old dogs that will never change."

"You don't think so—no chance?"

"No chance. Get those pills and you can go home."

"Well, maybe."

Good ole Evelyn. Such a good friend. I have to really think this out though. I really do have this nice feeling for Dr. Ashley—Cove. She doesn't know about that. I really like talking to him even though I get nervous. Only known him for a short time and if I leave the hospital maybe I won't see him anymore. I'm confused. He makes me scared. Maybe it's just because he's a man. No. It's something else. But, I really want to get better. I don't want to be full of pills. I don't even know what a psychoanalyst is, or does. I think he's a doctor. Nick said he was. I know I couldn't lie on a couch. Not in front of a man. So maybe he's just a psychotherapist. If he is, then that makes him second rate. That's what Evelyn says. If that's true, then maybe I could see Cove outside and I could sit up. Also if he's second rate, that would be all right because I wouldn't have to tell him everything. Only what I wanted. Then I could keep things smooth and easy and nice, no hassles. Oh God, I hope he's the second-rate kind of psychotherapist. I have to watch my step. Even now I sense a fear of him, though he looks and acts kind. Have to be very careful from now on. He has not put me down. In fact he has made me feel nice, in a way. But he said I should cry more. That made me very nervous—yes, I have a great fear of him. But I need him and I want him to talk to me. Somehow he is some kind of answer for me. I defended him, sort of, in front of Evelyn. She doesn't know how nice he is. But he is a man. We both know what that means. (I wonder what that does mean.) Evelyn, what does that really mean?

Thursday, March 13, 1969

Cove is coming in to talk to me in about an hour. Go to the bathroom. Get uneasy before he comes, so I have to do all these things. Put the water, Kleenex, cards, ashtray, cigarettes, paper and gum over here on the bed. Get a face cloth all soapy and wash the bedside table. Move all the stuff off the tray over the bed and do the same thing. Let's place maybe just one book on the tray. Maybe Ardrey's book. Then just the ashtray and cigarettes there. Put all the knitting away and move the chair near where the needles are sticking up. There—that section is ready. Put all odds and ends inside drawers, pick up Kleenex's, etc., stick waste basket under bed. All neat now. On to the bed. Remake it smooth but go into bottom drawer and get the heaviest blanket. Go to the bathroom again. Neatly tuck in the blanket so when he comes I'll be all covered up. Don't want him to see any part of me, even leg or foot. Fix pillows so I can sit up. Can't ever lie down in front of him. Go back in the bathroom and start grooming. Oh, I look so awful; well, no matter, do the best I can. Another half-hour left. That damn supper tray always louses things up. Can't possibly eat when he's here, so I either eat fast as it comes in or I push it back out and don't eat at all. Don't know why I can't eat with him around. Oh well, get toothbrush ready. Have to do this now before he comes. Bathroom again. Damn. It feels like at college before a big exam. How come I have to do these things? He seems so understanding. He seems so nice. He doesn't seem mean or aggressive but calm and serious. But he scares me so much. Damn. And then, he really doesn't know what kind of a shithead I am. He doesn't know and he'll never find out.

Sunday, March 16, 1969

They are out in the hall. The three of them. Don and Nick and Cove—talking about me. They all want me to go home from this safe hospital. I don't want to. Why are they so insistent? They sent the kids up to see me yesterday. How beautiful they look. I feel awful and guilty leaving them. But I still want to stay. Why can't they leave me alone?

Don comes in and holds my hand.

"We miss you so much, honey. We want you home. I want you home. We'll work things out. Please try."

He has a dejected look about him, so Carol feels extra guilty about being sick like this.

"I don't think I can handle things, Don, I choke so often. What will happen to me?"

"Well, we've been talking and it's really up to you, honey. What happens."

"What do you mean? You mean about Dr. Ashley? Oh honey, it scares me. Scares me so I don't know what to do."

"You have two choices really. You could try to fight this anxiety with drugs. Or you could continue with psychotherapy."

"Psychotherapy? This talking? Do you think I could still talk to Dr. Ashley when I'm home?"

"It would be your decision, please think about it. Oh darling, please come home as soon as possible. I'll rub your hair and feet and we'll try so hard, together."

Don sits at the foot of the bed, and they both have a light in their eyes. He rubs her feet and her tenseness decreases. Foot rubbing does that to her. It is a signal that they will work together no matter what her decision.

When he leaves she thinks about psychotherapy and going home. I do feel a great need to keep talking to Dr. Ashley. I wonder if I dare do that. Maybe it won't be too much—Evelyn says if it's only psychotherapy, then I can sit in a chair. It might not be so bad. I can tell him what I want to, and together we can figure out what the problem is. I don't have to get involved. Not like with the others. And then, of course, that feeling has come back far too often. That feeling that Don and I can't deal with. I certainly won't tell Cove about it. But maybe I can figure it out, if we talk. That feeling—just the day before I went to the hospital—I forgot it was that recent.

It started with that argument I had with Don about my drinking. He just didn't understand at all. How could he? I'm taking these amphetamines all the time. I hide them from him. How could he possibly know the only way to get anything done was to drink? No other way to come down from that awful feeling they give me. Oh God, the amphetamines. How can I stay off them? Never mind. I'll deal with that later. So Don doesn't understand. I'm so unhappy and he's picking on me. I'm trying. Don, I'm trying, so leave me alone. But he doesn't. Don't drink, don't drink. And that feeling starts to come over me. It's slushy rain and snow—the usual for New Hampshire in March. I grab my parka and run out the door. I walk fast over to town. I hesitate at the church. I am tempted to see if Father Ryan is there. Oh shit, what could he do? Anyway I don't know what's wrong. I head up past Gardener & Evans and over to Lynn Avenue. Heart pumping despair all around with that terrible adrenaline. Walk down to Haverhill Motors, turn on that road and walk fast. In the country now by the brook. She notices, then, that she only has on her sneakers and her feet are freezing and it's raining, and snowing very hard. If only I could lose myself, get away, never come back. She goes right to the brook and thinks about the brook. What would happen if she went into it? She'd freeze and drown—the water was very swift and because of the thaw, the ice was soft. This thought scared her. The sight of the cold water made her shiver. She was always so afraid of icy water like that—she ran to the other side of the road. Her eyes never left the ground. Afraid to look at the brook. Feet were numb but it wasn't enough, not nearly enough. She was immobilized, not knowing what to do about the feeling, so she went to a fence post and picked up a tree limb. It's hard to make herself do this at first because she knows it will hurt. After the first time it isn't so hard because her leg has turned numb. She hits herself with the limb over and over again. But the feeling is still there. Won't go away easily this time. She runs to the next fence post and figures if she is real, real good she could really hurt her hand, the bone sticking out of her wrist. Misses the bone the first time. Just bruises. She thinks about the barbed wire but dismisses that. Must not have any cuts. Then people would know. Just bruises, where no one can see. Unless it's a good broken bone. Only then it could be explained. Four or five more times so it hurts plenty. Have to punish myself, have to hurt myself. I'm a bad person. She falls at the bottom of the fence post and sobs. It's done now, she's paid a little bit. Now she can go home.

I'm so scared thinking of this. Must never tell Dr. Ashley about these feelings. Must never tell him about the amphetamines either. Never tell anyone.

Wednesday, March 19, 1969

Got everything ready for when Cove comes in at five-thirty. Knitting needles are in place, I'm covered up in bed and the desks are washed and cleaned. I'll tell him my decision to go home and to continue with psychotherapy. I'm not choking so much, so maybe I can handle things. He comes in and doesn't sit down for a while. He stands by the end of the bed. He has some papers in his hand. He talks about me going home.

"I know that you've been troubled and in a great deal of distress. I think that you can handle your problems if you have some help. However, this is not an easy thing and there would be a tremendous amount of hard work involved. I want you to understand that there are no real guarantees. Do you understand what I'm saying?"

"Yes, I think so," and she thinks, no, not really—hard work? Where? It sounds scary. Hard work? From me? Won't see me in his office if I don't make some sort of commitment. Maybe he doesn't mean that. I have to go on seeing him. I make a decision.

"Yes, I want to keep talking to you. I'm sure, because I can't seem to cope too well."

Cove smiles.

"Fine, fine. I hope we can work things out. Now, I have signed your discharge and I would like you to take these pills as prescribed. They're Thorazine, which will ease your tension. No drinking with the pills."

"Okay."

"I have made an appointment for Friday night at seven, March twenty-first. Is that convenient?"

"Sure."

"My office is in my home in Chester."

"Don can take me."

"You may go home when Don comes in. I'm glad you're excited. Take care now."

"Thanks, Dr. Ashley."

Oh Jesus, oh God help me. I'm on my own and feel all over again I'll choke. Jesus help me, I don't hurt myself or my family. I am now in the hands of this doctor who lives in Chester. Pray to God that nobody ever really finds out how bad I am and that I get better fast. Dear God.

Thursday, March 20, 1969

So glad to be home. Don and kids so glad to see me. So far, so good. Somehow got to get back to status quo. Afraid of what people are thinking. They know I've cracked up. How will I handle this? Afraid of appointment tomorrow night with Dr. Ashley. Don't have much confidence. Feel like I've been hit by a train.

Think I'll go for a walk so I don't wake anyone up. Get my parka and boots, hat and mittens, and start up toward the hospital. Feels good to walk fast. Turn right at Lincoln Field and enjoy the snow. I go down South Main Street. It's so quiet. Only the milk trucks with their lights on. Kind of miss the night nurses and our coffee chats. Keep walking past Hank's Novelty and stop at the bridge when a nagging feeling hits me. It hits my arms and legs. They start to tingle. Suddenly I'm tired like I've never been tired, and I'm choking again. What do I do now? Go home? What do I do at home? The panic is coming after me, attacking me. I'm stationary, stuck on the bridge. I grip the sides so I won't fall down. Don't, please, let this happen to me—please don't. Someone help me. I'm stuck. No one is here. Oh God, please. Now Carol, you are on your own. Don't think, don't think of anything. Just remember you can call Dr. Ashley if you have to. You won't die. So put one foot ahead of the other, like so, and head for home. Keep going, keep going. That's it. Now don't think. You can do it. That fear comes out of nowhere, striking down bad people, the guilty.

I get past Carpenter's house; the adrenaline pumping but the energy gone. The energy is replaced with dead heaviness. Something is moving around in front of our house. It is Ki, at the front steps with our dog Hennessey. She is sorting papers for her Springfield *Tribune* delivery. I momentarily forget my fear; I push it away so I can talk. Ki is having trouble with Henny about pulling the sleigh with the papers in it. Once, coming down a slight hill, Henny's harness broke and the sleigh hit her back legs. Now Hennessey's afraid to pull it at all. That sissy of a St. Bernard. Such a baby. We laugh at her.

I forgot for a little.

"Want some breakfast, hon?"

"Yes, sure would. Glad to have you home, Mom."

I gather myself together. I have escaped for now. But I have learned a valuable lesson. I must never do that again. I went too far from the house, and I was attacked. No more walking like that. Too dangerous.

Kids have gone to school except Peter and Tommy and now what do I do with the choking? Can't stop it now, it's taken me over. Don has a trial, can't call him. Evelyn doesn't come during emergencies and Katy is out of town. Oh Katy, why are you gone? Katy always makes me feel warm even if it's cold outside. She makes me feel nice when I'm a shithead. She makes my kids feel warm, like special kids. She makes us feel like people. Respected. Oh, why has she gone? Peter can go in there and plunk down and she plays great games with him. Peter, he reads to Katy. He's three and I didn't know he read. I bet Katy taught him. She says he taught himself. I'm pacing now. Have to get someone for the kids. Call Rita Frye—choking—Rita picks me and the kids up for the day. Choking has me panicked. Want to go back to the hospital. But Rita has Peter and Tommy. I'm watching her with them. They are a little afraid of her. She's a good woman; her house is neat but it is cold in here. Cold. She doesn't hug my children. If Katy were home I would go to the hospital. But my children here? No. I will stick this choking out, this day. I'll hold them and make them warm.

Friday, March 21, 1969

Afraid of appointment now. In the afternoon, get in the car. Have to check out where he lives. Funny-shaped house. Isolated spot in the country. Looks formidable, hostile. Don't like this house. Turn around at Apple Tree Road, go back again. Can't even see the house going the other way. Turn around again. The driveway is plowed, so I know someone lives there. Probably his family. Ha, ha. I am being so dumb. But I don't care. He scares me. Go home and call Evelyn.

"Where were you, Carol, I tried to call you?"

"Just out."

"Well, I've got the scoop for you. Billy boy is a psychiatrist, a doctor. He works part time at the Counseling Service, part time at Wharton College, part time at Middletown Mental Health, has private patients. And get this, will you, get this. He is the psychiatrist for Foxcroft Farm. A private retreat for rich, crazy weirdos. How about that?"

"Oh wow."

"Don't let him get to you at your appointment tonight now, and be sure to remember everything that goes on. I'll call you tomorrow."

I decide to drive myself. I walk the path leading to Cove's door. I push the bell. He comes down some stairs and greets me. He leads me to his office. It's a section apart from his house, like a separate apartment. The waiting room has a couple of chairs, a table by the kitchen section—sink, cupboards, bathroom. Then there's this big room. Has a couch in it. But not a couch couch, you know, but one of those uncomfortable things that you pile junk on. That's what he had done, stacks of magazines, papers, leaflets, letters, neatly piled on the couch. Then there is a Ping Pong table. It must be used because there's no rug on the floor and paddles are on the table. I follow Cove into a room off this room. It has double doors built right in. For privacy I guess. This is his office. Two chairs and his desk and his chair behind his desk.

Just an office. No couch. Papers piled around. I sit down. I have my thermos of water. When I drink water, it helps my choking. I feel very vulnerable and I have trouble talking. I mean, now I feel very shy. He asks me how I've been and I say fine like it's a social answer. Then he doesn't say anything, which means, how are you really. I talk now mostly about this choking and how it scares me. He is glad I didn't go back into the hospital. He says that took guts. Me? He is very kind. He builds me up. He says not to try to do too much all at once. He asks about Don and the kids and my friends. I tell him I have a wonderful friend, Katy Reczec, and lots of acquaintances. Don't tell him about Evelyn. She's my special friend. No need for him to know everything. Wants to know about our social life, what we do for fun. Tell him camping, fishing, tennis, plays, dinners, football, sewing, decorating, painting—and drinking. "Oh yes, drinking. Well, you see, well, our crowd drinks, the pressures, you know, and a little flirting here and there by me, you know, nothing serious. Don has already punished me for that, but I deserve it so it doesn't matter, you see. Means nothing."

"What happens?"

"Well, sordid details don't matter really, do they?"

"No, not really, if you understand why you get into fixes. Do you think you drink too much?"

"No, I mean, I don't know. I mean I have these feelings that start me off and then I want a drink and things go downhill—you see?"

"What are these feelings?"

"I don't know."

Cove sits back and looks at the bookcase. He doesn't say any more. I don't say anything either. I can't say any more. I'm getting scared again. I feel tight. I can't say any more to him because that's not how it's supposed to be. I tell him things I want to tell him. I don't want to get all tense. Why is he making me all tense? Can't we just sit and talk like regular adults? And besides, I don't know why these things happen and I don't know what these feelings are. So how can I tell him? And anyway, talking like this makes me uptight, so I'm not going to say any more.

But he doesn't say anything either. The silence just gets louder and louder. I can't stand it anymore so I try to focus my mind on his diploma. I read it and think of Wharton College. But it doesn't work. The silence is just awful. I say again a little louder, "I don't know." It's broken now so he sits forward a little and explains some things to me. I sit sort of dumbly there with my head down. This is scaring me.

"Sometimes, Carol, when problems are bothering you, you push them away. This is more painful than if you face them. It makes you uptight."

I hear him all right but I'm not going to say anything. Of course I see a connection. But he's making me uptight. I never had a God damned facial twitch before I talked to him. He's causing me to act like this. I won't talk to him anymore. Not tonight.

"Eventually all these feelings must come out. . . . You told me that you were drinking too much."

"Well, it eases the pressures."

"Do you ever think it creates more trouble than it eases?"

"Yes, of course, but it's like something has to give with me somewhere. There's this pressure that builds up and I—I—something happens to me."

"What is that?"

"I don't know, don't know."

"Do you think we should try to find out what happens to build up these feelings?"

"Oh, I don't know—I don't know."

I get mad now because he is much too direct talking like this. Nobody else ever talked direct. It's too scary. I sit like a dumb person. I go home soon, having made another appointment. Drive too fast. I'm running away from him.

I have an urgency now to find out what kind of disease I have. I want to find out how I'm supposed to feel if I have x illness, what Cove does if I have x illness and how he's supposed to cure me. I've got to find an answer. It's getting too mixed up and involved, so I want to put me in a category and I want to put him in a category and then we get the answer. I can walk only one block now because any further is dangerous. But I'm still driving. My body is a dead thing eaten away with this fear, a lump. I have my friends though. My pep pills to get me out of bed, my tranquilizers, my water. Always carry my thermos. And eventually, toward the end of the day, my liquor. Cigarettes too. With my little aids I journey down to the bookstore and I buy all the books I can. And as the new ones come in I scoop them up. First I read Freud, and I read Reich and Jung and Carl Rogers and Szasz and all of them and it is meaningless to me—awful. And I keep on reading, all the time trying to find out who Cove is and what kind of sickness I have and what pill to take. I am relentless in my search and my frustration mounts. Nowhere can I find myself and I can't find Cove either. Oh yeah, I see little pieces of both of us running all over the page. But there's no package deal. I eat these books like candy. Where am I? Where is Cove? We're here, it's just I haven't got the right books. Oh shit, it makes me mad. What does Cove have in my file? So much I want to know. Where do I fit? Cove is taking a form now of someone that doesn't fit. He isn't Don's friend or my friend or anybody's. But he acts like a friend—he acts like an enemy too. He's taken on the shape of being shapeless. So I have to find out more about him. He's too vague and undefined, like my illness. I get on the phone.

"Evelyn, I can't figure out who Cove-babe is. He's not a friend but he's not an enemy—or whatever. I don't know what to think."

"It's simple, Carol. Hasn't it occurred to you that when let's say a woman pays a man money for services rendered and the services are solicitude, kindness, empathy—human services. . . . What's that called? Think."

"I never follow you."

"God damn, Carol, you are paying him money for his attention. He's a high-class gigolo with a Peeping Tom complex."

"Oh God! Bye, Evelyn."

Can't find answers through Evelyn.

"Cheryl? Carol. How are you? Thought I'd just chat."

Cheryl is skeptical about psychiatry so I have to be careful. But

Cheryl likes me. I tell her about the hospital. I'm crazy. Joke. I can be funny when I want to. I get the information. Cheryl's cleaning lady is also Cove's cleaning lady. She says he has a wife and four sons, one of whom is a doctor. Oh, all this great information. Also Cheryl says that Cove is very particular in his house. That's all she tells me. I wonder what that means, "particular"? I'll think about that. I can't ask her any more because she'll be suspicious. Have to act normal. I'll find out more somehow.

Friday, April 4, 1969

Get hold of yourself, Carol. Don't let things get out of hand. Calm down. Get back to sewing and decorating and everything you do. Forget, forget. Start your lists. Keep moving. Evelyn has tickets for the play tonight, at the high school. Pull yourself together and go with Don. Make people see you out. Whole. Don't be afraid. Just a play. Uneasy funny feeling in legs. Take a tranquilizer. Take water jug. Nothing can happen. Sit down in seat. Good seats. See, everyone, I'm back. I'm all right. Don turns around and talks to people, so I do too. Turn to the back right and there's Charles and Frieda Dudley. Hi, how are you? (Do you think I'm crazy?) Then, oh Jesus save me, there's Cove. Cove is right smack absolutely behind us. There with his wife. I mumble a smile, I mumble a hello and my face flushes and I get dizzy. Want to get out of there. Want to get away. He can read my mind. I hate him. No way to escape. Why is he here to torment me with his phony smile, his phony hello? Oh he's phony all right. Probably telling all his friends I'm crazy. I face forward. Can't move. Want my water but it's on the floor. Can't move. Lights go out. Don holds my hand. He knows my fear. He holds me tight. I make it this way to the intermission. Quick we head for the back. Don says, "Let's go home." He helps me with this fear. We make love.

What is this fear anyway? What has happened? But it has happened. I am in the power again of this kind of man. After Father Anthony, after Melvin, I had said no more, no more, ever again. Yet here it is. Not the good kind of man like my Don. But the kind of man that makes me act weird. Who makes me do strange things. How did this happen? Cove-babe, Cove. Oh, he's making me feel this way. He has this power over me. He and his phony smile and his phony being nice to people. I know what he's like. He's a devil. Now he's taken a shape I recognize. It's not formless. I am completely in his power and I hate him for this. He didn't warn me or tell me he was creeping up on me with his power. But I am firm. I am resolute—he will not get me. He will not break me down. Now I know what I am fighting. I will keep my appointments. I have to keep them. For some reason that is part of his power over me. I want to see him. But he will never ever get to me. I will not cry.

Thursday, April 10, 1969

"That was nice that you and Don could go see the play. I noticed after intermission that you didn't return. Was it because I was sitting behind you?"

"No, not at all. I was tired, that's all. So we decided to go home. Nothing to do with you."

"That's good."

I have to be very careful now that I know he's dangerous. This makes me pretty tense, however, being on guard all the time.

"Do you think you could tell me why you hate men?"

I sit with my head down and I don't look at him. What a stupid question. I'm angry at him for asking that. Where did he get that idea? Why did he say that?

"I don't hate men. I love men. Of course I do."

"When you were in the hospital you expressed to Don that you were afraid that you might end up hating your father. He left me this note."

"It's because you make me feel funny. I mean, you ask these questions in a way that makes my body act . . . I don't know."

"All the time, Carol, you say, 'I don't know,' and it really is sort of a cop-out."

"I—I—I did have some experiences with men that, that weren't too g-good. If that's what you mean." I am stuttering—oh dear God, my body's not working properly. Never stuttered before in my life. Feel ashamed, like a damn fool. "When I was in college I started looking around for a religion. Every Sunday I went to a different church. For a while there I went to a pentecostal sect but their spontaneous prayers made me uneasy so I didn't stay there long. I wanted something firm, solid, because I was having trouble —troubles."

"Troubles?"

"Well, I had these feelings—that maybe I was bad. So I wanted somehow to make amends for something."

"For what?"

"I never really knew what for. Original sin maybe. That's it. I was born with original sin, so I had to get hold of myself somehow and, and—anyway I gravitated to the Catholic Church. I met a priest. I went up to him and said I wanted instruction. I saw him twice a week and I got more and more into the Church like a fanatic. I read all the Catholic doctrine, like *Imitation of Christ*, even wrestled with free will and sin. Sin was my big thing. I was so zealous it was awful and obnoxious. I was obnoxious. The priest was really nice, though. This was when I was in college. I was baptized in the Catholic Church."

"Sin was a big thing?"

"Oh yeah, that didn't come until later, after college."

"Don't let me interrupt."

"Oh no, no. It's okay. . . . Things didn't get funny until later anyway. After college. I went out West for a year. That's when I met this other priest, Father Anthony. He wasn't so nice. I was, how should I say, naive? We would sit in his office and he'd tell me about sin. All I was thinking about was sex, it seems. I was going with Don and I loved him. We were spending quite a lot of time, you know, fooling around. It was great. But as I talked to Father Anthony I started feeling guilty. Father Anthony was about twenty-five years old and quite attractive. He started lengthening our sessions to two hours and then at his house, not at church. He asked me intimate things about sex. I don't know how I got into it.

I initially went to talk to him about sex—sin. Anyway, it was a gradual thing. I had met Don, was going with him and loving him but also gradually loving this priest. A strange kind of love. It wasn't good. He had a power over me. But it definitely was turning toward the sexual. Father, I always called him Father. Even after, well—after my parents found out. . . ."

"Parents found out?"

"Oh yes. They had a fit, especially my mother. They didn't like me Catholic. It was disgraceful to them."

"Were you doing this to get even with your parents? For something?"

"Oh, I don't think so, I mean, well, I never thought of that before—I don't know. . . . I felt Father Anthony had a power over me."

"What kind of power?"

"Oh, I had to know where he was all the time. I knew all about him. What he ate. Who he talked with. His license number. I cultivated Mrs. Merrit, his housekeeper. I went to every mass he said, every day. Yes, it was sexual all right. Thinking back, it really was. He started treating me differently. I thought it was because he didn't like me. He didn't joke around with me as he did with others. Closed up in his room, he started asking me sexual things. He'd say sex was a sin before marriage and I'd say, 'But it's so much fun, it doesn't feel wrong.'

" 'What do you do?' he'd say.

" 'We fool around. . . .'

" 'What do you do when you fool around, like last night? What did you do?'

" 'I'd hug Don and he'd get hard so I'd put my hand inside his pants.'

" 'Go on, go on. . . .'

"That's what it was like. So obvious now, the poor guy was frustrated as hell and a virgin. But all this did was confuse me. It was mixed up with sin and God. I loved Don the good way and this priest a bad way."

"How did you work this out?"

"Oh, it got worse and worse. You know, I really, really loved

THE LONG JOURNEY HOME

Don. We were making plans to be married and I just couldn't get enough of him. Or him me. But I had this Father Anthony thing at the same time. I'd go to mass early in the morning, see Father A., meet Don, go to work, hold hands, make plans, make love. I mean fresh from Don I'd rush up to Father Anthony's and I'd say I've sinned. It was like I was rubbing his face in it. But also he made me do it. He told me to. He then said that my confession should be made in his apartment. With the door closed. He wanted all the details. Then he started holding me, giving me talks on purity. His Sunday sermons now all revolved around purity and sex. The evils of sex. I was beginning to feel sex was wrong, so I cooled it with Don."

"Did Don understand this?"

"Well, he knew something was going on. But how can you really accuse a priest? It's hard to do. I mean he was very uneasy with the whole thing and he knew a toll was being taken on me. I was again then starting to hit trees and . . ."

"Hit trees?"

"Well, ah, sometimes I get a feeling in me that like maybe I'll explode, then I hit trees."

I've got to be pretty careful with this because I slip out with things. Careful, Carol.

"But when I stopped physical stuff with Don, then Father Anthony started. And you know, you know I really was an innocent. I thought he didn't really know what he was doing. I was a mess. Somehow it was me that was the sinner and not him, or else how could he be a priest? I had this feeling and I was in his room. He ordered me over to him. He was sitting in his easy chair. He told me to kneel in front of him and he took off my clothes. And then he touched me. But it was different. He didn't kiss me. He turned his head away. And he was rough. I didn't feel any pleasure at all. I'd turn to stone. I don't know why I kept going back. But I did. And it was always the same. He never kissed me. Once when he was holding me I know that he kissed my hair. I felt it. So I held onto that fact. I had something on him. I felt like a whore, a sinner. One time we had been together on a Saturday night. It was quite violent. On Sunday morning, I mean the very next day, his sermon was on the evils of sex. I couldn't believe he was saying this. I just stared at him—does he actually know or believe what he is saying? I got very hard inside and angry. After church I waited until everyone had left. I went to the back of the church and I screamed at him, 'Shit!' That was the worst word I knew. And I never swore. He looked stricken. Like he didn't know why I would do such a thing.

"Dr. Ashley, I haven't ever told anybody about Father Anthony, and thinking back on it is very strange. I still can't figure out how that man could live such a lie and even seem to believe it himself."

"Maybe he isolated the part of his life that he couldn't accept, and, in that way, he could carry on."

"Well, the whole thing took a great deal out of me. I was doing things to myself that had to be stopped or else. . . . I mean, I wasn't careful of myself, like I would fall downstairs. . . ."

Easy, Carol, easy with that. He mustn't know.

"Fall downstairs?"

"Well yeah, you know. I slipped. I wasn't careful. I confronted Father Anthony one night and demanded that he tell me what was going on. I wanted him to make a decision one way or the other. Was he a priest? Did he love me? How could he treat me so if he was a priest? Was he going to marry me? He couldn't answer me or make a decision. I think now that he loved the priesthood and loved women too. Must've been terrible for him. But it was also terrible for me. I was so mad, an awful tightness came over me and I tore out of his room and I slipped and fell down the whole flight of stairs. I was hurt. I twisted my knee, so I felt better. My anger was gone. I used to get angry like that when I was a kid, so I knew what could happen. When I get angry I'm not any way near careful of myself, so I end up not looking and things like that. So I made a decision—of course this had gone on for quite awhile, in fact, all year; that's how involved it was—I made a decision to marry Don eventually. Instinctively, I knew that he really loved me the right way. The good way. Also, summer was coming and I had to leave Arizona. There. That's the story of me and Father Anthony. Awful, isn't it? Took me a long time to be able to go into church, any church, and not want to throw rocks at the altar. I still don't trust priests too much. Took me a long time to realize that God just didn't have much to do with me and Father Anthony. I'm glad I told you. I'm not proud of it. Those were bad things I did."

"Those weren't bad things. It was a situation that is very understandable. You were a young girl wanting order, acceptance and love. Sounds like you needed love very much."

"Yes."

"Were there other experiences that you had that were what you'd call 'different,' not good?"

"Yes. There were two others, when I went to graduate school at Georgetown, but they weren't as bad. My feelings about Melvin were pretty bad but I didn't get so careless with myself as with Father Anthony. Melvin was really a nice guy. The thing that was bad was having to know where he was all the time. Also like I didn't have a will of my own. I hate that feeling. I did Melvin's laundry. I would have done anything for him. Only in retrospect did I feel that he was using me. Not loving me at all. I didn't feel that at the time. I was consumed almost with, I thought, love?"

"Don't you think it was love?"

"I don't think so now. I was so miserable all the time."

"What do you think it was?"

"I don't know. I know that when my mother found out I was going with Melvin, and that Melvin was a paraplegic, she had a fit. I laughed."

"Melvin was a paraplegic?"

"Oh yeah. Wheelchair and all. Had a neat car with hand controls."

"Did it bother you that he couldn't walk?"

"Oh no, not at all. He could do everything. We bowled and went out and he necked with me. I was so naive—so stupid. He took me to dinner and was working up to a real seduction. I was ready, happy and in love. It never worked out. I didn't know what to do. Melvin told me what to do. But he couldn't. He was testing himself.

This was the first time after his accident. I wanted to marry him. It didn't matter to me that he was crippled. It mattered to him though. Very nice man. He let me go very gently. He went away to law school."

"Tell me about the other man."

"There isn't too much to tell. It didn't feel right, that's all. I had the same feelings with Izzy that I had with Melvin and Father Anthony—these feelings that I was a slave, ruled over. They could ask me to do anything. Good, bad or awful. I would do it. Izzy was nice. He was black and was in the language school. I spent a lot of time with him. He was in charge of the Latin department. Nothing ever happened. But it was because of him, not me. I was ready. He had strong religious convictions, and he never took advantage of me. But he could have. It was all in me. The feelings in me."

"Carol, did it ever occur to you that you might have picked these men for a reason?"

"No."

"Let's look at them. A Catholic priest, a paraplegic, and a black. Doesn't that strike you as a little strange? All three of them have a unique quality. Out of the ordinary. Why do you think you chose them?"

"Nobody else liked me?"

"Is that true?"

"No."

"Did other men ask you out?"

"Yes."

"Were your parents upset about Izzy being black?"

"Oh, yes!"

"Do you think it possible that you had found a very effective way to punish your parents?"

"I don't know."

"What would have been worse?"

"I could have gotten pregnant."

"You didn't get pregnant. Did you take precautions?"

"No. Sin, you know."

"So it's only good luck that you didn't get pregnant?"

"It sure is. I wonder why."

We sit quietly.

"Maybe next time we should go into these feelings you mentioned where you're 'not careful' of yourself."

Freeze, freeze, freeze, freeze—said too much already. Said too much—ease off, ease off.

"We worked better together, Carol. You were much freer talking with me."

I'm smiling now. I like him.

Monday, April 14, 1969

I think about Cove quite a bit now. He doesn't seem real to me. It feels like I love him. Think too much about him. He's unreal. Didn't ever want to get involved this way again. But I am. Just got the paper, run through all the local news. Must find out about Cove. I'm in luck—Methodist Church news, a meeting at Cove's. Are they the ones that don't smoke, drink, play cards? Or is that the Baptists? I'll find out. So he goes to church. And I got his license number too, S670, his VW bus was parked in his yard. Now with careful planning, keeping my ears open, I should be able to know where he is at any given moment. Pure luck I saw him drive by downtown. I can never tell him I am doing these things. It is too stupid. Carol, stop thinking, stop thinking. I'll make out a shopping list and go to the Grand Union.

"Anybody for the store?"

Kids hop in and off I go. In the store a new fear hits me. What do people think of me? What are they saying? They know I've cracked up. Getting tense. Such a normal thing, shopping. But my legs start getting weak and my throat starts closing. Oh my Jesus, here it goes again and I can't stop it. Oh my Lord, I can't bear this feeling. I'm over by the soups and I just wheel about-face and get in line. The kids don't understand. Don't care about them. Just have to get home. Waiting in line, waiting. Can't do it. Can't. I leave the cart and gather up Peter and Tom and head for the car. Get my thermos, take a pill and drive home. I don't know what's happening. I'm not getting better. It's not going away. Can't take a chance on shopping. Oh Christ I'm getting worse.

Thursday, April 17, 1969

All tense, scared. Am waiting out here for Cove-babe. Can't sit down. Walk around, all around the Ping Pong table. Around and around. Wonder who he has in there. Wonder if he treats them the same as he treats me. Oh, got to be careful tonight. Talked an awful lot last time. Radio is going out here, probably so nobody can hear what's going on. Quietly I go in his cupboards. He's got his doctor stuff stored in there. Door opens from the house section, and I jump, still walking. A boy comes in, high school age, and smiles and says hello. Me, I smile, my phony cheerful self, and say hi. I don't look crazy. The boy gets some ginger ale out of the refrigerator. That must be one of Cove's boys—he does have a real life! I'm too wrapped up in my thoughts about Cove. He doesn't seem human to me.

I go in and sit where I'm not directly in front of him and maybe he can't see me as well. The farthest chair. I can't seem to talk at all. I'm just not saying anything. Cove isn't playing games. He didn't even ask how I was doing because I always say fine.

"You made a remark last time about your not being careful with yourself. Could you tell me about it?" Cove turns to the side and waits.

I keep my face down now. I don't want to talk to him about this. I can't think. Mind goes back, flashes, when Mom and Dad had the Fryes for dinner. A dressy affair. Mr. Frye was my swim teacher. I loved him. I talked to him and he really liked me. That's why I was such a good swimmer. My Dad was jealous of Mr. Frye. I knew he was because they both said mean things about them before they came. Mrs. Frye took me bird watching and she was an actress. Mom and Dad hated the Fryes. It seemed like they always hated people I loved. I heard them say, "He's Jewish." I was ashamed they said this. They were all talking and laughing downstairs. I was at the top of the stairs listening. That feeling clogged up my blood. Made my heart pound. The Fryes were my friends. Mine. Mom and Dad would talk bad about them when they left. I couldn't stand thinking this. I was at the top, then I fell to the bottom. I hit the landing, bounced and went the last three steps to the bottom. It shocked me that I did this but I felt better. I wanted to cry now but of course I never cried. But I felt like it. The Fryes were worried that I hurt myself. So was Dad. But not Mom. Mom gave me her funny look and wouldn't speak to me for a long time. I wonder if she knew.

"Sometimes, sometimes, I get uptight and . . . I don't know."

"What were you thinking, Carol?"

"Sometimes I'd get frustrated and I'd go to my room and throw things around. Then I'd feel better."

Thinking now how I took my radio and I threw it at my foot and I did this over and over, and I took all the pieces and pressed them against my body, until I could cry.

Remembering these things is too much for me. My mind has a yellow darting light and I close my eyes tight and put my hand to my throat. I am choking and breathing hard. I want to say something but I am choking and my breathing is too fast. Cove doesn't say anything. It lasts about ten minutes. I can't look at him. He is sitting behind his desk all safe. And I'm not safe. He talks real soft then, so I look up.

"It's very difficult for you, Carol, and I know this is scary. I know it is, but I think we both know it's necessary."

"I hit trees. I've smashed them all my life. I made myself fall downstairs to hurt myself. Only way I can cry. Only way."

I tell him that, oh ugly! Now he hates me—like my mother. Now he'll leave me, throw me away. Shouldn't have told him.

"Do you think your frustration builds up to such a level that you can only break out of it that way?"

"Yes," very quiet and ashamed.

"It seems like you were a lonely girl."

"I never thought I was, but now I'm thinking that I had no one to really talk to."

Sit for a while. Cove swings his chair to the side to his appointment book.

"Think you'll be able to drive tonight?"

"Yes."

Cove doesn't seem to hate me.

Monday, April 21, 1969

I don't want to go out very much anymore. I'm afraid. Shopping scares me, and the car too. It's hard to pretend I'm all right when I'm not. I sit a long time in the house. I feel I'm being eaten with something evil. Don and I went to the Hydorns the other night and I panicked. We had to leave. I am so sorry. It doesn't do much good to be sorry. Maybe I'll start some oils. Get out the equipment and it frightens me. It's awful painting. I'm painting awful things. I have no control. I take the two I'm working on and throw them down the cellar. Can't paint anymore. Have a drink, calms the panic for a while.

"Hi, Evelyn. Nice of you to call."

"How's Billy treating you, Carol? What's going on?"

"I don't know. It just seems to be getting worse. I'm scared all the time and I can hardly do anything."

"That's not good. You should be better. What does he ask you, Billy, that is?"

"Oh we talk about childhood and problems and things. But it makes me so uneasy. I have anxiety every time I talk. I don't know."

"Maybe he's no good."

"Oh I think he's good, maybe too good."

"Talked about the Oedipus complex yet? That should be great fun."

"Oh Evelyn, really!"

"What's he like? How does he act?"

"Oh, he's really nice but I just get so scared sometimes, I can't talk."

"They're trained to do that, Carol. You know?"

"Well, I don't think he likes that part of it."

"Have you hit transference yet?"

"I don't know. . . ."

"That's when you fall in love with the therapist, only it's not him you love, but someone from your past."

"Well, not me. Not me. Never."

"You just wait. It's called transference neurosis."

"Come on. You've got to be joking."

"Well, I've been reading. Doing my homework. I have a good book for you. I'll bring it over."

"Okay."

I'm so uneasy talking like this. Evelyn is a smart lady. I'm confused. I look in my books. Transference does say something like what she said but it doesn't fit. Oh shit, nothing fits. . . .

"Katy, hi, Carol. Katy, I'm getting worse. I know it. Cove might be . . ."

"Who?"

"Dr. Ashley might be making me worse. I'm always upset when I talk to him. Maybe he doesn't know anything. Evelyn says that . . ."

"Carol, Dr. Ashley is a professional. He knows what he's doing. If you get anxious, then it must be because it's best for you. What are you doing?"

"Nothing. I can't seem to do much. I'm tired and I . . ."

"I'm going to get a sitter for the kids. I'll be over in a half-hour. Let's ride our bikes."

"I don't think . . ."

"See you in half an hour."

Once on the bikes my adrenaline starts moving. I have my thermos of water. We ride. I'm not so scared with Katy. I could go on and on. Katy begs for mercy. We're not on a marathon. Okay. Reluctantly.

I've come out of it for a while. But, Katy—both Don and Katy— are worried.

I take Peter for a walk. It is late afternoon. I can only walk this far, from my house to the municipal building, one block. I have my water. The Counseling Service is in the municipal building. On three afternoons Cove is there. I see his car. I make a game out of it. Peter laughs, he thinks it's funny. The car's locked. I see the knobs pushed down. I go right up to it and I check to see if any- one's around. Then I kick the tires. Hard. Three or four times. So does Peter. We walk back to the sidewalk and stand a minute. Then we turn around and walk home. I glance over my shoulder. Maybe he'll come out. Sometimes when we walk down his car isn't there. I always panic. Where is it? Where has he gone? Is he sick? I hate doing this. I hate checking his car. I don't know why I do this. It's a power he has over me like the big men. The bad men.

Wednesday, April 23, 1969

I'm scared of talking to Cove tonight. Throat's all tight. I'm wait- ing, Cove, for you to hurt me. Somehow I know you're going to hurt me and I wish you'd hurry so I could be done with this fool- ishness. Oh please don't hurt me like the rest. Please help me. I walk up the pathway to his door. I open the door and walk up the stairs. I'm early. He has someone in his office. I'm very quiet. He doesn't know I'm here yet. I'm tense. I walk quietly around the Ping Pong table. I look in the cupboards. My green cup is there. I keep my green plastic cup there all week in among his doctor things. I fill the cup with water and set it down. I have an urgency, a need. I don't know what it is so I keep walking. I go over to the closet door and look around. I open the door and look inside. There are winter coats. I put my hand in and go through them. The big tan parka. My heart starts pounding. I know it is his because I see his season skiing ticket. I put my hand on the coat shoulder. I feel like crying. A lump is in my throat. What am I doing? I take the coat off the hanger and put it on. I'm standing there with his parka on. I feel safer. I want to go in the closet and go in the corner and stay there with his coat on. Then I could cry. But I can't. Oh this is so stupid, so awful. What am I doing standing here? What if someone came in? Quick take it off and put it back. I want to keep it but I put it back and go sit down. No one saw me. It's okay because no one knows. I felt safe for a moment but now that's gone.

I have to pull myself together and stop this idiotic behavior. I push down that lump and I get angry at myself and at him. I hate him. I won't talk at all.

The door opens and two old ladies come out. Very old. He comes out and smiles. I force a smile. He is very nice to the old ladies. He is afraid they might slip on some ice. He walks them down the stairs and out to their car. I can hear them talking. This interests me somehow. I wonder what he's trying to prove being so concerned about the ladies. I am still angry. This disconcerts me. His kindness to them. His natural concern. If he is nice to them, will he be nice to me? Maybe he really is just nice. Is he? But he's a phony. I feel it. When he comes back upstairs he still has a nice expression on his face. It would really be rude of me not to speak. I'm well brought up.

"Hello, Dr. Ashley. Nice night out, isn't it?"

You won round one but I'll be very careful. Remember your power.

Head down, won't look at him. He doesn't say anything. Me, I keep hard inside waiting. We sit like that. I keep thinking of his coat—oh shit.

"Carol, if you are upset, do you think you could talk about it? What's troubling you?"

"Nothing's the matter. I'm not thinking anything, nothing."

"You are very tense. Can you talk about it?"

Don't want to think but his words set my mind moving. That yellow light goes in my head. The one that clicks and hurts with remembering. I remember when I was little.

"Tell me." Silence.

I keep my head down, and since the quiet is making too much noise, I decide to say what I can. Maybe a little.

"When I was little I learned to skate. We had a nice big rink in our neighborhood and we all learned to skate by pushing chairs. I was proud of my mother, she skated too. Those were such great winters. Cold and crisp, with that new ice. Such wonderful times."

"Do you know why you thought of that?"

"No."

So we sit quiet again. I am cold. I want his coat.

"One time I left the rink and I walked in the snow past the DuBois house over to a hill. The hill was wonderful, sheer ice. I thought it would be great to skate down the hill. About halfway I fell and everything exploded in my head. I saw racing lights and all colors. Then I remember lying at the bottom. My head hurt. I wanted someone to help me but nobody was around. When I got to our house I started to throw up. I didn't know why because it was my head that hurt, not my stomach. My mother saw me. She helped me into the house and that's when I got afraid. I got scared. Scared of my head and scared of my throwing up. I must force myself to stop. My mother had her methods when we were sick and so I never let her know. She always gave us enemas for everything. I was so scared of those, so I never let her know when I was sick. I straightened up then and said I was all right, just tired. I crawled into bed. My head hurt so. I was afraid to tell her I was hurt. I stayed in bed, I covered my head. I was waiting for her footsteps and hoping Dad would come home. But nobody came. I was about seven. I was so lonely. I almost cried then."

"You were little and hurt and you felt lonely because no one was helping you. And you were scared of your mother?"

"That's how I felt—you know, I was sort of hoping that my Dad would come home and, well, help me. When he knew I was hurt, he'd help me."

"Did he this time?"

"I don't know, I don't remember. I got better. I think it's just my mother thought I had the flu, you see."

"Why didn't you tell her that you fell?"

"Oh no. I never would. Oh no. My mother always got mad

when I hurt myself. I never told her. Dad helped me sometimes, though—if he knew, he helped me. You see, Dr. Ashley, it's just that I wasn't good, you see? I mean I was a bad baby."

"How were you bad?"

"Oh I was. Believe me, I was." Laughing a little because it sounds stupid—I want him to understand.

"Mom said I always cried for food. Even when I was just born I always cried the loudest. Screamed, she said, because I ate the most. I wanted all the milk. I wasn't good. Oh it sounds so dumb but I really do feel it. She made it very clear. She said my very first words were, 'Dennis did it.' They laughed at that tale because I was sitting in a playpen and I had the wet diapers and I said that Dennis did it. . . . I don't know."

"Are any of your children like that? Are any of your children bad babies?"

"Of course not! Sometimes my kids are exasperating but not bad. I know babies can't be bad. But I really was. Somehow I was. But not altogether, I mean my Dad helped me when he knew. I mean he rescued me, no, I mean he loved me. They both loved me but somehow, sometimes he made me feel safe."

"How did he do that?"

"Well, if he wasn't there, I would dream that he'd come and hold me, if he knew I was hurt. I knew inside he would help me if he could. I was special to him."

I started feeling like crying but I stopped it. I put my head down and wouldn't talk any more then. I thought of Cove's coat in the closet. It comforted me when I had it on. My Dad did that when he could. If he didn't know, then it wasn't his fault. I don't want Cove thinking badly of my Dad. He doesn't know him, he doesn't know that Dad would help me if he could. Cove might make Dad seem bad. Can't talk to him about Dad again. Ever. Cove doesn't know, doesn't understand. Dad loves me. He takes care of me when he can, so leave me alone, Cove, leave me alone, you make me feel like crying. I don't want to be hurt. Please don't talk to me about Dad.

"This is hard for you to talk about, Carol, but it is better if you do."

Don't want to talk to him anymore. I want to get home quick and check the kids, my babies. They need me to love them. I don't want them ever to be afraid of me. I hold them a lot. How could a baby be bad?

Saturday, April 26, 1969

Opening day of trout season. I'm getting too bogged down with this therapy business. I've got my fishing license and I'm going to have a good time. Don is watching the kids, he wants me to have fun like before. I'm going to Clearwater Brook alone. I don't know anybody else who fishes. I've got my thermos of water, my thermos of martinis, my gum, cigarettes and lunch. Plus bucket and gear. I will have a good time. It is beautiful here. I always forget how beautiful. Nobody is around, the brook is high and running swift. I want to fish the junction of the New Hancock and the brook, so I go and look. I have to cross and there's no way. Too swift. I'll head downstream. Oh, I feel a little free now. A feeling I haven't had in a long time. My tackle is in fine shape so I enjoy the casting. I think it's too early and cold for much, but it doesn't matter. This is like it used to be. I am whole again.

I don't know why I put up with Cove anymore. He just upsets me and makes me act funny. I don't like the way those sessions are turning out, I try to say some simple thing and it gets all twisted around. He puts a funny meaning on things. Why can't he leave me alone? How come I don't feel like an adult? Jesus, I stutter and act like a God damned fool. And then his jacket. How come I'm acting like that? Jesus, it feels like I love Cove. Damn him, how the hell could I love him? My line has snagged. The current is too swift. It won't break. Damn, I'll break it. With a flurry of anger I pull the monofilament. I wrap it around my hand. Before it snaps, the line cuts my hand. Jesus, what a cut! What's the matter with me that I forgot so soon how to break a line? Shit. I don't care. This anger is ruining things. The brook looks more forbidding. I'll show it, I'll show it. I gather my stuff and head for the bend. I go past the fallen tree and wonder how to get across the breakwater. It's covered. Should I chance it? Why the hell not? Shit on them all. If I fall, just remember to fall to the right, into the calm, not the swift, deep. I don't care. I don't care. My feet are numb, I only have on sneakers, but I am committed. As I head across I'm not scared. I'm too hard inside. The light hits the breakwater beneath my feet in such a way that I can't see where I'm stepping. The water runs swiftly up to my knees. I inch along, inch by inch, balancing. If I fall, go to the right, the right. The right. God damn Cove, I hate him, not love him. I'm never going to tell him anything again. Oh yeah, he has me coming to him. I can't stop that now, that's the trap I fell into, the power he has over me. But I'll never tell him anything anymore. If I love him it's an evil power he holds over me that makes me. I'll never tell him. Him and his being nice to people, old ladies, and his phony concern. It's more like hate if you ask me. I'm almost across and I fall over to the rocks. I am exhausted suddenly and my feet frozen. I made it. Now no one can get me. No one can ever find me over here. I'm separated by the water. An island. I find a hollow in the rocks and settle myself. I take off my sneakers and socks and hold my feet for warmth. I've sort of forgotten about the fishing now. It's way too swift anyhow. The water's too high. I'm settling in for thinking. It's comfortable. Maybe I'll never leave. I get my lunch out and pour a good-sized martini. I look at my hand. It's stopped bleeding but the cut's still open. I'm a little scared of my hatreds. There's that one side of me that is a worry wart. The side that worries about me. The other side seems stronger, the hate side doesn't care about me. The day gets colder. It is getting late. I stand up to go and urinate and I sort of wonder anew. What am I doing on the island? All of a sudden, that fear comes over me. How the hell am I going to get back? I do care about myself, see? I have to get back. The fear makes me weak. I can hardly see where I should go across the water. I'll have another drink. Sometimes that takes care of the fear. Don't want Don to know that I got way out here. It's not safe. Drink it all, okay, okay. Good. I gather my gear. I have new courage in my hate. That damned Cove has made me act this way. Well, I'll show him. No more simpering. I am strong. I can do anything I want. I don't think it's really fair, God, that I was born. So I am bitter at you, God. I was born bad. When everyone thinks babies aren't born bad. Ha ha! We know, God. I am the exception. I am bad so I have to pay. I will pay and pay and pay until I am dead. And if they don't make me suffer, then I will make myself suffer. It is the only way. I plow over to the underwater rocks. It doesn't much matter really whether I fall. I begin to slip. I bump my ankle. I lose my bucket. It goes swiftly downstream around the bend. Dark red. That could be me going. But no, that's too easy. Have to pay more first. I get to the safety of the path and I look back. It is all dark and swift. How did I ever do that? I am charmed by the realization that my death isn't going to come going swiftly downstream. It's going to take cut hands and bumped ankles and bruised face and pounded arms and all those messy, half paths of self-destruction. The inexorable chopping away of myself in chunks of flesh and bits of blood here and there. I go to a rock and I bang my fists on it. See? See? Always like that. Nothing neat and swift like my bucket. But I have to do it. I have to pay for my crimes. What are they, God? Please tell me what they are. I feel them, so how come I can't even glimpse what I pay for? Oh my God. Now I am crying. Lying in a heap by the river, I am crying and sobbing. I don't even know what my crimes are. I don't even know what I'm guilty of. I'll never know.

Thursday, May 1, 1969

He's not going to get me anymore. I bang his outside door. I stomp up his stairs. I get my water and I bang the cupboard. I don't sit and wait. I stand. If I let go at all, he might get me. That lady that comes out, I wonder if she knows his power. What problems does she tell him? He probably likes her better than me. She's younger and prettier. Let him talk to his stupid other patients. At least I have his nine o'clock. Before, if I had his seven o'clock or eight o'clock, then I always had the feeling I had to hurry. And that someone was waiting. Now Cove-babe has me at nine o'clock. He doesn't let anything interrupt a session. No phone calls or anything. There's no diversion, no getting away until I'm done. He told me before, he said I waste lots of time by not saying anything and then just before the hour is up, I talk. That way I keep him for almost two hours. He says maybe I do this on purpose. That maybe I manipulate him. Shit on him. I don't give a damn what he thinks. I sure as hell don't do that on purpose. What am I supposed to do? Panic on the exact minute to time things right? Shit. If he's too wishy-washy to time things and to kick me out in an hour, that's his problem. That's it, he's wishy-washy. I notice that when I get twitching too much, he backs down. He's afraid to push me. Well, it's a good thing he doesn't, that's all I can say. I don't know what I'm doing. I'm scared again so I have to get hard inside like this or something awful will happen. I sit in the chair and I don't speak. I don't look at him, so I don't know what he's doing. Got to keep my wits.

"Carol, you say that you had a good childhood. You start to tell how you felt as a child and then you get very tense and you lapse into 'I don't knows.' "

Silence.

I'm not going to talk. I'll just listen. I look at my foot. I concentrate on my sneaker. I need new sneakers. I ripped them on a rock when I was fishing.

"Why do you get upset when you talk about your father?"

Oh God, why isn't he quiet? Why doesn't he leave me alone? I'll talk about something else. So he'll leave me alone.

"I eat all the time. If I can't diet, then I drink. I can't stop eating or drinking."

"You eat and drink too much. Why?"

"I'm hungry."

Cove sits there looking at me. He keeps going after me. Silent.

"I don't know! I don't know!"

I'm getting mad. I don't want him to see me mad. He bothers me. He's after me.

"Why can't you talk about your father? You changed the subject."

Oh—I've got to make him stop. I take my hands away from my head. I leave my head unprotected and it feels like he might give me blows to the head, but I have to take a chance. I grip the sides of the chair so I don't explode. I grip them as tightly as I can and shut my eyes.

"You say you don't get along with your mother but she probably loves you. You say you love your father and then you stop. You stop talking and get all tense."

"Leave me alone. Just leave me alone! I'm mixed up, you mix me up. I can't talk good because I go blank. I'm confused."

Those lights go in my head. I can't stand the pressure anymore. I have to get out of here or I won't be responsible. I have to get away from him. I raise my fist. I clench my fists together hard and I raise my fists. What am I doing? Mustn't lose control. I raise my fists at him again. He's hurting me and I have to get away from him. I get up fast and I open the door. I forgot the second door, almost ran into it. As I open it, he's talking.

"You don't have to leave like this, running away won't help you face things."

I hate him. I tear down the stairs. I am shit. I make myself fall the last few steps. I've got to hurt myself now or I won't survive. I get out the door and I tear away. Don drove me, so I don't have the car. I don't care. I run as fast as I can until I see a car coming. I decide I have to get off the road. I go into the field, I head for the nearest tree. I run behind it and I start smashing it with my fist. Over and over until I'm too tired. My foot is in a puddle of water. I don't care anymore. . . .

My anger is gone. I have paid a price. I walk down the road again. I know that Don will be after me. It's all right now. I am quiet. Don can hold me and I won't be afraid for a little while.

Wednesday, May 7, 1969

Somehow I am losing control during our sessions. Nothing is turning out like I planned. This psychotherapy is getting messy, like my mind. I thought I could shut off those feelings but it isn't working right. I raised my fist at Cove. Why couldn't I just talk calmly like regular people? I'm scared now, I've got to stop this pacing and

I can't. My throat is closing up. I'm going to die again but nobody believes me. "Just plain old anxiety." I am bitter because it feels just as bad.

"Katy, can you come over? I'm dying and afraid."

"I'll get sitters and be right over."

Katy will help me. She doesn't seem afraid of me.

"Katy, I can't stop this pacing, this anxiety. I really want to go back to the hospital. I have to go back."

"Why don't you call Dr. Ashley, Carol, talk to him?"

"No, no. I can't call him."

Someone has taken the kids for a walk. I am talking to Katy as I race between the dining room and kitchen. Back and forth. I want the hospital. Can't call Cove. Afraid of him.

"Help me, help me."

"Oh Carol, I know how afraid you are, but let's take a look at you and figure what to do. I really have to laugh—if we could harness your energy, we could make a million dollars. Do you want me to call Dr. Ashley?"

"Jesus, look at me. Just look at me! I have to laugh too. My God, my body. What can I do with such a body? I can laugh. I wish it wasn't me. I've got to go to the hospital. I've got to do something. Call Dr. Ashley, but I can't listen."

"Why not?"

"Don't know. Scared."

I go upstairs. I go from one room to the next. She's calling and I don't want to hear. I'm scared to talk to him. Katy comes up and says she's talked to Cove. Cove is on the phone and wants to talk to me.

"No, no, can't talk to him. Can't."

"Okay, Carol, okay. Come on downstairs. We'll figure something out."

"I have to go to the hospital."

I go to the bathroom and shut the door. If this is what going crazy is, I've gone crazy. There's just no place for me to turn. I crouch on the floor and cover my head.

"Carol, take my hand. There is a place for you. Let's go."

"Where, what? The hospital?"

"Nope, here's a pill and here are your hiking boots. Let's go. I'll get your water and things. Don't forget your hat, it's pretty nippy."

"Did you talk to Dr. Ashley? What did he say?"

"He said to take another pill and that we should take a hike."

"You're kidding? What for?"

"Sounds like a good idea to me. Let's go."

"Well, okay."

So we start off from North Street and I'm going fast. Katy is chatting with me. I'm scared. If Cove thinks I should take a hike, I will.

"Carol, a hike is all right, but do we have to run? I mean, hey slow down."

I'm walking fast, very fast. Like I'm trying to get ahead of this choking. Katy has on her new boots and it's hard for her to keep up. After all, she doesn't have anything chasing her, like me. I have a little pity and race ahead and then come back. Race ahead and back. We head out past the hospital. I give it a look and wonder how come I'm walking past. I should be strapped down and full of shots. Katy says a hike is better, isn't it? I have to laugh. I laugh and laugh. Oh no, I can't have a regular doctor who wants me in the hospital. Oh no, I have to have Cove. Cove wants me to take a hike. Oh hell, this is funny. So a hike it is. We go past Sandra Ketner's horse farm and keep right on until we hit the dead end, King Notch Road. We have to decide whether to go right, the Chester swamp road, or cross country to the brook. We decide. Cross country, across the fields, thickets and rocks to the brook. We've been gone quite awhile. It really is a hike now. I am slowing down. Now it's fun. We decide to follow the brook back until we are adjacent to my house on North Street. We hit the railroad tracks and follow them for a while. I have a cigarette and we take a breather. This really is wild country. We talk about how lucky we are to live here. We plan a Memorial Day camping trip. I feel bigger now and not so scared. My throat has stopped closing up on me. We go about three or four miles and I can see we are getting near home. I am reluctant to go home, to leave Katy and the wild country. Suddenly, this seems the safe place to be. Not the hospital. As we pass the back of the hospital, I thumb my nose at it. Katy laughs. I laugh.

Katy and I are tired. My legs are shaking. I lie on the couch. She covers me up. She says to sleep, she'll handle things.

"When you hike, you really hike! I bet we lost weight! How about that?"

"Hey, Katy, thanks."

I sleep.

Thursday, May 8, 1969

I'm ready for my appointment. I'm subdued. That anxiety attack scared me a lot. Me running out of his office scared me. Maybe he can help me. Maybe I won't get wild. Maybe I can just talk.

"I'm glad you didn't have to go to the hospital. It's better to handle things at home if you can. How do you feel?"

"I feel all right, I guess. I'm scared now. Those attacks scare me."

"I know they do. About last time, do you think you can figure out why you were so angry?"

"Um, well, well . . . I-I think I felt that you didn't understand about my Dad, I wasn't explaining right how things were so I got mad. I was frustrated or something."

"Who were you mad at?"

"Well, nobody, I wasn't mad at anybody. Maybe at myself for not explaining."

"You shook your fist in the air, as if you were mad at somebody."

My arms and legs start getting funny now. Oh Jesus, my throat is beginning—if I keep talking, maybe it'll go. . . .

"It was me, I was mad at myself I guess. I'm sorry. Sometimes I feel like pounding something."

Does he know this? Have I told him? I can't remember. It doesn't matter, he knows now. Oh hell. Here I go again.

"Do you think that you felt like hitting me? Not yourself, but me?"

"No, no! I mean, why would I? Why? I mean you sit behind your desk and you just talk so you don't, you haven't . . . Don't know."

"You said that you thought I didn't understand about you and your father. Maybe you think I really do understand."

"What do you mean? What are you saying? Please, Dr. Ashley. I don't know, I'm mixed up again. Please leave this."

"In previous sessions you have asked me to leave this subject alone. When I do, you accuse me of being wishy-washy. You seem relieved for a while and then you seem to get angry that we haven't gone into things further. And then when I do push you, you get so panicky, and you make me feel cruel. So, no matter what I do, it's wrong."

"Well, I think what you're saying is true. You do seem cruel, and you do seem wishy-washy."

My head is down but I am listening to him. A funny feeling for this man to talk in such a direct way. I didn't think that he had any emotions. He says he doesn't like to push me—does he really feel? I wonder. His words are so, so—direct or, or . . . ? He doesn't seem real. I'm nothing to him. A bug to squash. Two hours a week, that's all, a job. Nothing. His power. That is real. I pick up my head and I look at him. When I first saw him he looked handsome. Now I can't tell anymore. He looks all different things to me. His face changes all the time now so I really don't know what he looks like.

"I guess either way you go, you can't win." I laugh a little.

"Do you think I should push you?"

"No."

"Do you think I should go easy?"

"No."

"Do you see my dilemma?"

"Yes. It seems like you have a real problem."

We laugh. For an instant, I see him as a real man with a problem in his work. A real man?

. . .

Silence for a while—we sit quiet.

"I seem to ask all the questions, Carol. Maybe we should talk about what *you* think we should talk about."

Now I'm scared again. I hate it when he does things like this. He gets me scared. I don't know what the hell to talk about. What the hell do I do now? Oh shit.

"I can't do that. Because lots of times I think of dumb, stupid things that I wouldn't mention."

"How do you know they're dumb?"

"Because they are."

"Why don't you let me be the judge?"

"Well, lots of times I think about what we talk about. And you seem to play an important part in all this. I dwell on you a lot. Of course, I'm mad at you. Sometimes I hate you, but it's hard to figure out why I would hate you."

"Why would you hate me?"

"Well, I come up with how mean and cruel and awful you are. But that's a problem because I see you sitting behind a desk. Just sitting there. Not doing anything hateful. So it's hard to square you in my mind. So much time I spend figuring this out. It's stupid."

All of a sudden I'm getting uneasy. It's easy for me to talk about hating him. It's the other. Never tell him the other. That's his power. If he finds out about his power, then I am lost.

"Is there something else?"

"No, no. Just thinking. Just thinking. I think it's that you put things in a bad light, you make things seem bad. They never were before—oh—your questions are bad, you see."

"They're bad?"

"They are, they are. I talk about a perfectly nice little memory and it gets twisted."

"Don't you think that *you* do this?"

"No, no. You do! You do this to questions, you always twist things up in my mind. You are the cause of problems I have."

"I am?"

"Oh, I know it's stupid. You see? That's what I mean about what I think is stupid. And I do stupid things. You make me do stupid things."

"I make you?"

"Yes, in a way. It's like you have a power over me. Damn."

"What stupid things?"

"Oh, I don't remember."

He just sits quietly. I have a debate going on in me. What the hell, might as well give him an idea of the dumb shithead I am. Give him a laugh. If he doesn't like crazy people, he shouldn't be in this line of work.

"Your car. I know about your car. I know that on Wednesday morning and Friday afternoon it's on Main in front of the Counseling Service. I know it's there. I go down and look at it. Sometimes I kick your tires. When it isn't there I get scared. I think you're sick. I hate myself for doing this. I'm such a shithead."

"Sometimes, you know, I have to park on Peters Road in front of Ralph's."

"What?"

"It's very understandable, what you are doing. You are finding out if I'm where I should be at the proper time. It's a security for you to know where I am."

"You don't think the car thing is dumb?"

"Not at all."

"Wow."

I'm subdued. Seems like he understands.

"Wow."

I smile, he smiles. I feel good now. It's okay what I do—it's all right. It's not weird. I'll be damned.

Tuesday, May 20, 1969

I'm sitting in the rocking chair in the kitchen, thinking. I am jumpy, and fear stops me from getting much done. This is hard to accept because I'm used to doing so many things. Don has taken the kids to Springfield to the dentist. I can't do that anymore. Can't shop either. Too scared, all the time. My truths, I have those. I hold them. Those truths about not letting "them" break me down—make me cry. I mustn't give in, let go, mustn't go easy, or things will collapse. It's taking all my strength to maintain these truths. And it makes me not want to see anybody, my friends either, they interfere with my thinking. Can't let go or something bad will happen.

The phone rings. I hesitate answering. Why should I? Nobody interests me. I can't stand the ring. I answer.

"Carol, this is Dr. Ashley."

"Oh."

My God, why is he calling me? I've done something wrong.

"I told you I was taking a vacation this week, but that there was a chance my plans would change and if they did I'd call you."

"Huh?"

"Well, I'm calling to say I *can* see you. I'm not going away. . . ."

"Oh yes, oh fine, okay, yeah."

"Would Thursday night at nine be all right?"

"Yeah, fine, sure—oh, thanks."

"See you then. Goodbye."

Clunk. Oh! He called me on the phone. He really did. I was just sitting there on the chair. I knew he'd never call, I dismissed it immediately because I knew he'd never call. "They" never call. That's one of my truths. But what happened? He did it. I just talked to him. Now I can see him this week. My truths, I have to let go of that one, the one where "they" don't do what "they" say. Cove did what he said. I feel warmer now, here in my chair. More secure. He called me when I knew he wouldn't. Something is happening to me. Things are not like I planned. Like the tide coming in on West Ridge beach, the water changing my foothold on the sand. The sand always shifting and moving, those smooth ridges disappearing under me, water throwing me off balance. I'm dizzy a little in my rocking chair, the motion, the thoughts of my foothold. I'm being swirled away, things are changing, no control, no control, tide sweeping me away. No middle ground now, no turning back, no status quo. It's going to be settled now one way or the other. There's no avoiding, no half way. If it isn't death, then what for me? I never dared to think of happiness. Now it flicks across the brain. It's going to be death, or life, with this kind of hope tucked away inside? Where did that come from? I smile because he called me. If this truth is wrong, some other of my truths could be wrong. If the tide shifts my feet and knocks me flat and changes and carries me away to something else, so what? It's better than now.

Thursday, May 22, 1969

"I was surprised that you called me."

"I said that I would, if our vacation plans changed."

Cove looks a little confused, wondering why I would mention this.

"But I knew you wouldn't."

"You knew I wouldn't? It seems like you don't trust men."

"Well, why do you say that? You always lump everything—I, I don't know—Love–hate men. . . . Never mind."

"You said love-hate men?"

"Well, these men that I, um, loved before, I told you, like Father Anthony, well, it wasn't easy love, like Don and me. It wasn't comfortable. It was too strong, too powerful. Swinging each way—all the time. Like I loved them too much, but it made me hate too much—they had too much power over me."

"It sounds like you felt controlled."

"Well, maybe. I don't know. . . ."

Quiet now. He turns to the side and puts his hands on his chin and elbows on his knees. He isn't going to say a word. I know him. He's going to wait for me. I don't know what to say to him. It's all so stupid. I won't say anything. I'll outwait him. My eyes are on the floor. The idea is to concentrate on something real that I can see and know. Then I won't be thinking of all this other stuff. I'll outwit him. I look at the leg of his desk. It's a dumb, ugly leg. Maybe it's an antique desk. The foot has a ball as a base, the size of a tennis ball. And around that ball stretch four awful clawlike talons, oh ugly, grasping and tearing at that ball, digging in as in flesh, only stationary, permanent. Ugly desk. It reminds me of the grasping hold these love-hate men have on me. Even when I was really little, a tiny little girl, "they" hurt me. Like Cove now. He hurts me by bringing up these memories in me. I hate him. I won't stop staring at the claws. I hate Cove. I want to see him hurt the way he hurt me. Even when I was little I wanted to see him hurt. I can watch and enjoy him being hurt because of how he hurt me. I was a blond, curly-headed little girl eleven years old and I was sitting on the green couch watching Roy Rogers. I had the pillow on my lap and my face was flushed. Dad was sitting in the green easy chair. He liked watching with me. I didn't want him there. He smiled funny. So I waited and waited for Roy Rogers. I wanted him to hurt, to get shot. I wanted him to groan and have the bad men punch him and beat him up. As the climax of the western built up and up, my face grew flaming and my pleasure increased and I pushed down on my abdomen under the pillow. My pleasure. I was seeing him hurt. I loved him. My hero. My hero. Oh, he's shot in the shoulder. My ecstasy. My joy. He is down. Now I can care for him. I will save his life. Then he will love me. I am on the couch. I want to be alone. Dad comes over, he wants me to rub his head. I want to take care of him, he looks sad, but I am paralyzed with that clawlike vise of fear. I want to cry, I won't cry. My cheeks get hotter, I race out, upstairs, what is happening, little Carol? Why do you behave this way, you mustn't worry. Do what you have to do. I go to the bathroom, I open the medicine cabinet and take out my mother's eyebrow pencil. I rub the end under my eye. Then I hit my fist on my eye over and over. I rub the black again. Now I can go outside. People will see me with a black eye and they will feel sorry for me and they will take care of me. I must get away from here, get away from this house. I run over to Mrs. Frank's house. She likes me. I tell her that my parents love me so very much and soon I will have glasses and braces on my teeth and even crutches. She looks at me funny, but she puts her arm around me. She is warm. I don't know why I said crutches. I'm very silly. I go home soon and I go to the desk in the living room and take out my grandfather's glasses. He died. I sneak them up to my room and put them on. Maybe someday I really will get glasses, then they'll pay attention. Then they'll see. I pick out one of my Lone Ranger books. I turn to the best section, where the angry men hold him down to try to take off his mask. I know they won't get it off but at that moment he is helpless and scared.

My eyes refocus on that claw and I find I am quite agitated. My chest hurts, my breathing hurts, Cove is looking at me. I hate him. He hurts me like "them." He does it on purpose. He is evil to do this, I can't look at him. I won't talk. But, I can't wait any longer.

"I love my Dad, you're making me think bad things. I love my Dad and I'm not going to have you do this. I can't have you do this anymore to me. I pay good money for you to help me and you make me worse like this and I can't take it anymore."

Then I can look up and look at him now. He is sitting square again.

"Can you tell me what you were thinking?"

"No. I can't go on like this, I can't."

"What, can't what? Say it, Carol."

"No, no, no—don't talk, don't talk, don't say anything. Stop."

I stand up. I raise my fist. I shake my fist at him. It's my warning. I'm giving him fair warning to leave me alone. Please, please stop talking. Rage at him boils in me. I don't know what to do with my body—my rage—outside my mind. I hit my face with my fist. Twice now, hard.

"Carol. Stop this."

Cove orders me, not loud. He orders me. That means I can stop. Someone cares now to tell me to stop. He doesn't want me to hurt myself. He doesn't want my eye black. I can stop. My rage goes down, my insides are numb, no feeling. Novocained body. No tears, nothing. The claw scares me like it was alive. I can't look anymore. I look at his face. His face, softer now, looks careworn, loving almost. I am dissolving and the tears come to my throat. But there they stop. He looks so familiar, his face so dear. His body, the body from long ago, the same, the same. I must get out of here fast, like long ago. This clawlike fear is chasing me.

I will come back, though, that is the evil power he has. I am drawn back forever. I am going to remember this hurt that Cove is giving me. I will make him pay. I want to see him suffer for what he's doing to me. I stay up late and I write the date in my notebook and I write down all the hatred I feel toward him. I write for three hours, in the quiet house, I write how I want Cove to suffer so then I can save his life and then he can love me. I feel very tired when I am finished and I feel a lot better. I crawl under the sheets and I hide there in my safe place, curled against Don, who protects me.

Thursday, May 29, 1969

Supper finished, Don and I stack and rinse the dishes. I'm beginning to feel scared. I have an appointment with Cove at nine. Don puts his hand on my cheek and neck and whispers to me.

"It's going to be all right, darling. It's going to be all right."

"Oh honey, it scares me so much." I grab hold of him and hold tight. "You know how I get scared before any physical exam?"

"Yeah—is it like that?"

"It's worse. He hurts me. It's like he's a surgeon with a knife. Only he doesn't tell me he's going to cut me up. Oh, it's so scary, honey. He doesn't tell me when he's going to strike. He twists the knife inside awful."

"Oh my darling, oh darling. I know. Maybe think of him cutting out a cancer. Huh? Think of it that way?"

"Maybe. I guess. I don't know. You love me? You love me when I'm so awful all the time?"

"Especially, my Carol, when you are like now. You are vulnerable now and you aren't hard as nails, like you get sometimes. I especially love you now."

"Please don't ever leave me."

"Never. Don't worry now. I'll run your bath and call you when it's ready."

"Thank you, my darling."

I take a hot bath, dry myself, put on bath powder and brush my teeth. I curl under the quilt and wait for Don. Now he is my protector, my husband. I need him, I need him.

"Does Dr. Ashley know what happens before your appointment? I must thank him someday—hmm. How about this, huh? No more attacking me. I think it's great."

"Well, not me, I mean this is okay but Cove isn't okay. He's—I'm so scared."

"I feel very close to you, sweetheart."

"Me too, darling."

Time to go. I pace around Cove's outer office. I fill my cup with water. I am very careful not to make any noise. I don't want him to think I'm listening. Well, I'm not anyway. I don't care what you do with your other patients. I hate them all. I want to be special to you, Cove, and when I see you acting so God damned nice to other patients, then I know I'm not special. So I don't care and I hate them anyway. Especially if it's a thin woman. Especially then. Well, you're not going to get me sniveling and crying and using Kleenex. No sir. I'm going to beat you. And I won't talk about anything I don't want to.

A couple come out. Jerks. I'm not going to smile at them.

I take my water and I sit in the chair by the wall. I put the cup on a Kleenex on his desk. He's pretty fussy about his stupid desk. Oh well, mustn't put rings on it.

Cove sits facing me. He starts right off, no pleasantries.

"Do you know why you started attacking and hitting yourself last time?"

"Things get too tense and I can't do anything else."

"Why do you hit yourself? Are you angry with yourself?"

"Yes, I am, I mean I guess so."

"Why?"

"I don't know. I'm a shithead, that's all. Well, sometimes I feel so overwhelmed that the only thing left for me is to hit myself."

I'm embarrassed saying these things. He can't help but hate me.

"Why are you so hard on yourself? Can't you have a little compassion for yourself?"

"You see, I begin to feel these things inside and I can't help myself."

"Are you afraid to feel these things?"

"Um, well, yes. You see, then I get all hard inside. Like a brick. And that scares me more than anything. Nothing can puncture the brick."

"You deaden yourself to all feelings?"

"That's it, that's it exactly. And then I hit myself. I have to. If I hurt myself—then the brick inside fades away and sometimes I can cry. Mostly I can't cry, but sometimes. Anyway I feel softer inside. I can feel again."

"Your feelings get so intense you shut them off? That's when you feel hard as a brick?"

"Yes."

"When you strike yourself, are you angry?"

"I feel nothing."

"Before, when you feel all these bad feelings, are you angry then?"

"I think so. Yes, I am."

"Who are you mad at?"

"I'm mad at myself. I'm the shithead."

"Anyone else?"

"Oh Cove, please, please. I know what you're going to say. I know you're going to say my father. And I don't want to do this, please, you have to understand how it was between us. I know that I have trouble talking with you—but—it's because you don't understand."

"I try to understand, but you block me. Why don't we try again?"

"Well, okay. I want you to understand. You have to understand or I get too cold. I loved my father. He was good to me. I loved him and he was nice, nice, a gentleman. He was handsome. I bragged about him to my friends. It's only that when I got older, I was uncomfortable near him. I loved him from far away."

" 'Far away'?"

"I didn't like to be near him. When I got older I don't think I was comfortable with either of my parents. It was always that way, so I think the whole world is that way."

"Your way of life?"

"Yeah."

"Why did you love him from afar? Why not close up?"

"He made me uncomfortable in the same room with me. I didn't like to look at him. I didn't like him looking at me."

"Why?"

"Oh, oh—please. I can't, can't. You don't understand, he was everything to me. He'd come home from work and I'd smell his hands, soap and tobacco, and he'd carry me to his easy chair and read me the Burgess stories from The *Herald Tribune*. Peter Rabbit and the Weasel. I was his favorite. He told me that, almost."

"This was when you were younger?"

"Yes, I was little. He played games with me, badminton and tennis, and he joked with me. The world wasn't around then, just me and Dad. We had a victory garden. Dad and me, we'd go through the woods to the garden and he'd work. I'd play. Scream and yell and yahoo and fire my cap gun. This one time Dad and I sat on the ground by some trees and ate ripe tomatoes. It was like we cheated, you know. The war was on and everybody was sharing the gardens. Juice dribbling all over. It was glorious. Dad said to me, 'Don't ever grow up to be a woman, Carol, stay just as you are.' I knew what he meant. I was a tomboy and you know women, how they are, I mean. . . ."

"Do you think that was a strange thing to tell a daughter?"

"No, what? What? Strange, no." Now I'm feeling funny, threatened.

"Wouldn't a father want his daughter to grow up to be a woman?"

"Well, well, of course, but you don't see. You don't see what he meant. It was clear to me. I mean he always, well, like I knew he was sad with Mom. He always tried to hold her hand, or pull her on his lap, stuff like that. And she wouldn't. I mean, he had a sad feeling, like he was hurt. I didn't want to be a woman either. I always was mad I wasn't a boy. They had privileges I didn't have and they acted like I acted only nobody got mad at them. I was a tomboy and my mother didn't like this. Neither did the other mothers. I could outfight anybody. When I was about four, I was playing with a doll. I was sitting on our front porch. There was a gang of older kids around. Boys. I put a piece of gum between the doll's legs to make it into a boy. And the kids laughed. I got mad. I took the doll over to the field and I pulled it all apart. The arms, legs and head. And I stuffed it under a pile of brush. I never played with dolls again. Ever."

"You wanted to be a boy?"

"Well, yes. Boys could do so much more. But then I also liked being a girl. I mean, to my Dad anyway. He didn't mind I did all the tomboy things but we both knew that I was a girl."

"What did it mean to you to be a girl?"

"I was special. Nobody thought I was special except Dad. And I knew it was because I was a girl. So I was glad in that way. When he said don't grow up to be a woman, I think he meant for me not to grow up to be the bad things a woman could be."

"Bad things?"

"Well, whatever. Not terribly clear what that is really. Maybe I got the feeling I was growing into a woman with 'bad things' when I was a teenager. Because then Dad seemed the same, but I was different. And I felt guilty toward him, like I was letting him down, but I didn't know, I got off the track somehow. . . ."

"In what ways did you feel different as a teenager?"

Slippery now, the ground is getting slippery and muddy, have to be careful. "I loved my Dad very much. I was so proud of him. He was handsome. All my girlfriends loved him. And he polished his shoes every day and sometimes wore black tie and tuxedo and had a stiff formal shirt. Handsome. But he still wanted to, he, he . . . I loved him but more like when he wasn't around. I mean, it was easier for me when he was at work and I could just talk about him. I mean when I was with him I was uneasy. He still wanted to, a, like hold me, or rub my back—like I was still a little girl."

"He wanted to hold you and rub your back?"

"No. I mean yes. Um—yeah—but don't, I mean. . . . I can't talk now. I'm too mixed up." Tensed up. Cove asked the question and it made me gag. He asked it funny. Arms and legs all tingling. Breathing too fast. Can't get a breath. Put my head back. Faster and faster breathing. Going to choke. I've got to get out of here. Why can't I breathe? Cove has made things bad again. He's watching me.

Can't get away from his eyes. Feel dizzy. Round light circling my head.

"If you slow your breathing, it won't be so bad."

"Get away from me. Stop! Stop!"

I put my head down until I'm not dizzy. I'm scared of Cove. I don't want to be near him. He's going to hurt me. I can think about him when I'm at home all right, but I can't be near him now. Have to get away. Jesus help me, Cove looks awful to me. I'm scared! Oh God, he looks like the dream I have. Oh Jesus, I have to get away from him.

"Try breathing slow and easy, Carol. Nothing is going to happen to you. I know this is hard but I think these are feelings you have to face and deal with."

"A letter, a letter. My Dad sent me a letter when I was in college and it hurt me. I never liked to read his letters, they made me feel awful."

"What made you think of that?"

"It just came back to me. I get so upset trying to explain to you how it was with Dad and me and I can't. I can't without choking. But I thought of those letters. Maybe they could explain how I was feeling. A letter would come in the mail and I wouldn't want to open it. It scared me the same way. I loved him but I couldn't be near him and the same with the letters. I hated them."

"What did the letters say?"

"Well, well, he usually enclosed a cartoon or two from *The New Yorker*. But his letters were too much for me. He said things like I was the only reason he had for living. Just awful things like that."

"I can see that might confuse and distress you. Did you keep his letters?"

"Yes, I think so. As a matter of fact, I think probably they're in our attic with my college stuff. Why?"

"It would be interesting if you could bring one in."

"Yeah. Well, maybe I can find them. Maybe not."

"You seem to be calmer now. You did very well."

"Yeah."

I love Cove now. He looks beautiful. I'll never tell him that. He'll never get that out of me. He looks familiar, he looks like my love. He doesn't hate me for being a shithead. When I stand up to go he comes behind me and smiles and he touches my arm. He touches me as if to say maybe I'm not such a shithead. Almost that maybe he might even like me. I don't know how that can be.

Wednesday, June 25, 1969

I see Cove tonight and he's going on vacation and I'm going to get serious with myself. I have let it go long enough. If I plan it right, then I can use him and he won't even know. I am in the bathroom and I have taken a good look at myself in the mirror. I have gone to the medicine cabinet and have taken two rainbows. Two. Now I need two and they don't last very long. Why do I have to make this decision while he's on vacation? Me, I will take a vacation from myself I guess. But it will be him. He's the one making the decision—even if he doesn't know it. I have to plan it right. If I have to sleep a long time it won't matter. Who am I fooling? Can't fool myself any longer. I am hooked on amphetamines. No one knows. Don doesn't know. I hide my pills in an old pocketbook so nobody knows. I was running out of doctors, now it could get tough with the new laws. Doctors aren't likely to prescribe them. I could call Mike for his black-market supply again but I'm going to do this first. It depends on Cove. I haven't told him about the amphetamines. Not a word. I just never told him. It started out all right when I wanted to lose weight. But that was long ago, and I lost the weight. And what happened? I want the high they give me. My mind clears and I'm optimistic and the world is right again for the short time they work. But now they're not working and if I don't take them my body is so heavy that I can't move my limbs and nothing looks good. What's happened to my nice pills? I can't understand. No more good feelings, just lots of awful jumpiness. So I have to drink so I can come down now. Drink that awful liquor and have Don mad at me for drinking. Oh, I see myself in the mirror. I have to face it someday and tonight I do what Cove says. I'm not going to tell Cove, but I'm going to sound him out ever so carefully so he won't even know. And damn him anyway, why is he taking a vacation? He's leaving me and I'll be all alone for two weeks. And not only that but the picture. Oh I'm mad about the picture. It's in a hospital brochure. Barbara Kelly is lying down on a bed with her hand stretched out to Cove and his hand is toward her. His left hand is on his hip and he has a worried look on his face. Oh stupid, ugly, dumb, disgusting picture. How dare he do that phony thing—and to Barbara of all people! I know all about her. It's sickening. He doesn't even know her and he'll end up liking her. And she isn't even a patient. And she has a pathetic look on her face. It makes me sick. And now Cove has to go on his stupid dumb vacation, meeting glorious sweet people and having sunny days every one. Oh, I hate him. Oh, I bet all his kids are perfect and he never has to go to the bathroom. And that's another thing. His glasses have slid part way down his nose so I can't see his eyes. I hate that picture. I hate him. I put it in my datebook by the phone with Scotch tape and look at it all the time.

I'll ask Cove if he'll prescribe a diet pill for me to lose weight. If he does, then I'll keep taking them. If he doesn't, then I quit. Forever.

I fill my green cup with water from his sink. I like the feeling that my cup is there all week, where I left it, among his doctor things. It gives me a feeling of permanence. Like he can't get rid of me as long as my cup is there.

I go in and sit down. Cove has on the same sport coat that is in the hospital picture. I feel a little mad at him for that picture, also I'm mad that he's going on vacation. I don't like this being mad but it's his own fault. Somehow he's made it so that I depend on him too much. I didn't know this was going to happen and he must have known because he deals with this every day, so it's his fault. He never told me.

"What was your reaction to last week's session?"

I'm not going to talk to him about last week. He wants me to talk about my father and I'm not going to. He's very tricky how he gets me talking. I'm forever slipping up.

"Can you see a pattern to our sessions? First a good one, then a bad one?"

I keep my eyes on the floor. I keep wringing my hands together. I'm mad inside and feel hard like stone. All this has nothing to do with my father or my mother. It's Cove who's making me act funny. It's his fault. I'm mad at Cove. No one else.

"Did you get a chance to look for your father's letters?"

"No, I didn't go in the attic. No. We have bees in our attic and probably bats. So I can't go there."

I broke my silence but only because it was negative.

"Do you think that there might be another reason you won't go to your attic?"

"No. I told you—bees and bats! That's the reason."

"I wonder if you are too frightened to find a letter from your father."

"No." Shit on him.

Silence.

I hate him for going away. He's not curing me. It's his fault. He's got this hold over me. He knew this would happen and he didn't warn me. So I have to come because I love him too. He didn't warn me.

"I shouldn't be doing all the talking and asking all the questions. You should be doing your share." Cove turns to the side and leans back.

"*Okay*. I'm not getting better. I pay you good money and now I want you to tell me what to do!"

I'm loud.

"In what way?"

"I can't get anything done at home and all I do is sit and think and I get very mad at . . . I'm wasting my life and I want you to tell me how to get out of this cycle."

"I can't tell you what to do, Carol. It wouldn't work."

"I don't see why not. I demand that you give me a list. List things, how I should act. You know how I should act, so why not tell me."

"If I told you what to do, you'd resent it. If things didn't go right you'd blame me. You have to do what you think is best."

"How should I act?" Louder now.

"I don't know how you should act."

"Yes, you do, you've read in books about what happens to people in psychotherapy. I mean, how mad I get at you."

"Do you want to talk about your feelings toward me?"

"No."

"Carol, are you upset because I am going on vacation?"

"No."

"It wouldn't be strange if you were. I'm not going to leave you, Carol. Are you worried about that?"

Silence. Silence.

"It seems that it's hard for you to accept someone's being nice to you. I'm not going to hurt you."

"Shit! I can't go on like this. I can't. I don't understand. I don't like the feeling I have toward you. I'm always churned up over you. You make me act funny. You make me swear and scream and act like a bitch. Other doctors, I never felt that way about them. But this, this . . . How come I can't act toward you like I do to regular doctors?"

"Carol, it's not the same. It's natural that you might feel differently toward me."

"Well, I want to end the whole thing. I'm not coming anymore."

"Would you like to discuss how you feel toward me?"

I shout at him now. No! No! Shit! I shake my fist at him and stand up. Cove looks at me and I see myself through his eyes. A bitch. I'm screaming at him and swearing. I'm doing it again. I'd hate a lady like that. I sit down. I feel defeated. Cove just doesn't understand all these things I feel about him. I don't either.

"I don't understand, Cove." I am weary. It's in my voice, my anger is replaced by weariness, defeat.

"Do you think that you might be so frightened of my going

on vacation that you want to reject me first so I won't be able to reject you? Does that make any sense?"

I bow my head. I'm so tired. It's hard for me to think.

"I think it's stupid and dumb for you to fly to Chicago. It's an awful thing for you to do. And I hate that picture of you with Barbara Kelly. I hate it. It's stupid. Never mind, never mind. I'm sorry I hate you. I don't hate you anymore. I, I—it's okay to go to Chicago, have a good time."

Silence. Cove wants me to go on. He has turned to the side. I can't continue my thoughts. I dried up my brain. But then I remember something. The amphetamines.

"Cove, I would like to go on a diet and was wondering if you would prescribe some sort of an appetite suppressant?"

Cove turns back toward me and looks surprised that I've changed the subject. My heart speeds up. I'm wondering what he'll do. He looks at his watch. It's late. It's time for me to go. Oh Cove, I don't want you to go. I love you. I want you to prescribe amphetamines so I can have energy to do things. I say nothing.

"I don't think it would be a good idea for you to have any diet pills. How about Weight Watchers?"

Shit. Damn. The die is cast. I've crossed the Rubicon. I have to follow through on my plan. Cove is going away but I have something good for when he's gone. I'm going to throw away the diet pills forever. I made the decision. Cove made the decision. I am a little excited about this. It is something positive, a good thing I'm doing for myself. All because of Cove. I've been addicted for nine years and now no more. Cove is good for me. He would be proud of me. One minute I'm an addict, the next I'm not.

I drive a little too fast on the way home. Don't want my good resolve to leave me. I head for my pills there in the old pocket-book. Don is asleep. I throw them down the toilet, all except one. I keep just one. I feel good with myself. Cove can have his vacation. He'd be proud, he'd like me if he knew. I snuggle next to Don. He'd be proud of me too. Sure wish I could tell them.

Thursday, July 17, 1969

I'm standing still now. I weathered Cove's vacation but I can't seem to muster my body into action. I feel stunned. I'm a mannequin. Can't move. Something is stopping me. I am frustrated. I can't talk to Cove. Something stops me from telling him my thoughts. This isn't good. Every night now I write in my notebook. I write all my thoughts down. My awful feelings. I can let them spill out on paper like Pandora's box. They are all about Cove, my God-Devil. They are wicked. I never read them over. The writing is the important thing. I feel better after I write them. I want Cove to know how I feel. Those things I can't say to him, I want him to know those things. I don't know what they are. I write them down and I forget them. But they are bad. I wonder if I have the nerve to give them to Cove? I couldn't. I put them in the car and go for my appointment.

"Hello, hello." His voice goes up and drops down a little at the end. He is pleasant. He smiles and seems glad to see me. I sure am glad to see him.

"Hi, Dr. Ashley, how're you?"

"Pretty good, pretty good. We had a good vacation."

Silence.

"Well, Carol, let's see. How are things going now at home?" Turns sideways.

"Oh, I don't know. It feels like I'm standing still. Almost paralyzed. I can't seem to get anything done."

"Can you get the meals?"

"Well, yes, most of the time. But I can't shop. Don has to do it all. It's really hard on him."

"How is Don?"

"He was really nice these two weeks. But it's depressing for me not to do my share of the work. I can't do anything. What is happening to me?"

"Before, you were burning your candle at both ends. Now you're burning your candle at no ends."

"That's exactly it. Nothing now, nothing. At least before, I knew that I was living."

"I think you've forgotten how painful it was for you when you were in the hospital. A lot has happened since then."

"I guess so. I have forgotten how horrible it was."

"It's like you are at an in-between place. You've left some of the past behind but you haven't reached where you are going. Sort of a no-man's land."

We sit quietly for a long time.

"Sometimes late at night I write things down on how I feel. You know I have trouble talking . . . and I was thinking maybe, um . . . you'd like to see . . . well."

"These things you write, do you have them with you?"

"Well, well yes, they're in the car. But Dr. Ashley, I mean these writings are gut notes and I don't remember what I said and they are bad, very bad."

"Are you afraid that I won't like you if I read them?"

"Well, yeah, sort of."

I'm looking down at the floor. I'm embarrassed but I think it is the right thing for me to do. I wouldn't have had the nerve but Cove talked nice and looked nice tonight. Not mean. He looks like my friend. He doesn't seem to hate me even though I'm bad, he is nice. I go down the stairs and get the papers out of the car. I'm afraid but I give them to him. They're on his desk. I can't look.

"Oh, by the way, Carol, did you go to the attic for your father's letters?"

"No. I told you I was afraid of the bats and bees. I really am."

Why did he bring that up? I get scared again talking about my father's letters.

"Maybe Don could help you find the letters."

"Maybe, I guess."

I leave soon. I can see a tough time ahead. I can see the opening of old wounds. What am I doing? Like picking at old scabs, scrapes, burns, snapping bones, cracking head, blood and punctures. I'll be sore and hurt. Maybe broken. Am I tough enough? Will I splinter? Maybe, maybe not.

Wednesday, July 23, 1969

I breeze through the dining room with my arms filled with curtains. It's about time I washed and ironed them, they're pretty bad. When I'm halfway through the kitchen headed toward the washing machine, I hear Don talking to Cove on the phone, and my insides flip. I hate him when he talks to Cove. I throw down the curtains and leave the room and stomp up the stairs to our bedroom. I feel overpowered. They want to keep me subservient, docile. They want me to be Nora in Ibsen's *A Doll's House*. They want to beat me down, keep me in line. Well, they're not going to win.

What's he saying to Cove? They're alike—they always act so nice and they're both so smart. I'm sick of it. They always talk rings around me and make me feel stupid. Well, well, I'm not completely dumb. I know some things they don't. I'm angry now and yet I'm alone too, the kind of alone you feel when somebody dies. When my father died. He died on me, he was trying to get me, I didn't let him even until the last, he never got me. Then he died. It was so easy. It's not hard to die, just one minute breathing air and the next gone away, corpse, not there any longer, empty shell never got me so I don't cry. I walk downstairs and watch Matt Dillon. Saturday night. Matt has amnesia, he has kissed a girl, he doesn't know he doesn't kiss girls but since he has forgotten, it's all right. See now, Carol, he didn't get you, even now he's being carried down the stairs on a stretcher. He's left you to get you, he did it on purpose.

I flop on my bed, my stomach hard as rock. I put my fist in my stomach, can't feel, can't feel. I get up and get my notebook. I ripped out what I wrote before and gave it to Cove. I must have been insane. He's probably read it by now and I can't remember what I wrote. Blank brain, can't remember. What did I write? Why can't I remember? I'm in for it. Oh Jesus. They're both after me and Cove is probably telling Don what I wrote. I hate them both.

I can hear Don on the stairs, he's coming in. No, he went right by the room, headed for David and Jim's room. I put down my pen and listen. I really want to know what they said about me. Did Cove tell Don that I'm a shithead? My anger subsides as my pen scribbles out the feelings. Don has opened the attic door and oh, I can hear him walking around for a long time. I am rooted for fifteen minutes, twenty minutes, thirty minutes. I know what's going on. Cove and Don are going to try to get me with Dad's letters. They don't know yet that I'm stronger than they are. If Dad couldn't get me even when he died, then Don and Cove can't. Let them try . . . now, oh, please, I don't care. I don't care. It doesn't matter, it doesn't matter what they do. I am alone.

Knock, knock on the bedroom door. Don asks if he can come in. No, I won't let him in.

"Go away, I know what you're doing. Go away."

"Honey, I want to show you something."

Fear. "What? What have you got?"

"Your old diaries from when you were a kid."

"Oh, oh really?" I open the door. Don looks nice again. I remember the diaries.

"No letters?"

"I couldn't find any. I looked through all our stuff. Probably you threw them away. But look at these great diaries. I bet Bill would like to read them. What do you think?"

"Oh, those diaries are really dumb, honey. They're so stupid. They're no use to anyone."

"Can I read them?"

"Sure, I mean they really are ridiculous. Here, look at this." I flip open to Wednesday, February 9, 1949, when I was thirteen:

Oh today was awful. I don't know why but I'm through with boys, I still love them, but I hate them. I'm all alone with girls that I don't like. I'm isolated. I don't think Ronnie and Jim like me anymore. I hate them. My motto "treat 'em rough." I wish I lived away from everywhere and all the boys hated me like Gail and so did all the girls. I wish I was just nothing cause nobody loves me. Jimmy doesn't (if he does, why doesn't he show it?). Neither do Mom and Dad love me. They aren't like other parents. They quarrel all the time and they don't love me.

Uh oh—trouble. I smell trouble. Gee, I can't believe I wrote that. The loving-hating business just like now. How awful, how depressing, how dumb. I feel stupid—didn't I ever grow up? I flip some more pages.

Sunday, March 13, 1949:
They don't like me. They hate me, but they all love Taza. Ronnie, Taza, Jimmy and I were talking. Ronnie told me Jimmy loves Taza. They only *like* me but I love them. Jimmy XXX Taza, Ronnie XXX Taza. Dennis XXX Taza. All of 'em. But no more. The boys aren't getting a hold of me. Nobody, nobody, nobody will.

Thursday, March 17, 1949:
Oh, I hate boys, all of 'em, period. Jimmy asked me to the dance and I accepted like a jerk for I feel something is going to snap. Jimmy did invite me but he doesn't like me, I know. I don't know what to do. Men are sneaky, lowdown, rotten-headed potato-brained bums, period.

Saturday, March 19,1949:
I just got back from the dance and I had a lovely time. Jimmy took me and Ronnie took Taza. Jimmy danced with me but he only picked me when Taza wasn't around. Jim really doesn't like me at all. He hates, hates, hates, hates, hates, hates, hates, hates me, but I love, love, love, love, love him.

There are three years of diaries Don and I read over. He thinks Cove would be interested.

I don't like to be reminded of that girl, Carol. I really hate her. I'd like to forget all about her—everything. She's dumb. She does stupid things. The diaries are mirrors to the past catapulting me straight back.

January 13, 1951:
Gee Gee kicked me in the head at basketball with her knee. My forehead is all black and blue. The swelling is going down. You should see her knee. . . .

January 30, 1951:
Didn't sleep much last night because my ankle hurt. I didn't go to school this morning but I did this afternoon because of Mom.

January 31, 1951:
My ankle is the same, wish it would get better because next Monday is our first game with Brentwood. . . .

February 1, 1951:
My ankle's a lot better. Mrs. Ford gave me rides today. . . .

February 2, 1951:
My ankle didn't slip out of place once today except at basketball practice. . . .

February 3, 1951:
Just got back from skating party. Jimmy didn't go so I didn't have much fun. Anyhow my ankle ached (still does).

February 4, 1951:
Tomorrow we play Brentwood High School at basketball. The nurse is going to retape my ankle so I'll be able to play. . . .

February 5, 1951:
Good news! We won our game 32 to 22. I made 17 or 19 points out of 32. No kidding. Rose made the rest. Rose was good, really good. It was just luck with me. Jimmy watched the game. I bet he thought I was a clumsy ox. I was. My ankle was all right until the last time out. Now it's murder. It throbs. . . .

I put the diary down and lay on the bed. Don rubs my head as he continues reading. I think about that girl in the diaries. She disgusts me. It's as if it's somebody else, not me at all. Just a cinema in color of that blond, chubby girl in the blue gym suit. She's very good on the basketball court but she puts herself down. She wants people to love her, to feel sorry for her. How come? Why does she go to such great lengths? Why does she act so? She has made many points during the game but there she goes. She's down on the floor, her left ankle has buckled. Down she goes. She's up, she's limping. Miss Hudson is talking to her. With two minutes to go, the game is over for her. She limps to the locker room. I can see her and I can hear her thoughts but I don't know her. The locker room is empty. She puts her hurt foot on the bench and removes her sneakers. She tests her ankle by putting weight on it. She is frowning. Is it because she has hurt her ankle? No, folks, that's not it at all. It is because she has not hurt her ankle *enough*. That doesn't make sense you say, well, you're right. No sense at all. She knows, too, that this doesn't make sense. She is as disgusted as we are. She has to do something and fast, before the game is over and the team comes in. We applaud what she does because she is so disgusting, she deserves the hurt. Let's punish her now. We don't love her. Let's gather around and urge her on. That's it, that's it, Carol. She's doing it now. She's doing it. She raises her hurt foot, pulls it back and swings with all her force, the foot against the bench. More now, more, more, until she can't feel it. Oh. She makes us sick. Sick. Will they love her now? Will they show her pity? Will her mother care? No! That's why she is so stupid. She thinks that now they will care. They don't. They will never care. We won't let her go, we'll keep after her. The girls come in the locker room and we can see that Carol wants to cry. Aha, we're not going to let her. We snatch the tears and dump them somewhere else inside her, like in her bowels. We'll keep them there a long time. I don't know if we'll ever give them back at all. Can't tell yet.

Thursday, July 24, 1969

I had to come for my appointment because of the power he has over me. But I am more scared than I ever have been. It's because of those notes that I gave him. I can't remember what I wrote. I'm afraid. Oh, what did I write? Did I say I hated him, loved him? I can hear him in his office with somebody else. He has the fan turned on here in the outer office so I can't hear. I don't want to hear. I want to leave. Oh Jesus, I have to go to the bathroom. The door's open. He'll hear me—I can't. But I need to go. Before my exams at college I always needed to go—fear makes this happen. When I was younger, too, before my dates I always had to go. Shame, shame. I'm ashamed. Jimmy rang our front doorbell. He sent me a rose corsage for the dance. Dad answered. I had blotches of red on my neck. I always got blotches when I was excited. I had to go to the bathroom, so I did. It was upstairs. I could hear Jim and Dad talking. I came down the stairs and saw them. Dad was joking. But standing right there, between us, like he didn't want me to go over to Jimmy. Dad says "Carol, go back upstairs and jiggle the toilet handle, it's still running." The blotches spread from my neck to my whole face. I had never felt that before, a new feeling. I wanted to take my fingers and gouge his face, destroy his mouth, rip apart his eyes and stomp him away, to kill, kill, destroy him. Stone, stone, no feeling. I go upstairs, heart beating fast, jiggle the toilet. Ashamed. Shame on me, I have to go to the toilet. Shame. Cove now, it's Cove. Cove must never find out that I go to the toilet. He must never know. But I am not thirteen any more. I am thirty-two years old and I feel hatred anew for myself for those feelings I have that I can't control. I can't make myself use his bathroom, yet I know I am stupid. Oh Jesus, what a mess. Out he comes with his stupid nice smile when all along he's read my notes and hates me. So the smile must be phony. Cove's phony.

"Come right in."

I slither into his office, head bent low, not looking. I slide into the chair by the wall. It's further away, he can't see me as well. The wall, too, protects me from him. The desk protects me. I bow my head. Face and neck all blotches of red. I put my hands over my eyes. Can't help it because of the shame.

"Carol, I think it took a lot of courage to give me your notes. I'm glad you brought them. So much of the time I wondered if anything we talked about was getting through to you. You'd sit quietly for long periods while I did the talking. It was hard to know whether we were getting anywhere."

"W-w-w-what?"

"It must have been hard for you—deciding to bring them in."

Cove doesn't hate me. I slowly take my hands away from my face. I sneak a look at him. I can come out now. He's making it easier for me to come out by swinging to the left.

"I don't remember what I put in those notes. I can't remember. I thought they were bad."

"Not at all."

Cove swings around and opens a small safe he has there in his office. He pulls out my notes. I don't know what he is going to do with them. They are like hot coals or like something obscene and ugly to me. I want to know what I wrote but not with Cove here. Oh Cove.

"You told me many things in your notes. You said that you wanted to talk about your father but were both relieved and disappointed that we didn't. Why is that?"

Silence.

"Maybe you forget things that are threatening to you, and erase them from your mind. Do you want to go over what you wrote?"

Silence. Me. I'm not going to talk. If I say anything, then I'm in trouble. Worse than I'm already in. I look at the floor.

"Are you afraid to read your notes?"

Silence. Cove is making me act stupid again, only it's different now. I'm not as protected as before. Before when I wouldn't answer him, he didn't know if I was thinking at all and now he knows. He knows I'm thinking about what we're talking about. It's harder to trick him.

"I-I-I w-w-w-want to-to know w-w-what I-I-I wrote." And then my eye twitched, I mean my right eye jerked and my whole head jerked.

"Will you read them?"

Silence.

Cove has opened the notes. No, I can't have him read them, no —no, please.

"Would you like me to read them?"

"No!" He knows I don't, he knows and he's doing this on purpose. Oh, he's doing this to hurt me. God damned shit. I hate him.

"Will you read them?"

"Yes, yes, yes!" I shout at him. The son of a bitch knows I can't have him reading them. He's tricked me.

Cove takes the notes off his desk and reaches over and hands them to me. I stand up because I can't stand what he is doing. I grab them from him and I throw them as hard as I can across the room.

"No!" I scream at him.

They scatter and flutter over by the lamp. I feel much better. Cove just sits there. He has put a candy in his mouth and he is playing with the wrapper. Crinkle, crinkle little wrapper. Shit, shit, shit. Cove baited me. Cove makes me so angry. He sits there playing with his candy wrapper and I'm dying. If I died dead on his floor bleeding and crushed, he'd sit there eating his candy and crinkling the cellophane and he'd say something like, "I think we should examine why you died, Carol, it might be significant." I sit back down. Cove leaves the papers on the floor. I sure as hell am not going to touch them.

"I thought maybe you'd do that."

"Then why did you let me, why did you push me so?"

"I wanted you to see how you avoid facing what must be faced."

"I'm scared, it's you in here. You're too close. I'm afraid. I can't have, you know—my throat hurts, you can't know."

"Know what?"

"I don't know, don't know—my thoughts. You can't know. Something, something, c-c-can't. . . . Someone leaning over me, me, no, can't get away. Can't, can't, no." Images come to my mind, my notes. I am stuttering uncontrollably. Cove read my notes. He's too close now, too close. He's bending over me. I'm in a bed. I shudder, my body convulses. A dream.

"Say it, Carol, say it."

No, no, no. I'm choking, choking, breathing in and out, gasping for air. Fast, fast, can't breathe.

"Say it, Carol."

"Can't breathe. Help me, Cove, can't breathe."

"Say it, Carol."

"Can't breathe." Lights dancing in my head, yellow lights. I take my hand and put it in my mouth and bite as hard as I can. I keep biting and tearing at my hand. I rip at it until the pain comes. Once I know I can feel again, the pain does that, then I can stop.

Cove stands up and comes around the desk. He's coming over to look at my hand. But I can't let him touch me. I can't let him near me. I throw my hand under my other arm and hide it. He doesn't come any closer. He's not going to get me. I won, I won, he'll never get me. I'm stronger than him, than both of them.

Wednesday, July 30, 1969

It's frightening thinking about my last appointment with Cove. I spend most of my time thinking about it. I can't figure things out. I feel weird, not normal. Cove has somehow got me mixed up. I mean, somehow he gets me to think things I don't like. I mean he's all mixed up with my father. I'm scared of him like that. It happens in his office often now. I wonder if he thinks I'm crazy. It's important that he doesn't. I wonder where the line is when you can tell if you're crazy. It's Wednesday, Cove's afternoon at the Counseling Service. I like to go down there twice a week to touch his car, see if it's there. Peter and Tommy come along, they're brown like berries. I wonder if Cove would like me if I lost weight. I want to be a normal person so much. I don't like thinking about myself so much. But thoughts, they churn away inside, bubbling like sticky, hot syrup, and when they spill over they're so messy. They touch all parts of me so I can't get away from them. Even at home, they spill out. Last night I had a horrible nightmare. I woke all hot. It was Cove. He was naked in a sleeping bag. Somehow he's making me think things by his dumb questions and now he invades my dreams. I don't see his car. I wonder if something has happened. His dumb car isn't around. Peter and Tom grab my hands. This is a bad place to cross. The North Street side of the municipal building is where Cove goes. I try to see through those basement windows. To get to the market it's easiest to go past these windows and across the lawn. I always have a little bit of fear that Cove might see me but that can't be helped. It's not like I'm spying. I sort of glance in the windows on the way by. Can't see anything. Where is he anyway? We cross Peters Road and go into Ralph's. I buy us orange popsicles. Good on a hot day.

On the way back across Peters Road there's a long line of cars. I'm startled, caught unaware. Right dab in front of me is the old S670 bus, Cove. He waves and smiles. He sees me eating popsicles with the kids. He sees me out walking on a nice day. I wave and smile. Oh glorious. I might even look like a normal person to him. It means a lot that he saw me doing what nice people do. Popsicles are so ordinary, so nice. Considering the fact that I might be crazy, I feel pretty good.

Sunday, August 3, 1969

We are camping at Clearwater Brook. I can't sleep. I'm trying so very hard to have fun. It isn't working. Katy and Paul Reczec are with us with their kids. I've been awake since four A.M. I take a walk to ease my jumpy muscles. Not working—something's the matter. Take a Thorazine. Fix breakfast for Don and the kids. Speak in clipped words as if I delay too long on them, something bad will come spilling out of my mouth. I hold myself in tight so nothing will escape. Everybody jokes and laughs and plans to go to the beach soon. A nice day. I don't like it. It assaults me because I can't enjoy it. Don and Paul and the kids all go down to the swimming hole. Katy and I finish up the dishes. I can't stop the fear. My limbs have begun shaking. Way off in the distance we hear a train coming. We know at the beach they will all be looking at the trestle and waving at the engineer. Train whistle makes me worse—I'm on the tracks and the train is coming at me—I see the light—my adrenaline flows and I can't move out of the way—here it comes, here it comes. But I'm only washing dishes, I'm not on the track. I scream and I can't stop. I grab the gin from under the table and take a big gulp. It isn't helping. My throat has closed. Katy comes over and holds me, she says she'll take care of things. She races off to get Don. I am rooted. I want to put my foot on the chopping block and take the hatchet and cut it off so I can feel. But I know this wouldn't be good. So I stay rooted so Don can rescue me.

Don comes and I keep saying, "I'm sorry, I'm sorry." He gets me in the car. Katy says she'll take care of the kids. I have to go to the hospital before it's too late. I feel a little better now I know that they won't let me take a hatchet to my body. Don calls Cove and I just wait in the emergency room.

I note if any doctors are around in case they have to do a tracheotomy on me when my throat closes. Nick Stebbins comes and Cove comes. I've calmed down now. I am ashamed to have let this happen. But I'm not sorry I'm in the hospital. It's not safe for me out there. I'm lying on the bed staring at the wall. Cove comes in and I don't even bother sitting up. I'm too low to even care if he sees me lying down. Cove puts his hand on my hand. I guess he isn't mad at me.

"What happened?"

I stare at the wall. Hard to talk.

"Is camping too much for you?"

"Yeah, I guess."

"Perhaps we should think about your going to the Springfield psychiatric unit."

"Do you want me to?"

"They might help you out."

"What do they do?"

"They have a program designed for people who are having difficulty working out their problems."

Cove wants me to go to Springfield Hospital. He and Don cooked this up, I bet. They can't stand me and now they're trying to get rid of me.

"You aren't going to treat me anymore?"

"Of course I am. Hospitalization would just be to help you over this crisis."

He's lying. He finally hates me.

Don and Cove talk in the hall. I don't care. They don't understand. I hate them. I go home soon and we wait for Cove's call. He's checking to see if there's a bed available. Don goes back to Clearwater Brook and gets the camper and gear. The kids will come home with the Reczecs.

I walk back and forth while Don's gone. I must be strong. What will they do to me there? They'll test me. They'll ask me the presidents. Quick, before I get too scared I look in Tommy's encyclopedia and write the presidents' names on paper. I try to learn them all from Nixon back to maybe Wilson. I can't concentrate, so I sit at the table and think of a sentence to help me remember. Never has there been a jackass known who is as enslaved by therapy as this ridiculous, horrible Carol in the hospital for the weird. That, I can remember. So the rest is easy. Never, Nixon, has there been a Jackass, Johnson, Known, Kennedy, who is as Enslaved, Eisenhower, by Therapy, Truman, as Ridiculous, Roosevelt, Horrible, Hoover, Carol, Coolidge, in the Hospital, Harding, for the Weird, Wilson. If they want more than that I'm out of luck. I also remember reading somewhere that to subtract seven from one hundred, and seven from that number, tests something or other. I was stuck on this because I can't subtract anything when I'm rattled. I figured that I can start with a hundred and subtract ten and add three. That's easy. I practice more on the presidents, memorizing my sentence. I can do it pretty fast now so I feel better. If they ask me proverbs I'll have to make up something. When Don comes in he says that Cove has contacted Springfield Hospital and I can go tomorrow morning. I sleep a little better figuring I have an edge on them all. I can subtract and I have the presidents down pat.

Monday, August 4, 1969

Don and I walk to the admissions office. We sit down and wait. I can't believe it, Cove and Don are actually going to leave me here. I suppose I should make a real effort to tell the truth and accept help. I look normal. Hey, admissions lady, do you think I'm normal? She asks me health questions and we laugh. They have a computer screen where my medical history is displayed for her to copy. It is quite fascinating until I see Cove's diagnosis—that hurts—it means I really am crazy. It's written down for this woman and anyone to see: "Depressive reaction, agitated type, moderate to severe. Passive-aggressive personality." Cove never used any terms on me. I never felt I was classified. Now I'm not unique anymore, I'm not special.

An hour later we are taken to my room. I'm ashamed knowing I have a passive-aggressive personality. I don't even know what it is. I have blotches on my neck. The nurse wears regular clothes, not white. She doesn't smile. She asks me if that is my suitcase. My old blue thing on the floor at my feet. She heaves it on the bed and opens it. I don't know what to do. I feel funny about her opening it without asking me. I have my things, my personal things that only Don has a right to see. I have gum and cigarettes and my notebook and pens and Preparation H and aspirin and combs and a note from Don—"I'll miss you"—hidden on the bottom; and my appointment cards going all the way back to March, when I started with Cove after the hospital. They are all together with a band around them. She is poking around my things. She takes the aspirin and Preparation H. She picks up my stack of appointment cards. I'm ashamed. Cove is going on another vacation and he gave me a time for when he comes back. I like to touch them. I like to see his writing. They made me feel a little safer. But now they don't. She asks what they are. I certainly couldn't kill myself with those, so she must just be merely curious—I don't know. I don't know how things are done here.

I say, "Well, my psychiatrist is going on vacation and he has given me an appointment for when I get back."

"Your psychiatrist is going on vacation?"

"Well, yes."

She puts the cards back and looks at me funny. I wish I knew how to act. She takes my razor and aspirin and Preparation H and leaves. I can't have those in my possession. I want to run after her and yell that she forgot my knitting needles. My knitting is in a little basket on the other side of my bed. But I don't think sarcasm would go with her. Why didn't she ask my permission? Of course,

I'm probably wrong. Here they probably do things different. Search and seizure rules and the rights of individuals probably don't apply. I begin to feel that I'm a nonbeing, an object. I worry about Cove's appointment cards. She scribbled in her notebook after she saw them. She doesn't understand that I've always done that with my love-hate men. I saved my childhood sweetheart's canasta scores, birthday cards, school work, things like that, anything that was HIS. It's the handwriting. I like the handwriting. Makes me feel close to them. Nurse won't know this. She'll think I'm weird. I have twenty-one appointment cards.

A nervous young man comes in and takes me to an empty room and gives me a physical exam. I think he must be a student but I don't know. I hope he is a doctor. He doesn't tell me.

When we get back to my room, Elizabeth, my roommate, comes right over to me. She looks scared too. Maybe everybody is scared around here.

She whispers, "Someone has burned down my house and every-thing I have is gone. They did it on purpose. I have no place to go. I am on the wrong floor. I am burned by the fire."

"How awful, are you all right?"

She comes over and stands at the foot of my bed. Don is rub-bing my feet. We are waiting for our first conference together. Elizabeth stares at us as if she doesn't really see us, so we don't say very much. She's maybe twenty-five.

The young man who gave me the physical directs us to the conference room. There are four men behind a table. They are sitting down and have pens and paper. Don and I sit side by side on the other side of the table. They aren't smiling.

"Why are you here?"

"Ah—well, I panic. Can't control my anxiety."

"What happens when you panic?"

"I feel like choking."

"Have you ever actually choked?"

"Uh, no."

I want to tell them that I wanted to chop my foot off. That I beat myself up and am scared I won't be able to stop. I want to tell them I'm scared for my life and I don't understand why I hurt myself. But my Don is here. My beautiful Don who loves me. It should be enough that he loves me not to hurt myself. But it isn't enough. It is wrong when I hurt myself. If I say it out loud for Don to hear, it will hurt him. He wouldn't understand and he will blame himself. I can't hurt him, so I can't tell these men. And that's the reason I'm here.

"Have you ever tried to commit suicide?"

"No."

I think now how I kill myself in little bits, a leg, a fist, then an eye. But I don't really want to die.

"Why are you here?" another man asks me again. They are young men, very grim.

"I don't know . . . well, I used to do lots of creative things that I can't seem to do anymore."

"What things?"—man number two.

"Well, like sewing, oil painting, um, wallpapering, rug hooking, stuff like that. And, uh, driving, shopping, like that."

"Why can't you do them anymore?"—man number four, black beard.

"Don't know."

"Why can't you sew?"

"Well, um, for example, it seems like my sewing machine jumps out at me and attacks me."

"Please repeat that"—number three has a Mickey Mouse T-shirt under his white shirt. I can see the ears.

"Well, I mean . . . no, I mean, that's just a figure of speech. I feel guilty because I can't sew anymore."

Oh shit, they're writing all this down and they think I think my God damned machine is attacking me. I've got to be more careful.

"Who is Dr. Ashley?"

"He's my psychiatrist."

"Is he really a psychiatrist?"

"Yes, he has an office in Chester."

Mickey Mouse and number two repeat at the same time, "Chester? Chester?"

"It's near Wharton."

"I have a notation here that your doctor is going on vacation. Is that so?"

"Yes."

The tone of his voice makes me uneasy. The questions seem accusatory. I must be imagining this. I'm scared, but along with scared, I'm mad. How dare they insinuate something about Cove? How dare they use that tone of voice? I haven't done anything wrong. Have I done something wrong? I don't understand the rules of this hospital. Who are these men anyway? Are they doctors? Maybe they aren't doctors or aren't any good, especially if they don't know Cove. I wish they had told me who they were. It's as if they have gauze masks. They're sterile. They have no names. I don't like anybody to be rude to Don. They didn't introduce themselves.

Mickey Mouse goes on now.

"Can you tell us today's date?"

"Well, August second, maybe third. Can't remember."

What a fool I am not to have noticed the date!

"Would you please list in order as many presidents as you can, starting with our present one."

Aha. They *are* doing the presidents. This is rich. I'll show these bastards.

Never, "Nixon," has there been a Jackass, "Johnson," Known, "Kennedy," who is as Enslaved, "Eisenhower," by Therapy, "Truman," as Ridiculous, "Roosevelt," Horrible, "Hoover," Carol, "Coolidge" in the Hospital, "Harding," for the Weird, "Wilson."

They are staring at me. I come to the end. I hadn't learned any more. I bluff, say casually, "Um, is that enough?"

"Yes, you may stop there," says Mickey.

I don't think they plan for people to know the presidents that far, so they look puzzled. Especially because I am so jumpy, itchy, and bouncy. Scared.

"Subtract seven from one hundred and subtract seven from that number and continue on." I do that easy.

"Could you explain what 'Birds of a feather flock together' means?"

"It means something like, ah, all you psychiatrists are alike." I chuckle a little. I can't help it. I think it's funny. They don't.

"Have you ever deliberately tried to hurt yourself?"

"Ah. . . ."

I want to tell them the truth or they won't be able to help me.

"Ah, well, I-I-I did, um, drop my sewing machine on my foot."

Don has been silent so far. Now he speaks. "No, no honey—that was an accident."

He explains to the doctors how it was an accident.

I bow my head. That day that Don and the kids were gone. Anger in me, anger against myself, picked up the machine and dropped it on my foot. Then I felt the pain. I felt something which was better than before. My machine broke. That's why I feel the machine is jumping out at me. I feel guilty and ashamed for hurting myself. The machine reminds me so I don't sew anymore. I told Don that it was an accident. If I insist now that it wasn't, then Don won't trust me anymore. It will make him look foolish. I wonder how I can explain this to them. I glance up. It doesn't matter now anyhow. They have believed Don. He is the sane one. I don't much care now if they do believe me. I feel muscles tighten, I feel like they don't like me. I feel closed in in this room.

They set up an appointment in four days for me and Don. They don't even ask if it's convenient for him.

Mickey Mouse shuffles his papers and organizes his notes. He might be their leader, I don't know.

"It seems that you have panicked because your doctor is going to be gone and you are using the hospital to babysit for you. What do you think?"

My face is flaming blotches. "That's just not true."

"Why don't you think about it?"

I bow my head. Bastards. They've shamed me. How can they

say that when they don't even know me? Why, we've just met. How can they say that? They can't be that stupid. Bastards. It's a slander on Cove. A reputable doctor doesn't send someone to the psychiatric unit unless there's a damn good reason. I take it all back, Cove, I take it all back. All psychiatrists are not alike.

Out in the hall I kiss Don goodbye. He looks very low. I'm sorry I'm here. I go back to my room. I'll take a nap. . . .

Elizabeth, my roommate, comes over and shuts the door all but a crack. She stands in front of my bed and looks out the crack.

"They are killing some babies down the hall."

"What?"

"Hear that screaming? They are killing some babies."

She peers out the crack.

I hear some groans down the hall. Elizabeth must think there are kids screaming. Oh Jesus, she's a fruitcake. I can't concentrate with her sneaking around. Jesus.

A while later I find out that they are setting up some kind of program for me. They have a schedule of what I do. A group walk outside. I can't go outside. Don't they know I panic? Will they make me go? I won't. I can't even get on the elevator without panic—I skip the walk. Then group therapy. I go to the room. It's too crowded. I'm afraid of crowds. I take the seat by the door. The door's open. I look at the woman next to me. The ash on her cigarette is really long. It drops down her front. The butt burns down to her fingers. She drops the cigarette. A man puts it in an ashtray. He tells me she can only have one cigarette an hour. She chain smokes and burns herself and her clothes. Someone closes the door. The crowd is too much for me. The shut door makes me feel like I'm suffocating. I go back to my room fast.

There is a note on my bed. I pick it up:

> Psychodrama   Thursday 1:30
> Conference Room
> Carol

I don't like the sound of psychodrama. I have no idea what it is. I don't even want to know. I decide then—the seed grows in my mind. I have to get out of here. Soon. Now. I'm not sick enough like Elizabeth and her burning house; and I'm too sick. Afraid to walk outside, afraid of group therapy and psychodrama. Fear. No place for me here. They're not like Cove either. They don't smile.

I watch TV for a while before bed. Can't sleep. They have a nice setup, a lounge with TV, a little kitchen to make snacks. All the patients wear regular clothes—the nurses too. There's lots of freedom, people walking around. A man asks me what I'm here for. I say I don't know. I go back to my room. The door is open a crack but the lights are off. There's Elizabeth again standing in the dark room looking out the crack. "They're killing the babies." I get ready for bed. I lie down. Elizabeth opens the door almost all the way. Then she goes behind the door and looks down the other direction through the crack by the hinges. Hell, I can't sleep with her standing three feet from me in the dark. It makes me feel creepy. I go to the nurses' station and tell the nurse that my roommate is standing behind the door. She says, "Nonsense. She's already had her nighttime medication. She's asleep."

She doesn't even believe me.

"Well, she *is* behind the door and it's keeping me awake."

I just stand there awkwardly. The nurse gets up and starts down the hall. What if Elizabeth has gone back to bed? God I hope she's still behind the door or I'll never get out of here.

She's in bed. That helps me with my decision. I'll leave here tomorrow. I'll talk my way out. I'm too scared here. It's too overwhelming. They have set up these programs for me and they don't even know me. I have no one to talk to, to get to know me. Psychodrama, psycho-drama. Even the name scares me. Reminds me of Alfred Hitchcock's *Psycho*. No. I've got to get out of here.

I fall asleep, exhausted.

Next morning, me to nurse: "Could you please tell your leader that I would like to speak to him. Now, if possible."

"Is something the matter?"

"No. Well—yes. You can tell him I have given his words a lot of thought. Thank you."

Three P.M. Mickey Mouse walks in. I smile, I calm down my limbs. I act humble, ingratiatingly so. I tell him what he wants to hear. I tell him.

"I am very wrong to take up a valuable hospital bed. You are right, you are right. The hospital is just babysitting while Dr. Ashley is away. I have to face up to this. And, especially, to my responsibilities to my husband and children. How silly of me not to have seen the truth. It had to be pointed out to me. Thank you. Thank you. I would like to be released immediately to make room for someone who is really sick."

"I'm glad we have helped you to come to this decision. I'll sign your discharge."

"Thank you so much."

I'm making myself sick. It's so phony. I leave the room gracefully and fast. Jesus, what a place! I call Don and I am checked out in two hours.

I was there just one day. Twenty-four hours. It was too much for me. I was too scared to stay. I didn't understand their rules. I tricked them all. I won over them. I am pleased with the way I talked my way out. How clever of me. I'll never go back. Don doesn't think I'm clever. He's not amused.

Wednesday, August 20, 1969

I feel pretty good. Cove is back from his vacation. I am in one piece. I have outwitted the hospital. I am clever. They didn't get me. I can see Cove now and we can talk nice, as it should be. I will go back to normal. It is warm, hot in his waiting room. He has exchanged the fan for an FM radio with silly music. The windows are open. Good to be back where I belong. With Cove. Out come Sally and Walter Stotz. I heard they were having problems. Now I know. We talk about the weather and laugh. Looks like a storm. They wonder about me. I wonder what they've heard. Oh, here's Cove. A haircut. He looks good. I missed him.

"It didn't work out for you at the hospital?"

"No, I hated it but I tricked them. I told them what they wanted to hear and I got out."

Cove stops smiling. "Do you think that was smart?"

"Well, yeah—I mean, I didn't like them. They weren't like you. They didn't trust me. They scared me."

"Do you think it was that you didn't trust them?"

"Of course I didn't trust them. They were not letting me even say things."

"I don't think you trust very many people, Carol."

I look at him. He's serious. He doesn't think I was clever. Now I can't tell him either. He stares at me. How can I explain. "Don was in the room and I . . ."

Pause. I can't tell Cove about the sewing machine either.

"Uh—they searched my luggage and, ah, uh . . ."

"They do that on all admissions, as a precaution."

Cove isn't listening to me now. He hears what he wants to hear. I forget that he's one of them. He disapproves of me. He hates me. I look at the floor.

"What did you go to the hospital for, Carol?"

Now he sounds like them. I get angry and tight. And loud.

"They didn't listen to me or know me. I tried. But they told me I was there because you were going on vacation. They said my duties were at home. They wanted me to go to psycho-psycho-drama, whatever the hell that is. . . ."

"You didn't tell them very much about yourself, did you?"

"No, but I wanted to."

"You didn't give the hospital much of a chance."

I'm frustrated with Cove. He sounds angry. Cove doesn't get angry. Now he is. He thinks I'm a shithead. I won't talk about the hospital. He doesn't understand. My cheeks are hot. I want to hurt him.

"They thought you were a quack."

Pause.

"Given the situation as it is, that you couldn't stay in the hospital, I guess we have a lot of hard work ahead of us."

Cove didn't even say anything about those doctors that didn't know him. He doesn't understand. If *he* doesn't, then no one will. I hate him and his God damned haircut. He thinks he's so great with his ordered life. He says he went swimming before breakfast when he was camping. Oh la de da. So perfect he is and his ordered life doing the beautiful people things. Shit, shit, shit.

"Why don't you go back to peeping in windows?" I guess I told him!

Cove laughs. That makes me madder. I can't even insult him. He's not human. I won't talk to him ever again in my whole stupid shitty life. I'll sit here and glare at him and feel nothing and I won't talk. It serves him right. I am stone so I can't be touched. I'll teach him a lesson.

Cove sits square at the desk, right in front of me, his arms on his desk. I'm in the wrong chair. Too near him. I was feeling good when I came in, now it's too late to switch chairs. He looks right straight at me, in the eyes. I glare at him. A battle is coming.

"Let's get busy."

Silence. I'm not talking, you shit, so go ahead, get busy. I'll beat you. I glare.

"Why do you think of yourself as a shithead?"

Glare. Go to hell, perfect Cove. Silence.

"Do you want to suffer?"

"Do you think all men are bastards?"

Glare, silence. Only you, you bastard Cove, who got to me. Bastard. Shit.

"Do all those men deliberately hurt you?"

Silence. Glare.

"Why do you get hurt?"

Nothing.

"Do you want to get hurt?"

Silence, madder, fury coming. Fury coming. Try to keep it back. Did this before. On a date. It didn't work, couldn't hold it. Hold stomach.

"Would you *like* to have more comfortable relationships?"

With who, with who, with who, you? Where, what? Can't, can't, too late. I was walking home from a dance with Jimmy. It was a summer night. I was fourteen. I wanted him to kiss me. It was only nine-thirty. I had a whole hour for him to kiss me.

"What can you do to break the pattern?"

Cove sitting forward, words loud, cutting my ears, like Van Gogh, slicing off my own ears.

Dad drove up in the car. He smiled at Jimmy and me. He said he'd drive us home. I stared at him. Bastard, fury. Don't talk to him. Get away from me. Don't spoil me. Don't spoil my kiss.

"Do you think there is a pattern to this or just a series of bad men by coincidence?"

Bad men? You are there staring at me. I stared at my Dad. He ordered me in the car when I wouldn't move. We got to the garage. No words, no reason. I scratched his face. I dug my hands into him. His face white in the moonlight. I hurt him. I'm sorry. I'm sorry. He made me do it. He's dead. Who is here? Who is this? Who is he?

"Why do you feel the need to be punished?"

Stand up—can't stop—hate him here, Cove, awful. Pick up my water, green cup. Throw it on the floor before too late—get away from his face before it's too late. Water running on the rug like blood down a face.

Sorry, sorry, sorry, bad girl. Have to hurt myself. Tear out, Cove after me, he stops. I slam door. Run down stairs. Fall—make myself fall last four steps. Have to. Feels good, the hurt. Cove on top of stairs. Go left, running up the hill. Go, go fast. Take a left. The storm has come. I see heat lightning. I want to get to the swamp. Chester swamp. Want to get to the bog and walk in the mud and rub it on my face.

I don't care anymore. I've run too far, too fast. I don't care about the swamp. There are too many mosquitoes and my energy is gone. Fury gone. Left only with shame. Shame and guilt and wondering. Do I want to change? Do I want to be happy? All I know is I don't like it here on this back road, my sneakers muddy from the rain. My knees hurt from the fall. I don't want the fury when it means I'm alone on an August night and tripping down a dirt road clutching my diaries from long ago. With my Don and children living, going ahead leaving me behind. Me, dodging shadows behind me.

Thursday, August 28, 1969

I've got to do something about this Cove business and these sessions. Me acting like a God damned fool. Acting this wild way more and more now in his office. I want to get away. Where can I go? Cove calls Don, and Don gave him my childhood diaries. Let's see now. Let's take stock. Dig in my heels. Slow down. Cove didn't get me to cry though, so I'm all right. I wouldn't give him the satisfaction. Have to go back to see him. I must be a masochist. But no. I have to see him. He's beautiful. Oh so beautiful. So nice. I want him to touch me. I think of him all the time. I want him to like me but he's not involved. He probably wouldn't notice if I missed an appointment. I want to touch him, but I don't want him to know about it. Maybe if he was asleep . . . if he knew about it, then he'd have too much power to kill me with. I'm more or less safe if he knows I hate him. Oh, did I tell him that? Yeah, I think so. I get mixed up. Boy, I really love Cove from a distance. That's it. But can't, up close. I am mixed up. I think of his body a lot. I think of him swimming. I wish there was some way I could love him or even watch him without his knowing. He must never, never know the love. That's like the crying. I am frustrated because I never can watch him in the office because he'd see me watching him. Sometimes I sneak looks. He has this green sweater that's furry. Most of the time he wears pants and sport jacket. And that boring, boring brown and yellow geometric-design tie. But I love his corduroy slacks. Sometimes I can watch him when he is concentrating on his nails. I used to hate that. He'd take his clipper out and fiddle with his nails. I felt then that what I was saying was boring or dumb. But I discovered that while he was doing that I could look at him easier, without being discovered. He has this brownish-blond hair that looks good when he's hassled, not so neat, more comfortable.

Don't know that much about his eyes. The color is hard to tell, maybe a cross between green and brown. See, it's hard to look that directly at him. I almost never do. Maybe I could catch the color of his eyes if we were discussing the weather or some such thing. The eyes bother me. His glasses drive me crazy. Lots of times they slip down on his nose just enough so the top of the frame blocks his eyes. Hate that, not seeing his eyes. Also, the light in his office sometimes hits his glasses wrong and all I get is a reflection. I think maybe I'll wear my sunglasses for my appointment this evening. I could just pretend that I forgot to take them off, then I could spend all that time watching him and he wouldn't know I was doing it.

I don't know what's going to happen. Oh Jesus, those stairs, maybe he didn't see. Oh, why do I do all these things? All that trouble with me out on the road, Cove calling Don, Don taking the other car, trying to find me. I'm not going to think of it anymore. That's in the past. I hate the past.

I especially want to appear very, very normal to him. Maybe he'll think I am. Don kisses me goodbye. I'm to call him when I'm done and he'll pick me up and put the bike in the stationwagon. I get on my bike to ride to Cove's. I think riding a bike looks normal. It's a beautiful evening. I am conscious of my "normalcy," and feel good. I have lots of energy. I'm going to see my beautiful Cove. I haven't been out all week. I have to walk the bike up the hill but speed down it. I park the bike over to the side toward the path. He won't see it, so I'll have to slip it in the conversation about my riding over.

The door from his house opens. A woman comes out, wearing blue shorts. Oh God, it's his wife. Cove's wife. Oh Jesus. I'm sure he's told her about how stupid I am and what a shithead I am. So now she knows what I look like. She says that Cove will be a little late. I panic now. His wife—he really is, I knew he was. It's all right though, being married. Unlike Barbara Kelly and those awful women patients of his, the wife is all right. I mean, I don't feel bad about her for some reason. He *is* married. It's all right that he's got this woman. That's the order of things. I relax when I get this straight in my mind. I smile at her. I say that there's no hurry because I couldn't gauge how long it would take me to ride my bike. She says, "You rode your bike out here?"

"Yeah, it's a beautiful evening."

We smile and she leaves.

Oh, I hope his wife thinks I'm normal. No telling what pictures she has in her mind about me. I whip off the sunglasses. I feel ridiculous with them on. So much for watching him. I've chickened out. I know his wife sings in the church choir. I check the paper every week to see where her rehearsal is. Jesus, I suppose she leads the perfect life like he does. Beautiful people, with church choir on Thursday night. I suppose he teaches Sunday school too. Jesus.

These feelings I have for Cove, the ones that make me want to watch him secretly, the ones where I see his neck, the lines of his shoulders, the slope of them. How his standing posture is a little hunched over, head tilted down, hands in pockets, listening very hard, absorbing what is being said. Something not right about these feelings. They permeate me. I want him to take me in, protect me. These aren't right because it's different from being married. I like being married. I love Don. It is right. But it doesn't eat me up, swallow me, like this does—like Cove does.

Don's washing my back in the tub. That's reality, that happened. That is my love. So what is this other? Where does it come from? Why does it take so much of my time and energy? Why Cove? What has he done that I feel this way? More and more. His hands, clean and long, purposeful. His hands always careful, no wasted motion. They know what they are doing. Meticulous. No grasping, tearing or drumming. Calm, like they could soothe. Oh, scary too. They could caress too. Yes. That's why they're scary. They know what to do. It makes me weak and frightened. And the fear makes me hate him. I hate these feelings for him. I don't know where they come from or why they are here. I resent them. Why do I have to spend so much time thinking of them? They make me weak, trembling—desire so deep it scares me. I desire him. I don't like to think so. I like to think I am strong. I know I love Don. It doesn't seem to be a matter of that at all—has nothing to do with Don. So I feel the feelings, like they've taken over the insides, without my control. And then there's the anger. I'm mad at Cove, all the time, mad at him. Does he know I have these feelings? No. He must never. But one side of me thinks he must be trained to know and he didn't warn me and it's his fault I am trapped. I'm furious at him. But I don't fight off the feelings so well anymore. It's because I don't want to. It feels good now, this desire. It's good in a wicked way. I want him. If I see him now I want him physically. I want his baby. Proof to me, something. If I had his baby, then it would be all right again. The feelings would go, disappear. He wouldn't have his hold anymore. His hands, his legs, shoulders, neck, head tilted down. They scare me. I wish I could tell him this, but I never can. It would destroy me. And if he is evil, then he will kill me. I can't take the chance. So I keep coming here. My insides feel his presence until I have to turn to stone. I can take the hate, the hate from myself, but I can't take the love feelings, the desire. I have no idea what to do with it, where to put it. I'm beginning to learn that the love thing has something to do with my crying. Now I'll never cry. The tears might make me so soft, I'd reveal something—the love or desire. It might get loose there in his office. Can't let it escape. It might destroy me, send me back even to the place these strange desires come from.

Cove comes in from his house. Takes a lot of strength out of me not to be completely honest with him. I fight against his pale yellow shirt, short sleeves.

"Hello, Carol, you look very nice tonight."

Silence. I love you, Cove, I love you, Cove. Don't talk like that, please, don't be nice to me because I can't take it. Head down.

Silence. Can't say anything.

"It was kind of a difficult session last week."

Silence. Oh Cove, Cove, hold me, please don't let me go. I love you. Please help me, help me. Don't talk nice, don't, because I don't feel strong enough to be cruel to you much longer.

Silence.

"Can you tell me why you were angry?"

"I was mad at myself for . . . I don't know."

"Mad at yourself?"

Silence. Oh Cove, I still think you're handsome and I love you even if you're making me think. I forgive you. Silence.

"It looked like you wanted to throw your water at me, not at the floor."

"I was mad at myself, not you. I'm a shithead."

I did want to throw water on you, Cove, to stop you, but I forgive you for making me want to do that.

"Were you mad at me because you thought I was displeased about your leaving the hospital?"

"No. I was mad at myself for disappointing you."

"Did you think that I would stop seeing you?"

Silence. Head bowed.

"Maybe the hospital was going too fast for you."

I wish Cove was an old woman. Then I could talk better to him. His maleness gets in my way all the time now. It makes me angry, and it also makes everything so confusing.

"You make it hard for me to talk with you."

I say this but I smile because it sounds funny.

Cove laughs and we both laugh.

"I'm hard for you to deal with?"

Cove laughs again. I put my hands up in the air, delighted that Cove laughs. If he didn't wear those pale yellow shirts he'd be easier to deal with.

"Sometimes you, too, can be difficult. Very difficult."

"Me?" We laugh again.

I say, "I sometimes wonder what you think of me, I mean, what you really think of me."

I'm a little weakened at saying this. My fear increases. I'm inviting inquiry into this scary area. I put my face down again. I want to know.

"Would you believe me if I told you that I think you are . . ."

I throw my hands over my ears and he keeps talking. I hum softly. Moonlight and Roses. I can't hear what he is saying. Mustn't hear good things.

". . . you can't accept good things about yourself or you would listen to me. . . ."

Moonlight and Roses . . . humming. Silence.

Don't wear yellow and don't be tan and don't look kind and don't say nice things. You're breaking me down. This way is worse than the other. Keep the tiger chained, vicious, all these bad feelings. Better, better, better. Feel lump in throat, a crying feeling. So much easier to hate you, Cove, than to love you. So much easier. It's better for me to throw my water on your floor than to throw myself at your body. Silence.

"Don brought me your old diaries, and I have read them over."

"Oh? They're dumb."

"I don't think so. In fact, I am amazed at them. I think they are worth talking about."

"You do?"

I sure as hell wouldn't mind talking about them if Cove wants. Nothing can touch me there, those memories are dead.

"It's okay with me, if you want."

"Some of your words are the same words you use today in running yourself down—'fat slob,' and so on."

"Well, it's only that it was as true then as it is now. That was the way I was then, fat."

Cove thumbs through some pictures Scotch-taped to the back.

"Is this a picture of you?"

"Oh yeah, it is."

"You don't look bad to me."

"Huh?"

"You don't look bad to me."

Oh, so that's the game he's going to play. The one-two get-her game. Okay. I'm adept at that.

"I am."

"We'll go into these next time." Cove smiles, and closes the diary.

"All right." I smile, warming at the sight of him.

We head for the door, I have my appointment card in my pocket. I call Don for a ride home. Warm August night. I tell him on the way, as I put my hand on his arm, that I'm truly sorry to have so many pent-up feelings with no place for them to go. It's okay with him. He takes his responsibilities seriously.

Saturday, August 30, 1969

I don't want to go, I don't like to go anywhere but I want to, too.
I will try, for Don. The hospital dance at the Inn. We go to
Dorothy and Allan's for a buffet dinner. I'm pleased with the way
I'm trying to act normal. People don't know what to say to me.
They know I've flipped and come to a standstill. They avoid me.
I wish so much they would treat me as normal but they can't.
There's a little circle of air about three feet around me, people
studiously not crossing the invisible line. Is it fear that what I have
is catching? Don sticks near me so I'm not alone. They talk to him.
It's going better. My, how nice everyone looks. Betty comes over
and asks if I'm feeling better and says how she thinks Dr. Ashley is
a nice man. At the mention of his name my blood starts moving.
She knows him maybe as a personal friend. They both live in Chester. I wonder how she knows him. Does he talk to friends? Does he
have friends? What does he talk about? What is his wife like? I put
these thoughts out of my mind. It's not true that he's like a regular
person. So I won't think about it. Don holds my hand the whole
time except when we sit down to eat. He's my connection with the
world that moves around there outside of my thoughts.

We all move en masse to the Inn. We're slightly late, for the
dance has begun. I'm glad because the ballroom is filled and I can't
be trapped in that crowd. They set up extra tables outside in the
other room and we sit there drinking and chatting. I am much more
relaxed. I have on my long red gown with a new necklace Don
bought me. I look nice. I cleaned the garage with him this afternoon, so I actually accomplished something. I got dirty and now I'm
clean. Almost like a princess. Another party comes in late and they
set up tables across and to my left. It isn't dark in the room like
in the ballroom. We see everyone coming in and out and get to talk
to people we know. I dance with Don. People must know I'm all
right, coming out and dancing and all. My dress is low-cut but
not too much. Don holds me very tight. We go back to our

table when it happens. May God help me, he's here! He's at the table out here in the light, the group that came in late. Katy and Paul are with us. I let out a strangled sound, involuntary. Don sees. He laughs. I want to get out of here, but it is too late. Cove waves. Cove has walked in here to the dance. How can I deal with this? Got to have a drink. Blood starts up and races like Clearwater Brook in the spring. I sit down with my back to them, change seats with Katy. Can't watch. Might be struck down. It's impossible for me not to react in this violent way. I can't help it. I'm so afraid. Spontaneity is gone. I pretend to talk and listen but I can't help it. I can't dance anymore. I feel my skin getting red. Blotches are appearing. Another drink. I've had enough to drink because the room gets a little hazy. Cove goes by. I see his back go by to the dance floor. He's with his wife, in a long skirt. I see his arm swirl off into the darkness. I can relax a minute. Collect my thoughts. Whew.

"Don, what am I going to do? Cove is here."

"Oh honey, don't get so uptight, for God's sake, relax."

Another drink. He doesn't understand. He's right, of course, but I can't. I'll just sit in this chair, I won't move. I won't dance anymore. I'll wait till Don takes me home. It's like with Jimmy, my boyfriend when I was young. He made my blood race downstream too. He had this same hold over me that Cove does. I wish now the dance floor was brighter so I could watch Cove dancing. There's a chance I'll see him and watch him and he won't know. There he is, there he is swinging away like a regular person, but what's this? What happened? I can't understand. How could he do this to me? Oh awful, awful. It's not his wife at all. He's dancing with someone else. My God! How can he? Not only that, but it's Helen Krump. How can he dance with her? I can't watch this blasphemy. He actually has his beautiful body wrapped around Helen Krump. Oh, what an ugly thing. I can't take it. Don thinks it's funny. And he thinks I'm funnier when I tell him. I think it's disgraceful. How dare he dance with anyone but his wife? How dare he do this to me? I'm very disappointed in you, my Cove. And you confuse me with these deeds. What are you trying to do? Why don't you go back to your office where you belong? Why don't you sit behind your desk? I want you to be like regular people but you aren't. What are you trying to prove? Are you trying to destroy me?

I have another drink. I sit and think about my beautiful Cove, prostituting himself like that. If I can't believe in him, what can I believe in?

Water, water, I've got to have water. I go to the fountain and gulp it down. The dance ends and another starts. I weave through the crowd, back to the safety of the table.

"Hi, George, oh Margaret, how nice you look. Hi, Evelyn, oh Evelyn tell me later. Well, hello there, Nick; sorry, can't dance, Herbie."

Collapse in the chair. Safe. Katy looks at me. Don looks at me. Tap on my shoulder. Can't move. Don't dare look. Tap again on my shoulder. Sit still. Don says, "Hi, Bill," and laughs. Katy says "Hi, Dr. Ashley," and smiles. They are facing me and my back is facing the tapper. He says, "Would you like this dance?" Me, I say sure, just like that. I turn around and stand up. I knew it was him all along. I wanted it to be him and there he is. Cove just asks me to dance as easy as pie. We go to the dance floor. It's loud music so what he says to me is carried away as by a howling wind. The sound deafens my ears. Is it real sound or is it my blood? Oh, Cove, this is not my fault. Don't you see I don't understand? His arm is around my waist and I feel it through my dress. It's a real hand. His left hand is holding my right. I have touched him. The very first time I touched him. Cove is dancing with me and he's looking over my shoulder. I'm afraid to touch him like this. I am afraid of him and I'm afraid of me. There should be his precious desk with the claw feet between us. Protecting me from him and him from me. My father had a tuxedo and it was handsome on him. He was tall, the shoulders are the same place to my nose. When I was little I'd go up to my Daddy's stiff starched shirt and go tap tap with the point finger. It wouldn't dent. I loved him like this. I put my left hand up now on Cove's neck. I caress the back of his neck. I touch his ear. When I went to the Fall Cotillion my Dad asked me to dance. I was very afraid. My ears heard the same blood storm. I didn't do the tap tap like when I was a little girl. I wanted to get away. I wanted to cry. Oh please, oh please, put back the desk. Oh please, let me go, don't hurt me, please. But it's Cove, beautiful Cove. It's not my father at all, how silly of me. Those drinks are mixing me up. Cove is here, and I love Cove. I have to do it, don't you see? There's no desk and he's pretending to be real. I pull him to me and I put my cheek on his with my hand on his neck. Poor Cove, poor Cove. But I can't help it. I can't stop myself. I have to see if he's real flesh. I have to keep touching him to make him real. But it doesn't work. I can't anymore. I let him go. I keep touching his neck but it doesn't work. I want to make him human so much. I want to make him a man who is just dancing. I can't do it. I've failed. He is still the God-Devil for me. I'm sorry, Cove. I'm sorry. But you tricked me. You almost tricked me into thinking you were a human man all by yourself but you're not. You're surrounded by my whole family. They come dancing down with their starched shirts in the vortex of the blood storm and they are going to hurt me somehow. And they've attached themselves to you. And even if you try to walk around like a regular human man, you can't. They've given you the same power. So that's why I have to touch you like that. Caress you. To test. I'm sorry if I embarrass you. I'm sorry and ashamed. But you tricked me. You might fool everyone else. But not me. It's back to the office for the both of us. Have to keep you there with the claw-foot desk between us. I know who you really are.

Thursday, September 4, 1969

"Were you all right after the dance on Saturday night?"

Head low. Ashamed. "Yeah," softly.

"This is such a small town, Carol. Things like this are bound to happen. I think I put you in a very difficult position."

I sneak a look at him. He looks okay now he's back where he belongs. I can take him better here in this office. It's funny because I never before thought the office was safe. But now I feel the safety. Anything that happens here is all right.

"I thought about it before I asked you to dance."

I don't want to talk about this. I want to forget the whole thing. Cove keeps on.

"If I hadn't asked you to dance, I think you would have felt that I purposely avoided you."

"Yeah, you bet."

"I was in a bind. I'm sorry if it embarrassed you."

I don't want Cove saying anything at all about what was right or wrong. It was me, after all, that acted like a shithead.

"I'm sorry, Cove, about—well, ah, you know."

Cove doesn't hate me for what I did. I relax a little.

We sit quiet for maybe ten minutes. If he's waiting for me, I'm not talking.

Cove turns to the side and reaches for my old diaries there on his bookcase. He puts them on his desk.

"Could we look at these?"

He picks one up. I pick another. Cove has marked some pages. He reads to me from the one in his hand. " 'Friday, April 8, 1949. Jimmy said he could beat me up, and I said he couldn't. So after school we had a friendly boxing match. I hit him in the jaw *hard*. Taza and I looked at him afraid he was hurt. I wonder why I hit him so hard. He didn't groan or anything, just stood there and took it like a man. Taza and I agreed that we both would like Rudy and not Jimmy and Victor but inside I can't shed him off my thoughts. He was so brave when I hurt him. . . . I wish Victor wasn't moving away. I love Jimmy now.' "

Cove and I look at each other. I feel funny inside.

"I've forgotten that these things happened. It's very strange to remember."

"Can you talk about this?"

"I think so. It's—it's like it was somebody else and not me. I see that little girl. She seems strangely familiar but it's not me."

"Can you tell me about this Jimmy and Victor that you mention so often?"

"Oh, Jimmy, was my boyfriend from age twelve until I left home. He could do no wrong. I loved him and I loved Victor too. I loved them in that strange way. In that section you just read, that was like a typical afternoon. It was always happening."

"You mean the boxing match?"

"Well, yeah, I mean I didn't really want to hurt the boys but I did in a way. I always thought of them as, as—like cowboy heroes—I wanted them to suffer—I mean, I mean. . . . I don't know what I mean.

"One time we went in back of Jim's house, Taza and Jim and me. He built a hut back there. He has such strong muscles. He smells a little bit like Campbell's tomato soup. I am afraid of him because I'll do anything he asks me and Jimmy knows this, the jerk —no, not jerk, I love him because he is different. We go in the hut because our mothers might see us. Taza's mom doesn't like her to fight. My mom knows nothing; besides we live across lots on the other road. Taza is the referee. I want to see Jim cry but I never will because he's so strong and handsome. I can throw Ronald's hat in a tree and he cries off to his mommy. I don't want to see Jimmy crying that way but the other way. The crying because of inside hurting. Hurting awful. That's what I want to see. Like the brave cowboy that is shot. Jimmy hits me some but not too much. He knows his power. His hands are gentle. I hit him in the jaw. I feel sorry about this but he is so brave. He doesn't cry. I know he must've felt the hurt. My insides get funny. We go outside and we tip my bike over in Jim's driveway. I like being at his house. It's a powerful house. Every window has meaning. I love everything about him. My stupid bike is broken. Jim knows everything about bikes. He's put his old green fender on mine. Mine got smashed. Jim hands me a link from the chain from his bike. He polishes it. Black on the edges with shiny loops. I keep it in my hand. I love the link. He gave it to me. Taza has to go. I push Jimmy on the shoulder. I love to touch him like that. He races around toward the back. We go way back past the hut to the dirt road Jim's made for the bikes. I can't catch him. Suddenly he stops and I go plowing into him. I fall over on the ground. He falls on top of me. I struggle to get away. He's trying to pin my shoulders. I turn this way and that. I can't get away. He has both my hands pinned to the ground on each side. He's going to kiss me. He knows he can. I'm going to pretend that I feel nothing. I stop struggling. We see Victor riding over. I'm mad. I want Jimmy to kiss me. But Victor is moving away. His parents are divorcing. We sit in the leaves and tell secrets. It's like they bind us together because Victor is moving. Jimmy, Victor and I. Victor lets his fingernails grow long. I don't like long fingernails but I guess it's okay on him. Victor whispers a secret thing. He says that he keeps his fingernails in a box. He carefully cuts them and puts them in a special box. Now he wants to know my secret. I tell him I was only kidding. I don't really have one. Victor is mad we don't tell him a secret. We wish he didn't tell us his. I jump up and I kiss him goodbye. And I run home across back lots. Jimmy and I never talk again about Victor.

"One time Taza called me all upset. Jimmy's dog was killed right in front of her house. Oh that's so awful, terrible awful. I race out of the house in the dark. I race to the back of Jim's house. I climb the tree. I can't see him. His bike is out front so he must be home. I crawl through the leaves up toward the house. Then go to the cellar window. There is a light on. Jim is down there. He is sitting on a couch. His head is in his hands and he's crying. My face is flushed. My stomach feels funny again. I push my hand up and down, up and down, on my stomach. I'm sorry, Jim, I'm sorry, but, oh, oh. This is my secret. Oh. I can't tell you about it because I don't understand it."

It isn't too hard telling Cove about this girl. I just think along and just tell him these things. I see her. It's like a movie with lots of voices crowding in. I'm a narrator, only a bystander after all.

"Do you think maybe that Jimmy was an ideal to you? I mean an idol?"

"I guess maybe. It was the first boy that she felt this way about."

Silence. Cove reads another. " 'Tuesday, Feb. 22, 1949. Taza and I are going to be blood sisters. I was trying to draw blood but couldn't. I asked Jimmy to prick me with a pin. He did and drew blood. I love Jim. I got fifty convertibles so Rudy and Taza were trying to get me to kiss Jim all day. Later he came up to me and said kiss me. I tried to kiss him. Oh, I hate boys, all of them, period. I feel something is going to pop in me. Jim, Rudy and Dennis got in my closet, the dirty bums. I'm sick of everybody (boys, boys), I only like Rudy a little bit. I ate over at Taza's, at dark we blinked our flashlights over at Jimmy's. He answered back. When I left

Taza's I talked with Jim. I'm still sick of boys, boys, boys. We talked about how loud our fathers snore. Things like that. Dad came after me. He always comes after me. I escaped through the back lots. I am listening to Bob Hope. Hi ya, Mort. Put money in the pot.' "

"I remember. It's mixed. Lots of love, hate. Seems so normal to that girl. Doesn't seem strange. The day before Taza and I helped the boys with the paper route. And I saw fifty convertibles. That means I have to kiss and marry the first boy that speaks to me. Jim was coming up Elmore Street, I knew he was, I had it all planned. Jim spoke to me, which meant I had to kiss him. So today Rudy and Taza keep after me to kiss him. After school, the four of us walk home. Jimmy throws ice chunks at my legs. I don't even feel it because my legs are too cold. I have blood on my legs from the ice. I don't mind the sight of blood, there. The boys might love me more if the ice chunks don't bother me. So I somehow don't feel it. Taza doesn't like ice on her legs so they don't do it to her. I chase Jim around Elmore. He circles through the woods and goes away. I don't care. . . .

"I go down Concord past Lenny's house. I think about Lenny and his mother. I shiver. Lots of things bother me. Things I don't know about. Lenny's house is off limits because of his mother. She doesn't go out of the house. Sometimes we sneak by at night and we see a cigarette glowing in the dark window. I hurry by. I feel like crying. I don't want to go home. I see our house through the back lots. Home scares me because all these things are so mixed up. One time Nina, Lenny's sister, told me her mother had bleeding from between the legs. We were over on the swing set. She said her mother had this. Nina had lipstick on her teeth. What a liar. I don't think Nina should talk about her mother that way. I hit her and ran away. Now my mother makes it hard for me to go home. For three days now I have bleeding between my legs. I thought I cut myself but I couldn't see any cut. I'm always cutting myself and bleeding from something but I can't find any cut. My mother catches me in the hall. Nobody is around. She has a strange look in her eye. She asks me if I want to tell her something. I wonder if maybe she knows that I kiss Jim or something bad I did that I don't even know about. My eyes go down, back and forth. I always do things wrong. I don't know. She has a straight line on her lips. It's something bad all right. She doesn't say anything, she just takes me upstairs and hands me two safety pins and this gauze bandage and says wear it on your pants and don't take baths and keep the box here, way back in the closet so nobody can find out. My face burns with shame. I am so bad. Bad girl. I am bad. My brothers don't ever make that line of straightness on my mother's mouth. Now I've done something bad. Maybe when I push on my stomach it makes me bleed. I don't want to be strange, please somebody tell me I'll be all right. . . .

"I don't want to go home. I go over to Taza's. I can't tell Taza about this now. I want her to still like me. I decide to make Taza my blood sister because I love her. If we have a pact she won't be able to leave me. We get the pin but now I'm afraid of blood. I'm afraid to jab the pin. That other blood scares me. Will I have to wear the bandage all the time? I'm afraid to prick my finger and so is Taza, so we go up in Taza's room and get her dad's flashlight and blink the special code to get Jimmy's attention. Jim's house is diagonally across from Taza's. Lucky Taza can do this anytime she wants. Five blinks in a row stands for "Jimmy." He almost always answers, which means he's watching for us. Jim and Taza and I stand in Taza's garage. I hold out my finger and he pricks me. I don't mind because it's another way for me to hold his hand. Taza's mother tells her to come in from the garage. I don't think she likes me too much because I'm always wrestling. She can whistle like nobody I ever heard before. She even whistles Beethoven's *Eroica*. We know exactly where she is because she always whistles. I wish I could do it. Quickly Taza and I rub our blood together so we're blood sisters. Taza is beautiful. I am so ugly. She knows so much more than me. She has talks with her mother too. They tell each other little things like what happened during the day. Her mother lets her pick out her own clothes, and she taught her about shaving her legs. Maybe I can learn some things. That's how come I like to hear what they talk about. Maybe I can unmix myself. Taza's mother bought her a bra. I want one very badly. She even takes her to the doctor when she is sick.

"Jimmy and I leave. I want Taza's mother to like me. We go toward the side and stand mushing the snow around to make ridges. I ask Jim if he gets along with his mother. He says yeah. Jim says that his father snores real loud. I say that my Dad doesn't snore. He wouldn't do anything like that. Jimmy wants to know how come my Dad always comes around when we're together. Like he doesn't want me to be out of his sight. I don't want to think about my father too much. I ask Jim if he's ever heard Taza's father play the mandolin? He says no. Taza's father leaves Taza alone. So she likes it when he is around. Me too. I ask Jim if he has a grand-mother. He says yeah, she lives in Colorado and she's pretty old. Taza has a grandmother who lives in Connecticut. Genivieve. Taza can even call her Genny. Genny bought me bell earrings for Christ-mas. They tinkle. Genny likes me because I'm Taza's best friend. I tell Jim that I have a grandmother but I never saw her. I guess my mother doesn't get along with her. I tell Jim my father's father was a policeman and people tried to change him from being that and he died. Jim tells me that his father can pee twenty-two feet. I think of my father then, how I stand behind my bedroom door and watch him naked in the bathroom. I don't want to think about this or anything about my father—he always comes to me and I watch him and I can't go home because they're there and she thinks I'm bad and he's always watching me and I want to be Taza. So I scream at Jim. Liar! Liar! Liar! Liar! And I leap at him and punch him. He holds my arms down to my sides and I try to fight him. A light is on us and we freeze in our tracks. Still, frozen. Dad. He has driven up the driveway and we never noticed and the motor is off and the lights are on. It only takes us three seconds and we leap apart. I go backward, backward. Always have this fear, fear of him, so I turn around and run across Taza's back yard, across the next yard, have to beat him home and get to my room. Jim tears away. I cross Elmore Street and run all the way. I make it to my room. It's always like this—me being afraid of things I don't even know about. I'm so bad. I close my fist and I hit my eye. Five times, ten times, then I stop. I go get them—the earrings that Genny gave me—and hold them in my hand and I cry. I put my face under the pillow and wonder why I am so bad. I feel better now so I can roll on my side. I unclench my fist and I look at them, so pretty. Golden little bells. The gold and sound make me feel better."

"It sounds like you were a lonely little girl."

"I dunno. I mean. I guess my childhood wasn't as happy as I thought."

"Did you hit yourself a lot when you were young?"

"Um—yeah—I mean when I talk about her it's like it's not me. Do you see?"

"I think so. It sounds like you were afraid of your father."

"Well, yeah. He scared me. When I was doing—when, I—well, sometimes. . . ."

"Does it scare you now to think of him?"

"I can't, can't think."

"What were you afraid of?"

Don't want to talk to Cove, put my hands over my ears but hear him coming through.

"Do you want to tell me about it?"

Starting to choke now—it was going all right—now he's making me choke, can't talk to him, scares me. Stand up because I have to get home fast. Am caught, he thinks I'm evil. He keeps staring at me. Watching me. I'm not safe near him. Don't want to see his lips form obscene words—yell at him.

"You're making something bad out of this between me and Dad. You're doing it, you're doing it! Stop it now. Stop it!"

I shudder, I gag in my throat so now all I can feel is choking.

"Help me, Cove. I can't stop choking. Please help me so I won't die. I can't breathe."

"Nothing is going to hurt you, Carol. Breathe slowly now, like this, now breathe slower."

I copy him. He'll save me. I watch how slow he breathes and he looks calm. He won't hurt me. I feel better. He looks nice again, looks familiar to me, not like the other. The other, when he carries the masks of them around. But now he's put them in his pocket for a while, it's Cove again.

"I'm sorry, Cove, I can't help it. Don't know how this comes on me."

"You said in those gut notes to me that you really wanted to talk about your father and that if we didn't you were sorry."

"I didn't say that, I didn't say that. I don't know why I would say such a thing."

"I have it right here."

Coves turns.

"No. No. I can't now. Is it okay if I don't?"

I'm too tired. I can't take any more about my father. I want Cove to like me. But he won't if I don't talk.

"You don't have to tonight, but I think . . ."

I interrupt him now. I can tell him so he'll like me and be proud of me.

"I gave up the amphetamines some time ago. I decided to give them up because you didn't prescribe them. And I haven't taken any since."

There, I told Cove. I shared my success. Now he'll be nice because he can see I'm really good.

Cove looks at me straight. He has a puzzled look in his eye. I forgot that I never even told him I was addicted. He looks wonderingly at me. I bet he'll even like me now. I'll bet he'll think I'm brave. And he won't watch me anymore. And he won't be out to get me.

Wednesday, September 17, 1969

Cove had another week off. Now he's back. The next time he has a vacation I'm going to cancel my appointment before. Then it'd be me not seeing him instead of him not seeing me. He probably went away thinking I was all better after I told him about the amphetamines. He said I should tell Don about them. Well, I'm not going to. I hate Cove. Maybe I won't talk at all tonight unless he's really nice to me. Oh God, I'm so glad he's back.

"I was reading in your diaries that you had clarinet and piano lessons."

He reads from the diaries: " 'Wednesday, October 5, 1949. Dodgers lost 1–0 against Yanks. I had music lesson and after supper practiced instead of in the morning. Then went over to Taza's. We listened to records. A new one, *South Pacific*, is very good. We went in Jim's woods and climbed, at least tried to climb, a tree. We snuck up and saw Jim in the window. He was pounding his chest and giving himself nosedrops.' "

"From when I was very little I wanted to play the piano. I saved pennies in a shoe box. When I was seven my mother told me she would pay half for a piano. So I counted my money and wrapped it. I had fifteen dollars. I remember going to the bank in the city. I was walking along, I could feel my underpants loose. The shoe box was in my hands and was heavy, so I couldn't hike up my pants. I saved for such a long time for this piano so I had to make a decision. Spill the money or let my pants fall. My pants fell.

"We put the piano in the living room and my mother painted it white. Sitting on the chair I could see out the window on my right. I started lessons right away. I loved them. Sometimes I looked outside the window and I saw the Browns' roses climbing on the fence. Piano lessons filled me up. My scary thoughts just vanished to the wind. My Dad always listened to me play. I got better and better. His face would look dreamy if I looked at him. I decided to practice in the morning, early before anyone got up so no one could watch me play. It was a habit to play every morning from six to seven. The world was new. Everything quiet except my piano. It was always fun for me. When I got a new piece to practice, I had a feeling of something nice to do. Like opening a present. I studied for eleven years.

"One morning I stopped practicing early and I pretended I was a little fairy and I set the morning breakfast table—as if no one would know who did it. I felt wonderful and whole. Then I would go outside at the dawn and I'd make a new circle in the driveway for our next marble game. When I was old enough and good enough I went downtown to the conservatory of music. My teacher was a little man. He wore a black suit with a flower. He never raised his voice. He taught me how to do things right. Just so. To get the music perfect. I like that. I like to do that now with wallpapering or knitting or with anything. Mr. Dannik was about five feet tall. He spent summers in Tanglewood. Once when I was studying Chopin my assignment was to go to the Bible and look up a passage about the right hand not knowing what the left was doing. That's how Chopin works. One hand moving around completely opposite the other, doing crazy things. I thought it was marvelous. I used to sit in the outer office with my homework in my lap waiting for my lesson. Once he stepped out and praised me for using my time in this way. I was very thrilled that such a nice man praised me. In the room were two grand pianos and oriental rugs and this little meticulous man. It made me feel clean and whole and special. Nobody could get close to me when I played. I took myself off and for that short time was happy. Almost like some kind of creation."

"That sounds really very nice. You had a special thing."

Cove is pleased I'm talking.

"Do you and Don have a piano?"

"Yes, Don plays quite a bit."

"You must still get satisfaction out of playing yourself."

"No."

"No?"

I bow my head. Hurts me to say this.

"I can't play. . . . My fingers shake, stomach hurts when I try. An invisible barbed barrier comes down between me and the keyboard. And when I listen to others I want to play so very much. It all comes back, the joy it was. But I sit down and my hands won't. . . . That's why I don't care about my hands anymore. I hurt them, bang them on things. I don't care what happens to them. They betrayed me. See how ugly?"

I show Cove my ugly hands. Ugly knuckles. Cove looks at me.

"How long since you've not been able to play?"

"I don't know. A long time. . . . I think since about that time— when my father was sick."

"Were you punishing yourself by stopping?"

Silence.

"You've never told me much about your father's death."

Silence.

"Once you told me that you didn't cry when your father died. That seems strange."

Silence. Too scary.

Cove switches around and grabs a diary and opens a page that is marked. I take a lot of gulps from my water.

Cove says, "Let me read you this passage: 'Friday, March 24, 1950. I wish I lived far away from here. Nobody loves me. Neither does Mom or Dad. Dad is mad and he never understands and he never will. The only thing good about today was that Taza taught me how to blow on my hands to sound like an owl. I can almost do the whole scale. A man, Guy Westfeldt, a friend of Dad's, is awful sick. He's been in a coma for two days with a hemorrhage in his brain. He has a fifty-fifty chance to live. But isn't that awful? He's Dad's age. Dad may be next. Oh, it's awful. I love Jim.'"

"I worried about Dad getting sick. I read the deaths in the paper to see how old they were. The people who died. Sometimes I maybe felt it would be easier for me with Dad not around. Sometimes I thought maybe . . . well."

"You mean—about if your father died. . . ?"

I start choking again. Hands go for my throat. I'm angry at Cove. He's awful, what he's doing to me. I start to tremble.

I came home from college to see my Dad, made myself do it. They came to the door to greet me wondering why I chose that day. Dad is sick, so sick. How can this be, no one in our family believes in sickness. No doctors, sinful sickness. He isn't really that sick. I haven't had to put up with his visits since his sickness—don't say that—bad thoughts, love him when he's away. Can't take him near. "Carol, go up and see your father, he's asking for you." Too much fear. I go to the top of the stairs and don't turn into his room, go to the right, to the bathroom. His door is open. Can't do it, can't see him helpless, inert penis, can't. Go into my bedroom trembling. Can't see Dad. Dad wants me and I desert him. He won't die after all, he'll never die. Go downstairs, they are gathered. "Did you speak with your father?" "Yes." Brother goes next. Comes down, looks at me. Father is dead all twisted on bed, dead on bed, leaving me, Dad leaving me with them, no one to love me ever again. Father did this to me on purpose because I didn't answer his letters. He did this because I left him. He needed me, nobody else loved him. His ears were ringing and his clothes got too big and he couldn't eat and I wouldn't go to him. I wouldn't soothe him; even dying, I wouldn't see him. Now dead, away, gone, body. I go over and I turn on the television. It doesn't matter that he's dead. Nobody will get me now, nobody will make me cry, break me down, no tears for me. They bring the stretcher downstairs, body dead, banging on the railing, tipping slightly. I turn toward TV. Matt Dillon gets shot. Glad he's dead, glad; he was going to get me. Now Cove is after me, it's not Dad at all, Dad is dead, it's Cove, he's the one. I hate to think of Dad this way. Cove is making me do this and Cove is making me love him in the evil way. I am so sad my father is dead and Cove is now my problem. He brings Dad in, to cover up all these things he's tricked me into feeling for him. My eyes flicker and the right one twitches. I gasp for air. Cove is watching me close, sitting forward on the chair, elbows on the desk. I'm a bug pinned to a board.

Cove then raises his hands into fists and he scrunches up his face into a tiny hard twisting thing and he doubles over into a ball.

"Look at me! This is what you do. This is how you look. This is what you do to your emotions, Carol. You twist them all up, then hold them down inside."

Cove looks ugly. That's how I look.

Gulping for air, twisting like a bug. Hatred for Cove coming from my bowels. Throat shut.

Cove tightens his body all up again to show me what I do. Makes me mad, doesn't he know I'm helpless? And he imitates me. Cove sits back and puts his hands together, fingertips touching. He puts his foot on the corner of the bookcase.

"You know, Carol, I think maybe we should take a look at where we are going and what should be done. I think the both of us should come up with a decision on the best way to proceed. We have spent many hours where nothing has been accomplished."

"We have? I'm so emotional, I don't see how you can say nothing is accomplished."

"You feel so many things and you think many things but you

don't let *me* see them. It doesn't work unless you include me. No wonder you have no energy left. You use it all up holding it all inside. You never learned to express sadness or disappointments."

"Well, I don't know what to do."

Cove is serious.

"You make me feel cruel, when I push you—and you say I'm wishy-washy if I don't. But it isn't my dilemma, it's our dilemma."

Cove waits, watching me. I've got to talk what I'm *thinking*. I can see the wasted hours, the loss of hope, the continual bad feelings. I put my head down in my hands and think. Oh, do I dare? Will I die? Can I do it? I don't think I have any choice. I must go ahead with this. If I say yes to him it's almost like a commitment to him and him to me. I don't want this surgery. It hurts me, but I say, "We've got to go ahead. No matter what. We have to, but I don't want to."

Cove and I sit quiet.

Cove turns and faces me straight. Green eyes.

"Tell me about your father, Carol."

"Oh, I . . ." Panic hits.

"Tell me about his dying."

"No! Ah. No."

Put my arms on my head, turning back and forth, no place to go.

"Stop! Stop! Please stop!"

Hate overflowing. Stand up, raise fist over head, bang down on precious desk, over, over, over again, bang fists, awful hands. Destroy precious desk.

"Talk about it, Carol—stop hitting—say it."

He isn't going to stop. He's getting me, big air-water bubble sliding past. Knotted throat, escaping to the outside, hits the outside and bursts into words.

"You! You! It's you. I love you, can't help it."

Hear words vaporize in air but hanging, hitting his ears. They escaped out of me like that and caused all the others to rush out, like throwing up—only it comes in tears. Strange tears. Never cry, never cry but I'm crying. Put my head in my hands bent over beside desk and can't stop crying. Nothing can make me stop. Water running from my nose and eyes, pouring on my clothes, and I still can't stop. Father dead and I loved him too much and I'm sorry he's dead. Oh my father, you died. I'm so sorry. I miss you my Dad, I loved you. I can't stop tears. Come rushing into present day. Cove, telling Cove. It's him I love, can't help loving Cove. So sorry, sorry, sorry. Dad loved me, gone now, dead.

Sobbing slows down, then mind goes back to dead, and my wailing starts the dirge music, the Indian wail, the mourners in black, the watchers of the dead, the souls of dearly departed, the funeral pyre, they join me, boost me up with their hands, rejoicing in my mourning. The tears making rivers, washing away unmourned souls of the past, washing them into the light, into the present so we can place them ever so gently, kindly and sorrowfully into the eternal grave. Can leave them there—where they belong.

Dominus vobiscum. Dominus vobiscum. So the crying stops and so do the dancing lights in the head and away the choking, gasping and twitching. Away the shame away, the hatred—flown away. Carol is finally quiet and Cove and she sit quiet.

"Are you all right?"

"Yes."

Thursday, September 25, 1969

Cove called Don when I drove home. He told Don that it was a good session, a breakthrough. A breakthrough all right. He finally broke me down. I felt no shame. How come? I didn't feel put down. How come? Don holds me, likes me—soft after crying—not hard concrete. Likes what Cove does. Me, all confused. How could I be wrong about crying? I had no choice. I just couldn't hold out any longer. Want to get away. Feel I have to go away somewhere. Shaky. Stops pulled.

"Don, is there any way I can get away? I feel loose, scattered, unable to stay here."

"Try to hold on, honey, we need you. Bill said this was a breakthrough. Maybe things will get better now."

"But I don't feel better, I feel worse. Something is happening. I don't know, something is changing, crumbling me away and I can't stop it. I'm really scared like I want to go away for a while."

"We'll think about it some more later."

"Okay."

I don't want to be so disorganized in my thinking. Thoughts flit here and there. Cove this, Cove that, Cove this. Dream this, dream that. Cove flitting in and out, first one face and then the other, mixing the pot, stirring it around, all scrambled. Want to bang myself around, a little for not getting supper, a little for no laundry and a lot for feeling bad and for creaking to a halt. Want to put myself out to pasture, just for a while, so I can feel some kind of control in my actions. Crying good for me. Somehow good. Can't face more of it. Can't face more of Cove. Why wasn't I destroyed? Have to go back now and see what to do. Mustn't tell him everything. Must always keep secret part of me from him. I must fight him harder. I can see that now. I wish I didn't have to fight so.

Wednesday, October 1, 1969

"You never really grieved for your father."

Cove, nice-looking, kind man.

"I'm mixed up about you and Dad."

"Can you understand loving your father and also being glad when he died?"

"Afraid, that's why I'm afraid of him—afraid of him touching me. One time walked through the upstairs hall. His bedroom door open, him standing there with no clothes. Eyes met, rooted, stared at each other. Afraid of powerful instincts coming at me. My naked God there with large penis. Too much for me. Couldn't handle—couldn't handle." Choking, gasping, inhaling too fast.

"Why do you think you have these powerful emotions after all these years?"

"No, no, no. Can't think, can't think."

I already cried for my dead father. Leave me alone, Cove.

"Carol, what happened between you and your father?"

"No! No! No!"

I stand up and shake my fist at Cove. Defiant.

"Don't say any more." I yell at him.

"I don't have a crystal ball, Carol. I don't know anything you don't tell me."

"Nothing, nothing. Ohh—can't think." Sit down.

"Did anything happen?"

Square at me.

"Don't know, don't know. Maybe ah ah, hurts me."

We sit.

"One time, ah, ah, Dad took me camping with my brother. It was real cold, and dark, and my brother was asleep. I couldn't sleep because I was too cold and my Dad hiked to the car and got a bottle of brandy and gave me some brandy to warm me up."

Skin jumping around, choking, Cove waiting for me, not letting me stop, making me go on, watching. Cove protecting me. Cove hurting me.

"I was in my sleeping bag and I was too cold so my Dad got in the bag with me—don't remember—nothing. That's all awful all."

"How old were you?"

"Fifteen years old, I woke up in the morning and I threw up behind a tree, I threw up and threw up behind a tree there—awful, I couldn't stop."

Pulse racing—can't catch up with the thoughts.

He keeps on.

"You told me once, Carol, that you had a dream of me in a sleeping bag."

"It was only a dream. Nothing to do with my Dad!"

"No connection?"

"No, stop! Stop!"

I stand halfway up. I clench my teeth and my fist. My heart and insides are pounding. Cove doesn't move at all. Cove sits right there. Have to stop Cove. Pain too much, going down the precipice—

fast, sliding, no control. I tear to the right and past the desk and I'm blinded in rage. I raise my fist and smash it down on Cove. Not enough. He grabs my arm, I scream, "No! No! No!" to make sure he notices me so he won't ever talk again. Rage at him. I hit him again, again, again. On his body, shoulder, there, have to smash him for doing this to me. Smash him with my fist for not loving me when I was little, for not protecting me from my mother. Smash him for looking at me funny in the eyes, sexual thing, smash him harder, harder for that. For making me want the baby, smash him so he'll never move. Smash him, kill him for dying on me. Smash him, yell at him. I hate! hate! hate! hate! hate! hate you! Smash him for making me love him. There, I got him. I got him. I can hurt him like he hurt me. It's flesh. I got him. Mind then stops dead, blank mind. Body grabs Cove by the legs. Slumping down to the legs, afraid to let go. Cove's hand placed gently on head breaks everything down and away. Makes the dam burst loose with tears. Long-time tears. She's exhausted.

Eyes flicker open. All out of focus. Things are askew. Everything sideways. I'm holding on to something. A hiking boot with a green sock. I'm holding it very tightly. Cove, human Cove. I crossed over the edge and I came back again. Cove makes it easy for me then. He asks me, very gentle voice, if I'd like to go back and sit down.

"Are you all right?" Cove nice again.

"Yes." Tired, tired, want to sleep.

Sit quietly for a long time, just thinking. Me and Cove—human.

"Cove?"

"Yeah?"

"What was that question you asked me?"

"I don't remember."

"Well, don't ask it again."

Thursday, October 9, 1969

I climb the stairs and go to the bedroom. I've made macaroni and cheese and banana Jell-O so I feel I can leave. Don is worried about me. I am worried too. I do nothing these days. The supper is a major chore. I put all my energy into the simple supper. I sit in the chair with the door shut. It's all I do now, just think. Rock and think. I have the kitchen knife in my hand, I'm a sad person. It's sad for me to think that I swear and scream and pound and hit. I don't like to think of me like this. My insides are hard. Stomach a knot. I have some kind of awful idea of cutting the knot out of my stomach so I can sleep again and care for my family. I dredge myself out of the chair and I look in the mirror. I see green eyes. Those are me. I wonder how come I hate to see myself? How could I hate this person so much? What has she ever done, really, to deserve such hatred? She doesn't look so bad now, does she? Have you no pity on her? Why is she so ugly to you? See how she rails at herself. But she can't help it. I hate the sight of her. Don't want to ever see her again. She's disgusting, gross, a bitch. Look how she can't do anything. Look at her disgusting body. She's evil. Has evil thoughts. She loves her father in an evil way and her mother hates her because her mother knows this, knew this when she was born. And she isn't any good for her children. If she loves her children, how come she can't take them to the dentist? How come she wants to be alone all the time? She wants to think about Cove. That's her doctor that she screams at, and hits with her fists. That's the doctor she loves in the evil way.

And her husband, taking care of those lovely children, what does she do about him? He goes and works all day and comes home and reads the little ones "Christopher Robin has sneezles and wheezles" and he tries to touch her and hold her but she draws back. The rock in her stomach. She isn't good or nice for any of them. She is bad for them.

She goes downstairs into the cellar. She pushes past the junk, past the sump pump into the back part, with the washing machines.

No good for anyone. She's no good. Awful. It'd be better if she died. Better for everybody because she's so disgusting. She slides down between the washer and dryer and curls in a ball. She holds the knife at her stomach but it slips down into the cobweb corner. She's so tired that her fingers can't hold it. She's so stupid she can't do anything right. Anything. She repeats over to herself singsong thoughts. I gotta get away, I gotta get away, I gotta get away. No good no good no good. Her eyes are a little funny because they stare and don't focus. She pushes herself in the corner curled and she thinks of a rhyme.

> *Rockabye baby*
> *On a tree top,*
> *When the bough breaks,*
> *the baby will fall*
> *the baby will fall*
> *the baby will fall*

And it goes on like that in her head. What a sad thing she is. But I hate her. She won't cry either.

And then she decides that her whole life is going to be like this, this is the reality, here in the cobwebs with the rock in the stomach. She's no good for anyone so she's got to die. Don will be better off, kids be better off, Cove be better off. Rid of her. Garbage. She relaxes a little now. She has the plan.

Someone is standing there watching her in the corner. Her husband. He squats down and puts his hands on her. That's the trouble with the plan. There are bugs in it. Don't want to hurt the husband. Can't hurt him so. He goes back upstairs. She can hear the footsteps cross the kitchen floor. He is dialing the phone. She can hear the children running around. Active noise. She thinks, can't hurt them. Maybe hurt self. Just a little so she can't carry out the plan. Gets up and walks to the top of the stairs, so tired. Lets all her muscles go limp the way they want to. Bounce bounce bounce, rolling down the stairs. No pain. Too fast for pain. Lying at the bottom. It's okay. The plan is gone, can wait. The pain has come, she's punished herself enough for now. Now can sleep. But no. Men are there. Three men—who are they? What are they doing? Putting her on a stretcher and to the hospital. Doesn't matter. Let them. So this is the way it ends up. Shame. Flaming, cutting shame. Deserved as it is.

Mad now I've shamed myself, mad I've shamed Don, don't want to see anybody. Dr. Stebbins there looking at my knees. I hate them. I kick at him to get away. I want to get out of here. Hate them all, these men. Important men. Hate them all because of the shame. Oh God. Cove is there! In the hall. He is watching me. Christ! Get him away. Why did they call him? Christ. He sees what a shit I am. I scream, "You didn't have to come." I fight them off. I hate them. All of them. They get me in a room and shut the door. Not a regular hospital room, more like a storeroom but has blazing fluorescent lights and chairs and a scale. Disgusting scale to tell how fat you are. Detecto!

Cove comes through the door, and another man. A big man. He has on white. Cove has on corduroys and those stupid hiking boots, trying to pretend he's a real human. I lunge at Cove. If he wants to be human, then okay. I'll tell him the truth. See, Cove, I want you. I want you. See, you made me love you. How do you like that? I plan on putting my arms around him to make him love me or maybe to hit him. I can't be sure which. I'm sure Cove doesn't know. He puts his hands up to protect his face. The other man. I don't know him. He just pushes me in a chair and tells me to sit. I think maybe they give me a hypodermic of something but I can't be too sure because I'm mixed up. I can't really hate this other man too much. He makes it very clear I'd better not move off the chair. I want to get out of here now. I've got to get out of this hospital. Cove talks at me. He asks me if I'll stay. I don't know. I can't think. If he leaves me here, then he's leaving me to do something awful like the plan, so I don't know what to do. Cove leaves, says he'll be back. I stand up quick. If I could make it to the stairs, I could outrun them. The big man just stands in my way, I make a half-hearted attempt to get by, but he really is quite nice-acting so I sit down, reserving all my hate or love or whatever for Cove.

Cove comes back. He says Don has gone home. That means I'll stay in the hospital. I stand up and yell at Cove.

"It's your fault I'm here! This is your fault!"

Cove tells the other guy to leave.

"You made me love you so it's your fault. I'm shit! I can't go on like this and I'll kill myself anytime I want and I hate you. I've got to get out of here."

Cove is standing. He's on guard. Like he's ready to get out of my way if I spring on him. We're both poised ready for action like before the whistle at the beginning of a basketball game.

Cove says that he can't keep me in the hospital if I don't want. He keeps asking me if I'll stay. I finally tell him that I'm going home. I'll walk home. I won't stay here.

Cove is in a dilemma now because he's thinking of practical things like how the hell is she going to get home? And will she go home, the state she's in? I have no idea what she'll do—so what do *I* do? But I don't care about Cove's problems. I walk to the door and Cove stands in front of it. He wants to be very sure that I'll be all right. I tell him I will. I tell him that so I can get out of here. But Cove hesitates because he doesn't believe me. He says he'll drive me home. He says that we're not going anywhere until I've settled down. So we both stand there a long time.

Oh why do I keep doing this? Why? But it's too late now. Cove and I walk to his car. I am pretty quiet and we're driving along when I get this whole helpless nothing feeling that I got back there in the cellar. I really can't go home, I really can't. And here we are gliding toward home and I'm not stopping us. I sneak my hand over and undo the seat belt. We're on Main Street. It's deserted. Late night now. I open the door slowly but Cove hears the click. I leap for the cold air outside, thrusting open the door all the way. Cove grabs at me and at the same time slams on the brakes. I struggle but he has me firm and I can't get out. Cove yells at me. Never heard him yell. Never did before.

"Son of a bitch!"

I don't even care he swore at me. He won't drive if I'm going to jump out. And he isn't going to fight me either so I get out easy as pie and I run down the road. He stays in the car. He doesn't know what to do and I don't care. I go past the bridge and go up Union Street until I find the road to the brook. I hide down there. I pick up stones and throw them at my legs. There's nobody around to do it for me. I see lights of cars up above. They're trying to find me but I escape. I run in the shadows, darting behind the trees. Don's car, Cove's car, police car. Once I stole some figs from the A&P and my mother spanked me and made me take them back to the manager. I was four years old. And once I stole a dime from my father's dresser and they blamed my brother and I didn't say anything. I can't think of much else though. So why did they call the police? I am so very tired. I drag myself over to the Inn and I count my money. Enough for a room. If I can just get on a bed, I'll be able to think better. An awful thing happens then. I can't sign my name. It's like how I can't play the piano. Now I can't sign. I scribble something but this really bothers me. I lie in the locked hotel room. No sleep. It scares me. I can't sign my name. I don't know who I am anymore. I don't know if I'm a little girl or a big woman. I don't know who I am.

Thursday, October 16, 1969

I have made a decision. I'll talk to Cove about it. It's really important that I get away somewhere. I have taken the shame and humiliation of last week. There was nothing else I could do. But I don't like to hurt myself and I don't like those awful feelings that made me act so crazy. I am terribly afraid of myself. I can't think of anyplace to go. Maybe that place that Evelyn told me about. That place Cove goes to on Tuesday. Foxcroft Farm. I have to go somewhere. And maybe it wouldn't be so bad knowing that Cove was their psychiatrist. Cove comes out, he is done with his other patients. I can't look at him. I was sure he was never going to see me again. I can't understand how come he doesn't hate me. Makes me want to do a whole lot better, even if it's not for me. Maybe do a whole lot better for them. Cove and Don. I keep my head down. Cove is very serious looking. I can tell when he's thinking real hard.

"I'm sorry, Dr. Ashley. I've been thinking—maybe I should go away someplace."

"You only stayed at the hospital for one day."

"I want to go somewhere now. I have to. I want to get better."

"What do you have in mind?"

"Well, I was wondering about Foxcroft Farm. I mean, is that the sort of place that might do me some good?"

Cove puts his hand on his chin. He looks thoughtful.

"It's kind of a rough place, but for some people it really works. It's not run by professionals, you know. The staff is dedicated and experienced but I'm the only doctor and I'm only there once a week. I couldn't give you any special treatment."

"Oh no, I didn't mean that. I wouldn't want that. Do you think I could do it?"

"It would mean a lot of hard work. I mean physically too. The guests and staff all live and work together."

"Could I come back to Chester once a week like I do now? I mean, could I continue seeing you?"

"Well, I think it might be worked out. Occasionally guests see their private psychiatrists if they want. We could talk with the director about it."

Cove looks at me hard. He sees that I am serious. He doesn't know if he can trust me.

"I could, of course, see you when I go on Tuesdays—like the others. You're serious?"

"Yes, I am."

"Well, I could call Timothy Kearns, the director, to see if they have a vacancy."

"I've already talked to Don about it. He wants me to go somewhere. He doesn't want to go through another week like last week."

"Neither do I." Cove smiles.

·   ·   ·

A gust of wind shrieks outside. Some leaves hit the window. For a second the lights dim. Cove sneezes. Three times. He has the strangest sneeze I ever heard, almost like he's choking. The wind rattles the window. I stand up and look out. Cove stands too and puts his arm on my shoulder. The foliage has been brilliant this fall but the leaves are dead now and falling fast.

Part Two

THE FARM

Monday, October 20, 1969

Gorge rising in throat. Winnie the Pooh lying on the table, suitcase open on the table. Children gone away visiting so not to see Mommy leave. Failure, the final failure, desertion of family. I could be dead, I want to be dead, but I'm not. Because of Don and children and because of Cove. I call Evelyn to go with us because of the gorge. I'm afraid it might overwhelm me and then I'd be dead.

We drive. Don and Evelyn talking, me holding onto my insides. Get to the farm, get there, want to get there where they don't know me, where I can't hurt anyone. Drive for two hours and turn up a hill, hard with the cold. Ski trails, waiting for winter. Pine trees, sky so blue. Up and up and up. To the top where it levels. A tennis court, blown with brown leaves. Far from anywhere, no town, no gas station, in the wild. Wilderness all around, dark deep forests. Okay. This is wild. But I am wild. This is okay for me. I have to be here. The sky, that's all ours—Don's and Cove's sky too. So I have a connection. No fences, no bars, no white coats. Pine trees, beautiful pine trees. And the sky.

We go in the main farmhouse. Big, white, rambling. Fireplaces making it warm. Fireplaces and dungarees. Dungarees walking around and talking; stocking feet, wool, and hiking boots lined up by the fireplaces. Me, following, head down, shuffling, scared. Don, Evelyn, dungarees, then me. Into a dining room. Big table filled with steaming food. Roast beef and vegetables and tomatoes and potatoes and salad and homemade bread. Take trays and fill plates and sit at empty places. They're expecting me. I take a chance and glance around and I fix this awful phony smile on my face. Just fix it there. I see regular people eating and it's all regular and Don and Evelyn and I smile because it's nice. I'll be all right. It's a good warm place. They have to leave me now and I walk to the top of the hill. I will do what I have to. I will get better. I feel warm tears starting in my eyes and at the same time around the other side, way behind, I hear men shouting. "Fuck, fuck, fuck, fuck," that's what they're shouting. "Fuck you." The warm tears stop now and a smile fixes itself like plastic cast on my face. I turn and go inside with the dungarees.

Tuesday, October 21, 1969

I have a private room. This woman, Helen Tarnish, shows me around the farm. She is pleasant. I don't talk. She takes me up a long path in the woods. I watch my feet walking on the beautiful leaves. Like Gretel going into the woods to meet the witch. The path winds around and we cross a wooden bridge with hand rails because the trail goes up a steep incline. I'm to live here, in Spruce Cottage. If it wasn't me, here, I would say it was beautiful. She explains that the house mother is on vacation; the other women here are guests, who are to be my cottage mates. We hear loud music. As we walk in the door I see its source. A girl is bent over with her head on a table. Two speakers are on each side of her head, touching each ear. It's so loud. I think she must be a deaf person. But no, nobody's deaf. The other girls blur in front of me. I'm dizzy. I want to lie down. The music has stopped. My presence is known. They all stare at me. They are young. My smile is still fixed. They don't smile back. They don't want me here. Helen introduces us but nobody listens to her. She is staff. I bend over to pet a dog. His name is Hermit. He walks stiff-legged. He doesn't like me either. I walk stiff-legged, frozen smile, into the room that's to be mine. It's a nice room but dirty. Helen is talking to me about the rules. Meals in the main house. Have to work on the work program. No violence, sex, drugs, liquor or suicide allowed. I won't do anything wrong. I never break rules. They must be for the animals in the other room. I hope they aren't crazy. I just want to be left alone. Maybe I'll like it up here in the wild woods with my door shut. I'll just stay in my room. Helen leaves. I make myself go out the door to get things to clean the room. The girls stop talking when they see me. Their eyes follow me into the kitchen. Dishes all over. This is a small kitchen for coffee and snacks. I get the broom and dust pan and a waste basket.

One girl is strikingly beautiful. She has jet black hair and olive skin. It is amazing. She has blue eyes. She has a beautiful body and beautiful teeth. I envy her. She is so beautiful. She is lucky. I can't function and I have left my home. Nothing can be the matter with her that is as bad as that. Her name is Madonna.

I spend the night cleaning the room. I skip supper. No hunger, no tears, no feelings. Maybe they'll forget all about me. I drop off to sleep late. I have dreams of wolves. Is it really just dreams? Maybe the dog really is a wolf.

My period has come. I take a sleeping pill. I curl into a ball and hide under the covers. Don and Cove are far away. My insides are raw, exposed. They feel this way because it takes up so much of my energy so as not to feel anything.

Morning; I stand in front of the mirror. I fix the smile back on my face and wait for somebody to rescue me. Someone named Lena does—Lena Mae Jogger. A friendly lady my age. Some of my perspective comes back. She has a child. I have children. It makes me more real. I am somebody after all. Lena lives on the farm with her little girl and her husband Gregory.

We walk down the path. I have missed breakfast and now it's the work program. That's all I hear around here. You've got to go on the work program. I'm to work with Lena Mae on rugs for Pine Cottage. We're to cut the shag rugs to correct size, then tack them down. If I can get my mind focused on this work, maybe I'll be able to loosen up a bit. Lena Mae chatters away. She measures and I help her cut them and tack them down. Maybe she'll like me. I still have on my shit-eating grin.

We hear a gong in the distance, down past the woods, floating up to us in the forest. Lena Mae says that it's the lunch signal. We pack up our things and follow another path through enormous pine trees. I see their beauty. I see it, but I can't feel it. So their beauty is superfluous, almost obscene. I try not to look at them.

As we wend our way down, we come to a clearing where we can see, almost like from an airplane, the main house, empty swimming pool, tennis courts, pottery house, chicken farm out back and the gardens in the distance. I can see the cars parked in the circular drives. I study the cars. And I see a bus. Jesus, Jesus. It looks like Cove's camper bus. I forgot it's Tuesday, and this is where Cove comes on Tuesday. How could I forget that?

I shift the old rug to my other shoulder. We are carrying it rolled up, each of us at an end. As we get through the trees, toward the house, that's when I see Cove. He sees me too. He looks surprised, like he didn't know I was here. Cove has on old clothes. Hiking boots, old pants, old sweater. He smiles. I bend my head. We get to the porch and put down the rug. I hope Cove is pleased that I'm here at the farm. I want him to be proud of me. Lena Mae goes inside and Cove comes over and talks to me. He says that he will have to say some things about me at the staff meeting. I say okay. We chat for a minute, as if we were regular people. He confirms my appointment for Thursday night at his house. Don will pick me up and take me back. Cove says that maybe it's not a good idea for me to stop at home, that I should try to think of the farm as my home for a while. I think he wants me to work hard, so I think I'll try.

I can't get over Cove wearing those old clothes. Timothy Kearns, the director of the farm, comes up to us and says he'd like to talk with me. He looks nice. He has a southern accent but I don't hold that against him. We go in his office and I stutter. Jesus! I'm stuttering again. I tell him about my panic. I tell him I'm afraid of everything and how I can't leave the house or get anything done. I don't tell him about Cove. That's private. Timothy gives me a nice feeling about myself. Cove and Timothy can both do this. He says that if I have any problems, I can talk to him anytime I want. Most of the staff live here on the farm in separate houses, with their families.

The lunch in the main dining room is strange. It's hard for me to realize that this is where I live now. It's a buffet with fantastic food. I have cottage cheese. All this noise, coupled with Cove here, has taken away my appetite. I have a good look at the people. I sit with Lena Mae. That's good because I can think my own thoughts as she chatters on. So Cove is actually eating. He's by the door toward the middle room. And people all treat him normally. They talk to him and sit by him, as if he's regular. How about that? I'm exhausted by all the things going on in my head. After lunch the staff has a meeting so it's easy to skip out of my work crew. I go to the library at the other end of the main house and look out the window. I look out until I see Cove walk up to a staff house past the pines. I watch him walk. I never really saw Cove walk before. Only in his office. And so now I'm watching him walk up the hill. When he's gone I sneak up the other path to Spruce and to my room and lie down. I'm so very tired. I've decided that I like to see Cove walk around like that. I like to see people treat him regular. I never will be able to, but I wish I could.

I walk to the main house in time for supper. As I walk in the door, I hear terrible noises coming from the dining room. I walk in and see two things happening at once. A large-boned woman is standing by the kitchen door with a butcher knife poised at her wrist. She's yelling, "I'll kill myself, I'll kill myself," and then, at the same time a big black has gone to a table and is in the process of tipping over the chairs. They're heavy so it makes a lot of noise. I am fascinated more than scared. I think it's fascinating because *no one* does anything. I slip into a chair next to a guy and ask him what's going on. He says, "Not much." He says lots of people do things like that, especially when the doctor comes on Tuesdays. He says the doctor is almost finished talking to people. He's upstairs in a sitting room. I look around wildly. He must be talking about Cove. My Cove. People keep eating, ignoring the commotion, so I get in line, take my food and go back and sit with this guy. He's nice looking, about my age—he must be staff. As Cove comes down the stairs the noise eases up. The knife is put back with the bread, and the chairs are picked up. I watch Cove in the food line. He glances my way. I pretend I don't see him. I begin to talk to the guy next to me. Maybe he'll be my friend in this lonely place. His name is Maurice. Cove will think I'm a regular person if I chat with people. Maurice asks me to his cottage after supper to listen to records. He likes classical music. Yes, I'd like that. He is a guest.

Tuesday, October 21, 1969

Cove has a therapy group after supper. Don't feel good about him doing things I don't know about. He's a high old monkey monk around here. Everybody talks about him and the stupid group therapy. I'm not included. I don't care. I go outside and sit on the porch. I won't get involved. This place is nothing to me. I go over and check his VW. It's locked. Maurice has been watching me. He comes over. I'm so glad to see him, and to be noticed. We walk up to his cottage. He puts records on. And he begins to talk. He is an artist. He might let me watch him paint someday. He trusts me.

"Listen, Maurice, tell me about this place, will you? I get so scared."

"Let me give you the lowdown about the staff. If you get mixed up on who's who, guest or staff, don't let it bother you. It's no wonder. Half the staff are former guests. That's one thing that makes this place click. There are no professional mental health helpers, except Dr. Ashley. And he's only here on Tuesday. I wouldn't be here myself, but I can't find the right kind of job, so I asked Timothy if I could stay on for a while as part of the staff. He doesn't know yet, so I'm still a guest."

"Can I ask what the matter with you is?"

"Sure, sure. I've had a string of bad luck, that's all. Can't stand the jobs I've had so I quit them. I'd like to sell my paintings. But I can't finish any of them. What's the matter with you?"

"I don't know. I can't seem to work either. I get real scared leaving the house. Anxiety, you know."

"Yeah, I have anxiety attacks sometimes myself."

"You do? I never met anybody like me before."

"Oh yeah. If you have one, come to me. It's better if you cry, then they go away."

"I've heard *that* before, oh yeah—easier said than done."

"Where have you heard that?"

"Oh well, I had some psychotherapy and that's what I was told."

Maurice comes over and he takes my hands and pulls me to my feet. He puts his hands on my shoulders.

"Look at me, Carol." He looks into my eyes.

"What?" I feel funny. I don't know what to do. I am flattered, but scared.

"If you need me, come to me. I will help you." He grips my shoulders hard.

I'm more scared.

"Uh, okay. Okay."

"We will be friends. I'm glad you're here. I can't talk as well with the other guests."

"Uh, well, all right." I squirm a little under this pressure. His foot hits the coffee table and he lets go of my shoulders. He turns the record and flops down on his bed, face down.

"Come over here and rub my back. I'm very tense. It's always like this on Tuesdays. Dr. Ashley comes and everybody acts up. I should be in group therapy but I wanted to talk to you."

"You're in group?"

"Yes. I get so sick of it though. They all have such problems. I wanted to listen to music with you. My muscles are tense. Come and rub my back."

My blood starts racing. I don't know what to do. Oh Jesus. What can I do? I walk to his bed. I sit on the edge and I put my hand on his back. I don't know why I'm doing this. What am I doing? God, how do I get into these things? I can't say no to him. Why can't I? I am rubbing his back. Oh Jesus, I'm rubbing his back. Cove is in group therapy and Don is home and I am rubbing Maurice's back. Well, no matter. It's not hurting anybody. It's their fault. They stuck me up here on this farm with nobody to talk to. And they live their perfect sin-free lives. So to hell with them. This

Maurice, he's not so bad. And we'll be friends now. Just friends.
He's lonely too.

I shift positions and straddle him. I give him a real back rub.

He groans, "Good, um, good.

"Would you like a drink, Carol?"

"I didn't think we're supposed to drink on the farm."

"Oh, nobody pays attention to that."

"Well, sure then, sure." I want to drink. A triple. Maybe it will
quiet me down. I'm all stirred up. Feel like screaming. Don't know
why.

I move over. Maurice gets up and we have three, then four,
five glasses of wine. It hits my stomach and warmth spreads around
my body. It hits the Thorazine and Valium and plays a fine fiddle.

I have to get out of here. It's almost ten o'clock. If I don't get
out of here I won't be able to get back to Spruce.

"Bye, Maurice, have to go—see you."

"Remember what I said, Carol."

"Sure."

What did he say? What in hell did he say? Run downhill, stumbling. Don't follow the path as much as go through the tall pines.
Head for the driveway. Stumble. Don't care. Get to Cove's car.
Stretch out my arms and lean on the side. Oh Cove, I'm so glad
you haven't left. Oh Cove, please help me. Will I be all right?

I go across the road and sit at the top of the hill in a clump of
trees. I put my head down and wait. I can see the porch. Cove
comes out, walks toward the car, gets in. As he swings around the
drive his headlights flash by me, but he doesn't see. And then he
drives down the hill. Away toward home. He's left me. They've
all left me.

I stumble up the path to Spruce. I hate to go in. Those girls
hate me. They are animals. Not one of them has spoken to me. I
go in. Roka Klein has thrown the phone across the room. Now
the one they call Madonna starts throwing everything off the tables onto the floor. As far as I can see, she is the ringleader. There
are five of them—Madonna, Roka, Queenie Miller, Maureen and
Gert. The music, acid rock, is playing as I walk through. I don't
feel safe. I get in my room and slam the door.

Suddenly it's quiet. I sit on the bed wondering.

The door opens. In flies Hermit. The animals have thrown the dog in my room. He's cowering in the corner. He stinks. Poor dog has tangled with a skunk. I see red. I see blue, orange, yellow. Furious at them for scaring the dog. I race out of the room screaming—loud!

"You God damned bastards! How dare you scare that dog! You shits! Animals! If you so much as look at me sideways or even whisper, I'll smash you to pieces, every one of you. You are the most vile, disgusting slobs I have ever seen. Do you hear me? I said, do you hear me? You're to absolutely, finally keep your disgusting God damned shithead selves away from me. Understand?"

They stop giggling as I start yelling. They have stopped dead in their tracks. Staring.

"Understand?" I yell.

Madonna puts her thumbs in her dungarees. She stands there staring. We are deadlocked in silence. The five against me. She strolls over to me, stands facing me, and says, "Hey man, where the hell you come from anyway?"

I relax. She is so pretty.

"Come from hell."

"Well, so's us."

"I'm Carol, how about we get some tomato juice and clean that poor dog."

"Tomato juice?"

"Yeah, it takes out the smell."

"You know a lot?"

"Some."

We all go to the main house. I'm not stumbling anymore. We sneak down the cellar. Madonna shows me how to get in the cage where they keep food. We make a lot of noise. We are legitimate. Going to clean the dog.

When the job is done we say good night and I go back to my room. I feel okay now. My frozen smile is gone.

Knock on the door.

"Come in."

Madonna and Queenie.

"We can't sleep. We was wondering if you could tell us how the hell you sleep in this fucking place?"

"Have a seat. How the hell do I know? I can't sleep either."

Wednesday, October 22, 1969

Wake up early. Go to main house in the dark. Write down feelings on paper. Am a little looser feeling than before. Go to kitchen and study big coffee pot. Put coffee on for the farmers. Put small pot on for me. Early time like this is time for me to gather my wits, assemble my forces. Now I go to the living room and sit at the piano. Put my fingers on the keys. Can't push down. Can't.

Watch Jud as he shuffles in. "Jud, why are you up so early? It's only six. Want some coffee?"

Jud mumbles. Talking about sex. He scares me. Has on a yellow hard hat and dungarees with suspenders. Pants are baggy, fly half down. Smelly, dark beard and wild curly gray hair escaping from under the hat. He sort of breathes in his words like slurping. Hard to understand him. Don't want to understand him. I won't sit near him. Then Jake Healy comes in. He's staff. He reads *The New York Times* and doesn't talk at breakfast. I'll try to sit near him. Ronnie Minkrob then comes in. Little pipe, lit. Small tiny shuffling lady. Very thin thin legs. Nose running. Grinning with her pipe. Then Gregory comes in with part of the woods crew.

The breakfast crew start putting out cereal, toast, jam, honey, silver. The cooks this morning are some of the guests. Miguel, the chef, is gone for a few days. Everybody gives their orders. Jake has a half cup of coffee, orange juice and scrambled. On it goes, like that. Woods crew have pancakes. They think they're the best. They strut. They think they have the hardest job. Working in the deep woods. They eat the most too. The elite of the farm.

We have morning meeting at eight o'clock. Everyone has to come to morning meeting. The book of work assignments is over on the corner table where the woods crew sits. Three staff members stand by the book, marking, deciding on our fate. We can request certain work if we want, then we'll be put on that crew. I'm in a dilemma. I want to work hard but I'm scared. So I don't say anything. They put me on the vegetable table for the morning. Ugh. Veggies for the vegetables. That's where they stick people who can't do anything else. The real sick. I work with Jud, Ronnie, Minnie, Alfred, and Frieda Fern. Frieda came back from her vacation. She's our housemother at Spruce, a staff member, about thirty. She has long braids wound around the top of her head. Something like a pyramid. On top of that she has stuck some kind of decoration. It's made of cloth. As she makes a point she turns her head and the little flag flutters, accentuating her words. I'll have to be careful of her. She's been watching me. She has a large backside and I can see that she has sewn a big red patch on her dungarees over her crotch from front to back. She says she is an Indian.

After morning meeting we go up the hill to the gym for volleyball. I love this. The gym isn't heated, so it gets our blood moving. The staff is very kind to everybody, they make sure even Minnie, Ronnie and Alfred play. Woods crew is fiercely competitive but most all of us have a good time. I feel a little bit more a part of things. Some try to get out of volleyball. The late sleepers are sought out by staff and routed from their beds with a lecture. There is one staff member who I watch. He is a slim, wiry man that everybody seems to like. John Vanderwater. I've seen him at odd spots around the farm, closeted with some guest in trouble, listening to his or her woes. I'll try to get into his crew this afternoon. I think I like him.

Vegetable table. Five of us put newspaper down, gather cutting boards and knives and sit. Frieda clips out her orders on how to cut potatoes, carrots, onions, apples, peppers, squash and tomatoes. She sounds as if it is something very profound that we are doing. She is watching me most because everyone else is basically inactive. She analyzes the way I hold the paring knife. Oh well, Madonna told me last night that she was angry that I listened to music with Maurice. I saw him this morning at the meeting but he didn't speak to me. I help Alfred with his knife on the potatoes. He acts mentally retarded but Madonna told me it's an act to escape work. I think it might be an act to escape something else. He has a doll in his lap.

After lunch the book is read again. This is when I request John's crew. I get it. Chickens. It's slaughtering time for the chicks. Madonna has a glint in her eye. So does Obie Smith, the black. They volunteer for slaughtering.

We have an assembly line going on downstairs in the summer kitchen. Six of us are lined up at the long table. It starts with the killing. Madonna and Obie are outside by the garage putting the chickens in a thing that cuts off their heads, then defeathers them. Then the chickens come to us. They are washed in big barrels. My job is to take stones out of the gizzards. We hear hooting and hollering outside but most of us can't look out the window at the slaughter. I concentrate my whole being on just this one job of slitting open the things and washing out the gravel. I disassociate this part of the bird from the whole bird. It makes me feel slightly sick. We work very hard. It's an awful mess. John is right to the left of me. He is compulsively organized but he gets fantastic results because of it. We push ourselves, doing this thing we don't want to do, because of him. He makes us proud to work. To accomplish. I haven't felt this way for a long time. It's almost a brand new feeling. It makes my skin and body feel very strong, even among the entrails. It makes me smile and laugh. These chickens are our food for the winter. Someone moves a chicken voice box in a certain way and it squawks as if alive. I jump and shudder. John puts his arm around me and smiles. I start to smile but it sticks. Something has happened. An awful feeling comes from inside. It's John that makes it. Oh my throat now, throat is closing off. He has his arm around me and it hurts me. The innocent touch like pain making my throat hurt. Want John to touch me, want him to. But it's too close, too much. Fear now of letting go. Fear of something. He's too close. I pick up my cigarettes, I race up the stairs, I race through the dining, living rooms, out the front door. I've ruined things somehow. Go to the tennis courts, hit tree there with fists. I was feeling and it was too much for me. I make a strangled cry like the dead chicken. My body is dead except for the throat. John comes to me from the house. He asks what is the matter, he tries to touch me, hold me. I push him away.

"I'm choking," I yell at him. My limbs are trembling and I am ashamed. But he is kind, he is nice, he is handsome.

"Let me help you to relax, Carol. Let me help you."

But John has taken on new colors. The colors of hurt. The colors of shame. I can't have him near me. He's too close.

I race away. I shout at him, "I'm sorry, I'm sorry."

He is a love-hate man now. Someone who I'm afraid of. Like Cove. And before that all the others. And before that, someone else.

Thursday, October 23, 1969

Don gets out of work early, arranges sitters for the kids and makes the two-hour trip to the farm. Tonight is my appointment with Cove. Don embraces me and I show him around. I introduce him to Madonna and my other friends. So glad to see him. We sit in my room and we hold each other. I wonder why I'm here. I feel distant from home and family. Now I have Don holding me, the distance closes up. Frieda walks in and sits down. We want to be alone. Frieda asks about Don's job. She asks all sorts of questions. She asks me why I'm here. I don't answer. My eyes meet Don's and he just shrugs his shoulders a bit. Frieda keeps talking. The flag in her hair bobs up and down.

We leave for Cove's. I put my head in Don's lap and put my hands in fists next to my chin. I forgot how scared I get of Cove. Don will pick me up when I'm finished and drive me back to the farm. I want to see the kids. It's hard for me to be so close, yet so far.

"Well now, Carol. How are you doing at the farm?" Cove has his suit on, like normal.

"All right I guess, it's taking me time to get used to it, some people are very sick. It's funny. I'm really much more relaxed when I'm working hard. It's when I stop I get scared. I even felt pretty good there one time. We were working on chickens and it was hard work but I was almost enjoying myself. It was a strange feeling. But it didn't last long because then it got spoiled. I don't understand—I panicked and had to run away. John tried to help me but it didn't work."

"How did he try to help you?"

"I don't know. . . . He, well."

Throat constricting, clenching, hands sweating.

"Tell me about it."

"Nothing. Don't know. Don't know."

"It seems to bother you."

"Well, all he did was put his arm around me and that's all, because the dead chicken was squawking and that's all. Scared me."

"Scared you? The chicken?"

"No. His arm."

Don't know—don't know. Had to get away. Get away. Sweat dripping from my head.

"He's like you, somehow. He's like you, and I didn't want him near me."

"Like me?"

"Yeah, scared of him. Had to run away."

Cove watches me, waits. He puts his chin in his hands, says nothing.

"Well, it scares me! You scare me, John scares me. Things are going too fast. Too many people doing too many things all too fast and it's all physical. The whole thing. Even all the work, physical, and all the touching. . . ."

"Touching?"

"Yes! Everybody puts their arms around each other and flings themselves around and wrestles on the floor and and everything is wild and loose and it scares me and I can't help but run from it!"

"It's too much?"

"Yes! Even the guests, I mean the other night I was rubbing Maurice's back, for heaven's sake, and I don't even know how I got in that position. I mean, I'm sorry. It's scary."

"Is Maurice like me, too?"

Silence.

"You said that John was like me in some way. Is Maurice too?"

"No. No. Maurice wasn't, isn't. I mean I'm not so scared of him. It's just I don't know how I get so involved so fast. He isn't like you at all. No."

"What about John and me frightens you?"

"I don't know, it doesn't make sense. No sense at all because you and John are really nice and Maurice is not so strong."

"You are afraid of strong, nice men?"

"No. No. Yes, I am. I don't understand. Makes me mad. I want to be like everybody else and be able to joke and put my arms about people and talk and even talk to you but I can't. You see? I can't."

"The strong men mean more to you than the others?"

"Well yes, of course. Yes."

"Yet you are more afraid of them, especially when they touch you?"

"Yeah. I guess. I guess maybe I'm afraid that they won't like me. So I run away. No, that isn't right." I put my fists on my forehead. I'm trying to figure this out. Cove sits quietly. He waits for me to think.

"I can't figure it out. I can see it. I can see me, but I can't figure it out. I am very, very scared of the nice men. And not of the others, but I can't figure it out."

"Is there more at stake with the strong men?"

"That's partly it. I'm afraid I'd lose, I mean, the stakes are too high."

"What are you afraid you'd lose?"

"Oh! Stop! I know it's stupid, you see, I see it's stupid, but I can't help it. You don't understand."

Silence.

I look at Cove. I can't understand why I'm so afraid of Cove. It makes my throat hurt and I put my head down. I don't want to be so afraid. I start to cry. He doesn't understand. The tears come so easily now, swooping down out of me as if I've always been able to cry. It almost feels good in a way. I'm feeling sorry for myself. I'm just too afraid to let Cove near me when I want to more than anything.

Cove's voice gets very low and it gets very gentle with me.

"I think I do understand."

And that makes me cry all the more because he is being so nice. His voice, soothing words like a loving parent. A safe refuge, an escape from the monsters in the closet and under the bed. No laughing, jeering, disgusted, harshness. No jarring, grating. No fear. Cove has come around the desk and has put his arm on my back. Cove, safe place from the storm, peaceful harbor. A parent who doesn't hurt.

Friday, October 24, 1969

The bus has left for town. Everyone goes to town on Friday night except one or two. I pace around the living room. I didn't go because I'm scared of the bus ride. Afraid I might panic. I'm mad at myself. I'm left here with Glory and Chuck. What a zoo! I'm trying to figure out about my crying last night. It's like all my feelings have come out of my body and have landed on top of my skin, ready for Cove to snatch them when he wants. I feel I'm in danger. I hope only Cove can see this. If the others here see this, they might pluck at me and eat me up. Glory has drawn some paintings of her diamonds. She has a sure, steady hand on her drawings. Diamonds. A thing that makes her eyes shine, her breath quicken. She looks at my diamond ring, which flashes in the dim light. Her pleasure seems almost orgastic so I put my hands in my pockets. Then she spies my stocking feet. My boots are in front of the fire. She groans in ecstasy and goes back and forth in front of me, darting glances at my feet and biting her knuckles in delight. I quick get on my boots so she'll stop this groaning. I feel constricted and alone. Glory isn't much of a listener. She talks loudly, halting every few words.

"Can—I—polish—your umm—diamond?"

"It won't come off my finger, Glory."

"Umm."

The distance from home to the farm seems so great. Now, my friends are the ones here: Queenie, Madonna, Maurice and John.

Those are the ones I think about. I'll wait until eleven when they come home from town. Maybe Madonna will play pool with me. I look at my watch.

I think of last night. I felt so safe. Now I don't feel safe anymore. The world in his office and the world at the farm. Two separate, distant places that clash in the night shadows.

Monday, October 27, 1969

Haven't choked since I saw Cove. Am nervous but haven't choked. I got through the weekend. It's hard because there are no work crews. Cove says that he has established in his own mind that I won't crack, and because of that, he's pushing me. That gives me confidence. I think all the time of Cove. I love him. I went and dug around in the pottery shed in a box of materials and I got some black embroidery thread. I have some linen and a hoop. I'm going to make Cove a tapestry for Christmas. It's going to be beautiful so he'll like me better. He'll be surprised that I'm good at this. He only knows me as a shithead. I had another dream about him naked in a sleeping bag. Makes me nervous to dream. So I sit listening to the radio, doing my embroidery.

Don came for a visit and we sat in my room and he rubbed my feet and we talked. I love him more than anything in the world. He's too good for me. I don't deserve him. He talked with Madonna and Queenie too. Madonna is having a rough time of it. Madonna is afraid that she's pregnant. She told us about when she first came to the farm. She got into trouble and people were chasing her and she broke her ankle, but kept running. It was a choice between the farm or the state hospital. I asked if she was scared. She said, "I never give a shit if I get hurt." I see me in her. She's a master at turning cold.

Yesterday started wild. Minnie was wandering around with her head tilted in a certain stiff way, sing-songing a lilting song about her love for Maurice. She followed him around about ten feet behind. Ronnie stood in the middle of the floor, drooling and chewing on her pipe. Jud followed me around mumbling awful things. It's uncanny, because he talks about "your father." I turned around and pulled his hat over his eyes and told him to get away from me. He kept following. And then Glory gets all hyped up because Roka Klein has taken off her shoes in front of her. It really makes me mad. Glory groans and Roka tells her to lie on the floor. She does. Roka puts her socks on her breast. She groans back and forth in ecstasy. Makes me sick. I go over and order her shoes back on. Jud bumps into me; he's following so close and we all bump onto the floor. Maurice comes over and then Frieda Fern. Frieda makes me nervous. She looks at me. Somehow she's mad because Don came on Saturday.

"Carol, will you examine with me why you are on the floor?"

"Shit!" I'm too confused. Queenie and Madonna walk in as a coal from Ronnie's pipe falls on Minnie's arm. Minnie howls and Alfred comes down the stairs telling us all that he has a doll from Uruguay.

Frieda still intent on me.

"Can you analyze why you are swearing?"

Madonna and Queenie pull me off the floor and Madonna yells, "Fuck you, Frieda." She's protecting me.

John comes racing in from outside. It seems that Obie and Gregory are having a fight. He gets Terry, a staffer, to handle the fight and yells, loud, "Stop!"

Everybody stops.

So we go bowling.

A bus ride to town for bowling. But I'm scared of bus rides. I see Timothy come in the door and tell him I'm afraid of the bus. He just looks at me and says, "Would you rather stay here with Ronnie?"

I made it on the bus. And I made it bowling. I even had a good time. It was strange for me to have a good time. I liked the feeling.

Last night alone in my room I started doing imitations. I can do Alfred, Frieda, Ronnie and Jud the best. Also Minnie and

Glory. I made myself laugh. Sometimes I feel swallowed up by their personalities. I wonder, How would I go about imitating myself?

We had main meeting. Main meeting is where everyone on the whole farm gets together and discusses problems. I get very anxious. All of us thrown together. I keep my eye on John and on Timothy and Terry. The strong ones. I watch how they act with people. I watch how the guests are relaxed with them. How John and Timothy and Terry put their arms around people and it all seems so normal. There's a lot of friendly touching. Back patting and embraces and hugs for encouragement. I am jealous of them. I think about this and it scares me so I have to leave. The crowd scares me. I pace around outside, mad at myself. I try to hear the problems. The woods crew is using too much maple syrup on pancakes, not using too much, but wasting too much. Another is the telephone. People aren't recording their long-distance calls and it's taking Jake too long to figure what calls are made and by whom. Another problem is the Down Yonder Café is now off limits. Friday night some guests got drunk in there. I can't hear the rest.

John comes outside and I tell him, "I'm okay. Just got scared." John puts his arm on my shoulders. I let it stay there. It's all right I guess. It's a little like when Cove touched me.

"Come try the meeting again, Carol, you're doing just fine."

"Okay, thanks, John."

"My wife and I are having a few people over tonight for hot mulled cider. Would you like to come?"

"Sure. Yes. Thanks."

Oh, I'm so happy. Oh I feel very nice. I went bowling and got on a bus and I let John touch me and now I'm going to his house like a nice regular person. Oh, I really like feeling nice. Cove comes tomorrow. I think I'll get my nerve up and ask if I can join group therapy. Things are going right. Madonna even got her period.

Tuesday, October 28, 1969

This is Cove day and I'm thinking about how to avoid him. It hurts me to see Cove. But I want to see him too. It's still strange to see him in old clothes, walking. I think the best thing is to stay away and make sure I don't see him. Then I won't hurt. I have cider this morning for my work, that's outside by the summer kitchen. We put the apples in the press and two of us crank it. The third washes the jugs and puts them under the spout to collect the juice. I'm signed up to work with Glory and Rachel. Which means I'll have to tell them what to do. Rachel is in another place from the rest of us, a dreamy place. I'll have to watch her or she'll catch her hands in the press. She follows me a lot. She wants to have a baby. She asks me over and over if it hurts to have a baby. I tell her no. What else can I say?

As I'm planning the day in my head, I skip volleyball. Too much chance of seeing Cove when volleyball is over. I stay in the library so nobody will see me. I hear screams from the kitchen. Minnie runs through with a smile on her face. She runs past me and out the door. What has she done? Laura Lee is on the floor crying. Jesus! Her shirt is stuck to her back. I go and help her to her room. Minnie threw boiling coffee on her. She was mad at Laura Lee for talking to Maurice. I help her off with her shirt. Laura Lee Jones is a nineteen-year-old college girl. She's working with the staff on a work and study program. She has three more months. Her back is blazing red but I don't think it's going to blister. She'll be all right. When she's calm I go to find John at the gym and he tracks down Minnie. She is sorry for what she did but she keeps smiling. John talks with her. She'll have to leave the farm for sure now. You can't hurt people like that. I wander back to the main house. I see Cove's car. I go way around it. I don't want to see it. I see this new guy sitting on the porch so I go sit with him. His head is in his hands. He's moaning.

"I'm choking, I can't breathe, I'm choking. Help me!"

"It's okay," I say. "It's going to be all right. I have the same kind of choking feeling lots of times, but you really aren't choking. It's anxiety."

"Help me, I'm choking."

"You'll be all right, you'll be all right." I put my hand on his shoulder.

"GO FUCK YOURSELF!" and he pushes me away.

John was on his way back through when he told me that Cove was taking a look at Laura Lee's back. I tear around to the back of the cider mill. My heart skipping. I see Laura Lee naked on her bed and she has a beautiful body. The body of a nineteen-year-old girl. How dare Cove look at her! He quit being that kind of doctor to be a psychiatrist, so he has *no right!* Jesus! I'm jealous! I was feeling so superior to these others with their men problems. Minnie jealous of Laura Lee and Rachel wanting babies and here I am jealous. Shit! And Frieda is jealous of me and my Don. Jesus!

I'll get even with Cove though. I'll get even. I won't go to lunch. I get Queenie to bring me some cottage cheese. Tell her I don't want to see Dr. Ashley. Tell her I hate him.

"You? We hate doctors but we didn't think you would."

"Well, I do, today."

"Anything else you want?"

"Well, keep an eye on things, on him too. Tell me what's going on."

"Sure, Carol, sure."

In the afternoon I choose horseback riding because it'll get me free and clear of staff so I can think things over.

It's cold out. Two horses are in the barn. One outside. He looks big. Am I supposed to ride that? Madonna is in charge. She has ridden twice before. But she has something Queenie and I don't have. No fear. I am fascinated. Madonna gets the other two horses out and gets the saddles. She throws one saddle over and kicks the horse's stomach as she tightens the strap.

"The horse bloats out his stomach, like this, see? The horse is trying to trick you, so you whack him and in comes the stomach, so you can tighten the strap."

I let her do the whole thing. There is no saddle or bridle for my horse. I look a little concerned so Madonna gets a piece of twine in the barn and somehow sticks it in the mouth for reins.

"Don't let him eat grass because then he won't mind you. And don't walk behind him because he'll kick you in the teeth."

They get on and ride away. Easy as that. I stand there and look at this horse. They tied the string to the fence, so I walk all the way around the other side of the gate to look at the horse. His eyes stick out. I climb the fence, pat his neck a little and mount. I feel good. I look up and see Queenie and Madonna galloping across the field. It looks so nice, this cold autumn day with the leaves all yellow.

I pull the strings to join the girls but nothing happens. The horse is chewing on the grass. I pull again. Nothing. I get a little mad and yell at him, "Move!" He stomps his foot. This terrifies me. He hates me. He moves across the yard about ten feet for another clump of grass. So the two of us sit there. Me and horse. Part of the landscape. I sit like this a long time. Now I can think. I let the string reins fall to the ground. I think the horse doesn't even know I'm there. Very quietly I slide off him and walk away. I never look back.

Later in the afternoon I wander around like everyone else. At four, Miguel, the cook, brings out homemade cinnamon rolls. Six of us sit at the table in the corner playing poker and eating. People wander around waiting for their time with Cove. It's set up so that if somebody wants to talk to Cove, they tell a staff member early in the day. I didn't set up a time because I'm mad at Cove. He's to blame for lots of things. I'm unhappy and he's to blame for that too.

I go to my cottage and get my embroidery and bring it back to the main house. I sit in the living room and work on it. Cove walks in and stands by the door. He motions to me with his hand.

I get all flustered and throw the tapestry back in the plastic bag. I don't want him to see it. He'll think I'm all better because I'm doing one of my creative things; and also, it's his Christmas present. He strolls over to me with a smile. I turn to jelly. I'm not mad at him anymore because he came to me. He likes me.

"Would you like to talk to me, Carol?"

"Sure, okay."

We weave through the dining room, up the stairs to the conference room. I can't get over how Cove looks so human. He's life-size, instead of Green-Giant size.

"How are you doing?"

"Can you believe that I haven't choked since Thursday, not once!"

"That's good."

"Yeah." I look down. "I haven't choked but I do get real uptight."

I'm uneasy because Cove might think I'm all better. The anger rushes back at him.

"You don't know what it's like living here. I hate it. I don't know why I'm here. I can't take it anymore. I'm leaving!"

"Leaving?"

"Yes. I told you I hate it here."

"In that case why don't you call Don and tell him you're taking a bus home. You can handle things from now on. Including your mother at Thanksgiving."

"Shit!"

"If you're ready to leave, you must be better."

"Bastard! Stop! Oh, I'm sorry. I didn't mean that. I'm sorry. I get so mad at you. You know my mother scares me. You know that."

"I want you to realize what you are doing and saying."

"But, this farm is so crazy. I mean, I'm getting all involved with people here and I don't want to. I could get into trouble. Don't you realize?"

"Do you want to get better?"

"That's a stupid question. I hate it when you ask that."

"Do you?"

"Yes, damn it. I'm caught in the middle here. Sometimes I feel like a staff member, sometimes like, I don't know my place here. Most everyone is younger. Shit. You don't understand."

"You shouldn't play mother with guests and you shouldn't play staff."

"What the hell *do* I do?"

"Be yourself."

"Shit! I'm sorry, I shouldn't swear so much. I do have a friend though. Maurice likes me. He will help me, he said so."

"Maurice?" Cove looks stern.

"Yeah, well, he talks to me. Oh, something else. I'm saving some pills."

"What?"

"Well, after last week I wasn't choking so much so I didn't take noon medicine and only one night medicine and I'm saving the rest."

"Are you testing me?"

"What?"

"Are you testing me?"

Silence.

"I don't know what you mean."

"Carol, you know that *I* prescribe your medications and I expect you to take them that way. If you have problems with them, ask me. We've been through this before."

Cove looks mad. I see a red mark on his cheek.

"You don't understand it around here."

"I think I do."

"Well, I asked Mark, he's the med man, to cut me down and he wouldn't. He made me feel stupid. So I'm saving the leftovers."

"Saving for what?"

"Don't know."

"You know that I'll have to tell the staff about this?"

"You don't have to. What I tell you is private, right?"

"You're putting me in a bind again."

I look down. I don't want him to be mad.

"I won't do it anymore." Subdued voice. "I hate this place. People hate me."

"People really like you here, Carol."

"That's because I'm phony!"

"Not because you're phony. They like you because you are considerate with them."

"Shit."

"Carol, stop putting yourself down. For heaven's sake, give yourself a break." Cove smiles at me now.

"Well, thanks for talking to me. I feel better. I'm not mad anymore."

Cove squeezes my hand. I'm not afraid now. Warm hand like regular person.

Mark, the staffer in charge of medicine, comes up to me after supper.

"Hand them over."

"What?"

"Hand over the pills."

"What pills?"

"The pills you hid. Dr. Ashley told me you have them. Hand them over."

"Sure, sure thing. I'll get them and bring them back."

I go to my room and get two Thorazines. Cove told on me. He told them. The shit. He had to and he really did. Shit on him and on group therapy. I put two pills in Mark's hand. That should satisfy them. I go back to my room and hide the rest in a safer place.

Friday, October 31, 1969

I get up early this morning and shower. I don't like to hang around Spruce any longer than necessary because of Frieda. Madonna and Brenda have already moved to the main house because of her. I go down there and make the big pot of coffee. I do this every morning now. People depend on it. Then I make the small pot for me and the old reliables that can't sleep. Jud, Glory, Jake Healy and lots of times Gregory. I set the table for Jake and Gregory.

Gregory is in charge of woods crew and always sits in the corner by the book. He lifts weights in the game room. I have a lot of energy and I like the feeling. Something has happened to me. I have this new energy that I didn't have at home. I want to work. I eat my breakfast next to Jake. I have a pancake with maple syrup to keep this new energy alive. I feel on top. Timothy sits next to me with his breakfast.

"How are you, Carol?" He has a red plaid shirt, a large grin.

"Oh, well, fine. How are you?" I'm mumbling. Why am I so stupid? Why can't I act normal?

"Frieda said that Don brought you your absentee ballot." He puts his arm on my back, like he does with everyone.

"Yes." I blush. I hate myself. This is ridiculous. I can't escape my social ineptness with these nice men. It's so obvious to me here at the farm. It's so stupid, I feel like a toad.

"We haven't talked much since you've come. Are there any problems?"

"Um, no," toad says.

"Well, anytime," prince says.

"Croak, croak," says toad.

After volleyball Lena Mae seeks me out. "I have spoken with John and we will take a walk this morning." She is small and pretty.

"Hi, Lena Mae, sure. How come? That's great. Can I get out of work?"

"I'm taking you off work program, gives us more chance to talk."

We head up the road past the horse pasture toward the lake. I wonder how I'm getting out of the work program.

"Isn't it hard working here?"

"It's good for me. I like it. I have some problems myself, in fact I'm a lot like you, Carol. I have anxiety."

"Do you have trouble sleeping and things like that?" I'm curious.

"I used to have a lot of trouble. It's better now."

We notice the trees are almost bare. There's a small stone chapel to the left of the road. It looks beautiful.

"In fact, Carol, I was wondering why *you* are here. How could you leave your family?"

"What? I had to."

"But why?"

"I couldn't function."

"But you do function. I watch you. It looks like you can do everything."

"But I can't. I mean, that isn't my only problem anyway. There's more to it than that."

"What problems?"

"Oh, it's very involved."

"Dr. Ashley told the staff that he was treating you. How come he wants you here? Doesn't he want you with your kids?"

"Yes, of course. I don't know. Yes. He does. I don't know."

"Does he mix you up when you talk to him?"

"No. I mean, yes he does but it's not his fault. I'm mixed up all by myself."

"Maybe you shouldn't see him anymore."

I look at Lena Mae. We stop.

"Why?"

"I think you should be home with your family. I think he's wrong. He's bad for you. That's why you shouldn't see him."

"How can you say that when you don't really know?" I feel funny as she talks about Cove. I won't discuss Cove with her. Ever. I feel as if this conversation has a point, a reason that I'm missing.

"Lena Mae, I have other problems that I'm working on." I won't tell her how I hurt myself. We're becoming wary, like two female animals. My mind has picked up the scent of danger. I must protect Cove. Nobody but nobody attacks Cove. Except me!

"What problems?"

"Well, for example, men. I'm afraid of men sometimes."

"You're exaggerating. I see you with Maurice all the time. Frieda tells me you go to his room."

"Wait a minute! We just listen to music. And what does Frieda know anyway?" I'm angry. Also I blush.

"I see you with Obie and Jud. You're not afraid of men. In fact, you're bossy."

"Well, I suppose you're right but it's, I'm—only afraid of certain men."

"Who?"

"Well, strong men."

"What do you mean?"

"I don't really know what I mean but take my word for it, I have things to work out before I can go home."

I won't say much else to her because she doesn't know Cove or me, so I just won't ever talk about that.

"What's between you and Maurice anyway?"

"Nothing. We talk, we listen to music."

"Frieda says you stay out late."

"I do stay out late. I can't sleep."

"I think you should talk to Timothy about going home. You don't belong here."

"Oh, Lena Mae. I explained to you I have problems. Besides I'm afraid of Timothy."

"You're afraid of Timothy?" She laughs so I laugh. I'll make it a joke.

"Well, sort of. Funny isn't it?"

"How could you be afraid of him? He's so nice and kind. Good looking too. Right after lunch I want you to talk to him."

Silence.

"I will march down with you myself if I have to."

"I'll talk to him."

What the hell am I going to talk to him for? I'm scared to, and I'll make a fool of myself. Lena Mae will probably forget. Oh, why do I open my mouth?

We sit on the chairs by the edge of the lake. It looks like it might be good fishing.

"I used to like to fish." Wistful Carol. Sad not to fish anymore.

"I hate it. Hate to bait the hook," Lena Mae says.

There are many things to work out before I go home. I must like to fish again. I must be able to fish again and I decide to, there! That's the reason for being at the farm. If I can only somehow throw away the garbage stinking up my soul. Then I'll be able to fish.

Lena Mae and I go back down the hill when we hear the lunch gongs. She has the power to yank me off a work crew and the power to tell me what to do. But she doesn't understand me. So her power is frightening. She doesn't want me here at the farm. I don't understand. I know that she spends time with Maurice. Is she jealous?

At lunch, we are all laughing because Glory is running around the perimeter of the dining room, bumping into things and making lots of noise. Frieda motions for me to come to her from across the room. What does she want?

"Carol, I see that you didn't go on work program this morning."

"Well, no. Lena Mae and I took a walk to the lake."

"I don't think you should have done that."

"No?"

"It's against policy."

I get confused. Frieda and Lena Mae are both staff. They disagree and I'm caught in the middle. "What policy?" I look at her. My eye rivets to her crotch. I can't help it. That's where she sewed the big red patch. It embarrasses me.

"It isn't good for you to get too friendly with the staff. I have been noticing you, Carol, and would also like to talk to you about your relationship with Madonna and Queenie. Have you left your own children to replace them with these girls?"

"That's stupid, I haven't."

"And you want the best of both worlds. Well, it won't work. You have your husband visit."

"What's the matter with that?"

"It's against policy. Husbands are not to visit unless it's a holiday."

"But—"

"It isn't good for you. I hear you pacing around at night. I hear you through the walls."

"But—nobody else has . . ."

She interrupts then. "And I see through you. I know you come out of Maurice's cottage, late."

"But nobody else has a husband. How can it be against policy? Nobody else is married."

"You mustn't get too close to guests. You mother them. You mustn't talk to them so much."

"Oh Frieda, that's silly. All you're saying . . ."

"You are very hostile. I see hostility in you. You don't get along with your mother and are overcompensating for this imagined lack of love by trying to be a mother to all."

"Shit!" My insides are getting hard. She is attacking me and my eyes just stay focused on her red crotch. I feel cold now. I'm detaching myself. I think she's very jealous of me.

"Your hostility comes out in your swearing. I know about these things."

"You?"

"Yes, I do. Now that this is settled, I wonder if you would like to come to my room for some wine tonight."

My God, she talks crazy. I look at her. Her flag is waving, her braids top-heavy. I feel put down, a kid, a jerk. Is she right? Maybe she's right. Maybe Don shouldn't come. He is too good for me, my Don. I don't deserve to have him. I had to leave my kids for a while. Didn't I? Oh Christ. Oh Christ. Laura Lee comes behind me. Frieda walks off. I see her head over to Maurice.

"Carol, could you teach me to knit?"

"Ah. Sure, maybe tomorrow—okay?" I see Laura Lee glance at Maurice and Frieda.

"How's your back?"

"Oh I, it's all right. I think I've forgiven Minnie for throwing the coffee. At least intellectually. But I'm glad she's gone. It makes me uneasy being here now. I don't know if I'll stay much longer."

"You're doing just fine." I put my arm on her arm. She smiles at me. She is a nice young woman.

Lena Mae interrupts us and takes my elbow and leads me to the head of the stairs.

"I want you to talk to Timothy. Now!"

"Oh Christ." She opens the door that leads downstairs to his office and gives me a shove. I am caught momentarily off balance and lose my footing. The door slams. I catch hold of the bannister and sit on the stairs. I sit there. The noise upstairs is blurred. I'm not going to move.

I put my head in my arms. Timothy comes out of his office. He comes up the stairs and sits on the step just above me. He puts his hand on my head.

"Why, hello there. What are you doing here?"

"I don't know. I really don't."

"Did you want to talk to me about something?"

"Well, everybody else seems to think I should." I light another cigarette.

"Do you want to?"

"Timothy, do you think we could arrange a time for me to tutor Queenie? I've talked to her about it."

"During work program?"

"Doesn't matter to me."

"I think that's a fantastic idea."

"Good." I pick my head up and smile.

"How're things going otherwise?"

"Oh. Confusing. Things get confused fast, don't they? So many people."

Timothy and I both stand up and start up the stairs.

"The people getting you down?"

"Yeah. How'd you know?"

"Get me down too, sometimes."

We part. I smoke. I smoke too much. My smoking has doubled. I don't know why.

Monday, November 3, 1969

I've decided to stay by myself for the rest of the day. I worked hard in the summer kitchen making bread and cookies. I took charge because Rachel and Alfred were with me. We joked and fooled around. Made sixteen loaves and a quadruple batch of cookies. Rachel got on my nerves. All her questions about babies. Makes me think of my babies. Uptight now. Emptiness in me. Big gaping hole in my stomach. Are they all right without me? Will they hate me for leaving them? Is Daddy holding them and kissing them? What am I doing here? I'm not going to get involved anymore. I'll just do my jobs and think things out. I'll be calm and easy. Then I'll go home. No more messing with all these people. I go to the small table by the stairs and sit with my back to the wall. Cove's embroidery is coming along. Too many people in here. I move to the library.

Jay is sitting in a chair reading. He doesn't live at the farm anymore. He has a job in town. He comes up the hill and stays over sometimes. He's in Cove's stupid group therapy. Skin Bradleap walks in. I like him. He organizes the dishes crew, which is an awful job. And he does it well too. He also does the store after meals. He sits on the chair opposite me and he flicks his cigarette ashes in the cuff of his dungarees and stubs it out on his knee. He grinds the tobacco into his leg. His leg is twitching up and down, up and down. I wonder what happened to set him off?

"You all right, Skin?"

He doesn't look at me but at Jay.

"What are you doing here?"

"I've come to the farm to see my dear friends and tell . . ."

"What friends? You don't have friends."

"I certainly do. I have Timothy and John and . . ."

"Shit you do. They just don't know how to get away from you," Skin says. I interrupt him.

"Hey Skin, Skinny, what happened? Did something happen to you?" I've put away the embroidery.

"I don't like *him* here." Loud voice. Laura Lee Jones walks in.

"What's going on?" she says.

"Nothing's going on. I'm Glory. See? See?" And he takes off Laura's shoe and falls on the floor, groaning. Then he jumps up and he races over to Jay and yells, "I am the Boston Strangler. I will take a broom handle and I'll ram it up your mother. I do glorious things!" Laura Lee is stricken with fear. She runs from the room. Skin is getting carried away. I can see he can't stop. He can't stop now and I don't know what to do.

Skin lunges at Jay. There is kicking and grunts and it goes on and on. A crowd gathers at the door. I jump at Skin and grab his shoulders and push him on the couch. I race to Jay. I yank him to his feet and push him out the door. I slam it shut. Skin is quiet. His face looks bewildered and hurt.

He says, "Do you like me? Do you like me?"

"Yes, I like you."

"Do you like me?"

It hurts me to see him like this. What happened? It was like he was pretending and then it wasn't pretend any longer. The crowd is gone. Skin has gone. Helen has taken him to her cottage.

Something has started in me. I feel like Skin Bradleap myself. What has started? I must do something. Fear is building. I want to cry. I have to cry but all I make are mewing noises. I must find those hidden tears in this God damned place before I get like him. Cove, where are you? Why isn't it Tuesday? Help me, Cove. Frieda walks in. I grab my boots and jacket and embroidery and I race out the door. I run fast up toward the big pines. It is dark now. I fall at the bottom of the tree and I take my fist and hit the tree. Over and over. But I can't cry. My hand is numb. Why isn't it working? Where are the tears? Voices come from the path. Frieda has Laura Lee and she has Maurice. Coming to get me. Slip on my boots and jacket. Hold my embroidery to my breast. Cove will help me. I run up, up, up into the hills. Only Maurice follows, and he catches me. He shakes me. I glare at him. Defiant. Testing.

"I have no tears. I can't find them." I dare him, but I don't know what for.

"Carol, let go, let go. I'll help you."

"Get away! Get away!"

Maurice raises his fist back. I see it coming, a flash of white in the night. It hits me on my face. Palm is open. The lights dance around. I fall down. He hit me. He hurt me. I stay on the ground trembling. He falls down beside me and puts his arms around me.

"I did it for you. I had to do it. Now you'll be all right. I didn't want to hurt you. You'll be all right. I had to do it to snap you out of it."

I listen to his words there on the ground. I gasp and gasp. I put my arms around myself. And I make noise when I gasp.

"It's all right. I'll be all right. It's all right." I don't want him to hit me.

"You'll be okay now. I understand these things."

I lie there feeling nothing. I don't tell him. I'm not sure I even want to know it myself. But nothing has happened. The urgency is still there buried under the words, under the slap. And so the fear comes flooding back. I don't dare move. I say nothing. Flashlights coming up the hill. Up and up. Finding us. Maurice the hero. Calming down the crazy lady. I lie there quiet. Mark has come with them. They give me pills. I tell them to take me to the cottage. They say Frieda won't be out again for the night. I look at Laura Lee and I wonder why she ran out on Skin. I look at them all. I have decided to do something I should have done in the first place. So I'm quiet now, subdued. They take me back to Spruce. When all is quiet I slip out and head for the main house. I go through the living room, dining room and kitchen. I open the cellar stairs. I have to do it. It's the only way. I put Cove's embroidery crumpled up under my arm so it won't get soiled. I let myself go then, tumbling down the stairs. I lie at the bottom and the tears come. I lie there and it feels good to cry. I finally found them. I'm so sorry I have to wrench them out of myself this way. But I had to do it. I'm sorry, Cove. I'm sorry. I put the embroidery to my tears. I'll make a pretty picture for you. I really will. It will be nice enough to put on your wall. You'll like me then, won't you, Cove? You'll like me then, won't you?

Tuesday, November 4, 1969

I am sore. I am cold. I am old. My head is hanging. I don't like myself very much. I am all alone. Nobody cares for me. I'm a nothing. A shithead. I go to breakfast and I don't sit next to Jake.

I sit by myself. This is Cove day but I don't want to see Cove. Cove will hate me if he finds out what I did. So I have to stay away. I have a cup of coffee. Don't want food. Skin has come in. He acts so strange. I don't want to see him. He's not himself. He's so loud and John and Steve, Helen's husband, are trying to calm him down. He bit the back of a chair. It makes me want to cry. What has happened to him? I don't understand. I can't look at him this way and am about to leave when John and Steve take him out. The room is hushed. Makes our hearts beat faster. Glory jumps up and grabs the bread knife and holds it to her own throat.

"Eeee."

We go back to eating. Tension is broken. This is normal.

The book is read. I am put on the front sewer drain. Terry is in charge. He is a large, nice, black-bearded man. If I got to know him I'd probably be afraid of him so I just stay quiet. No talking. He's given me a good job. I stand in the truck with the hose and wash the dirt off the gravel. The rest of the crew shovel the gravel neatly on top of the pipes. We are out front. The larger sewer crew is out back. I'm all wet and cold but I like it. It's doing something good to my mood. I see Cove drive in about ten, so I sit down in the truck until he's gone inside. The hose has a powerful force. It hits the stones and makes them bounce around. The sun hits the water and makes rainbows dance. The mud leaps a little, then goes off in streams into the ground, leaving the gravel white. What a marvelous job. I love standing in a truck. It makes me feel as if I know what I'm doing. I always think people in trucks know what they're doing. I'm smiling when Timothy drives up in his car. I wave to him. He steps out and leaps up next to me.

He asks me to take a ride with him to the polls. I leap down. Feel young again, not so alone.

We tear down that mountain. He talks so sensibly, talks to me as if he's talking to himself, being kind to me, giving me the kind of advice he gives to himself.

"Try not to take the guests' problems so seriously. Don't take them as your own problems. Don't let Skinny's sickness bother you so much. You won't get swept away. You're doing fine. Don't let Frieda get to you. Maybe you'd like to move to the main house? And also, Maurice. Might be good to be careful there."

"Careful?"

"Let me put it this way. It would be easy for me, around the farm so much of my time, to get fond of someone—Laura Lee, for instance. Young girl, beautiful body. But I don't. It's not worth it. I'm careful. Get what I mean? He's attractive, you're attractive."

"I don't think that I—well." No psychoanalyzing with Timothy.

He goes to vote and I think how amazing that he knows about me. How does he keep track? I really don't feel alone now. We head back to the farm.

"I was wondering, Carol, what do you think of Mark? He's so fat—I wonder why."

"I don't know." Timothy is asking me, a guest, about Mark, who is staff. I am very flattered. He's confiding. I don't think he thinks I'm crazy at all. I like that.

Lena Mae has asked me if I'd help Miguel with lunch, so I go in the kitchen and help him with some chicken he's frying. Miguel likes me. He asks what makes everybody so crazy. I say I don't know but it sure isn't the food. The food is great. He knows it is, too.

I stand by the sink rinsing out some utensils. The sun is streaming in. I turn around and there's Cove. Just standing there in the sun. Cove. His face looks tired and his face looks old. Oh. A shot of overwhelming love goes through me so bad that I want to cry. He is a part of me now. I don't want him old. Oh. He's going to die of cancer. I love Cove. I want to run to him and put my arms around him. He has on his green sweater. I don't know how to deal with this. It just struck me so fast. I turn around and run out the back door. I run past the chicken farm up the green pasture. I lie on the ground and look at the clouds. It's so hard for me to know that Cove is human. I start to cry. I think about his hair. I think he's letting it grow longer. It looks nice. Cove looked so nice in his eyes. I don't know how I could think that he'd hate me. It hurts me to love him like this because it makes me so afraid. Afraid like something awful will happen. Some powerful, awful thing will scrunch me and hurt my head. So I better stay away.

Maurice comes up the hill. I see him winding up the path. He lies down beside me and we watch the clouds. He says that Lena Mae put him with me for the afternoon. They all know I'm up here on the hill. Lena says Maurice's supposed to cheer me up.

"Well, go ahead, Maurice. Cheer me up. But actually I feel all right now. I heard that you're leaving soon. What are you going to do?"

"I'm going to live with a friend. She has a house and will try to help me get a job."

"What about your painting?"

"I'm in a dry spell. Can't paint. I'll be back to the farm to visit. If you ever need me, call." He hands me his number. He rolls over on top of me and then rolls off. He laughs. I wonder if Maurice will be all right. He certainly is attractive. But I sense something. It happens every time I'm with him. Something. Like maybe he'll get a broken leg. Or end up with a patch over his eye or a car will run him over. He seems clouded by a limited vision. Or maybe a vision too far. Maybe it's just fear that I see in him. Like in us all. Or maybe he doesn't like women.

Madonna and Queenie bring smuggled supper up to my cabin in the woods. They are delighted with my Tuesday games with Cove. They admire me for staying away from him. The more I say nothing about it, the more they admire me. The only thing is, though, I really want to see Cove. I want to tell him all these things. I want to make sure he's all right. He's at the farm and I can't see him. Now that it's seven-thirty, I know that group therapy has started. I can leave my room, go to the main house and not see Cove. I wonder what they do. I don't like Cove with other guests so I get mad at him all over again. Shit. I get some coffee and flop down in the dining room. Shit. Frieda comes over and asks about me moving to the main house. I mentioned it to Maurice. I'm a little embarrassed but I say that since I spend so much time here, it makes more sense.

"What are you running away from?"

"Nothing." You turkey.

"Am I threatening to you?"

"No, Frieda." I think you're crazy.

"Are you jealous because Maurice talks so long with me? This is called transference."

"For heaven's sake, no!" Jesus, what a looney.

"You're going to have to realize that Maurice is leaving. And face it."

"Sure, Frieda." Actually I'm glad he's going.

"Maybe we'll be better friends now that he's going."

"Maybe." But we never were friends.

John walks in the room and sees us talking. He comes over.

"I'd like to talk to you if I can, Carol."

Frieda looks cross at him. Does she think I'm her prize patient? Oh, my heart beats faster. What have I done? Have I done something wrong? I like John so much, I hope I haven't done anything. John takes my hand and he leads me in the kitchen. He whispers. "I just thought you might like to talk. I notice you've had a few rough days." We go to the far side of the kitchen and sit at a tiny table in the dark.

"Thanks, John. I have. I'm not very nice. I'm mixed up. I get funny when Dr. Ashley is here. Skinny getting so sick, that fight in the library. So alone."

"You're not alone. We love you. We know some of your pain. I really care. You had quite a time last night."

"I don't know what happened to me. I couldn't cry."

"Maybe we should try to laugh more at things. You always seem so tense."

"I am tense. All held in." John grabs my hand. I hold onto his hand very hard. We sit and talk in the dark, and he lets me hold his hand very hard.

"I would be glad to rub your back, help you relax."

"I can't."

"I know. I sense you can't. That's all right."

His offer to rub my back is very nice. It seems he thinks I'm all right somehow. It makes me think of the network of nice people here, in the background, walking around caring for me. Noticing me when I'm unhappy. I think I'm alone and I'm not really alone at all. I clutch at his hand. I want to tell him about the stairs. But I don't have to. He knows about all of us guests and yet still lets us hold his hands. It doesn't matter how awful we are. The staff, they walk around and work and notice us. And it doesn't matter what we do. When we're ready they'll rub our backs and make us calm and let us sleep.

Wednesday, November 5, 1969

It's four-thirty and I'm up. I take my usual shower but I don't go to the main house. I sit in my chair. I don't want to move from the chair. I'm sick of it all. I want to go home. I'm not going to work. I refuse. I need answers. I need questions! I don't even know what questions. But I know I'm not going to move. I'm lead, heavy, my head weighs a ton. I hold up my head with my hands. A granite mountain of weight. Too much for my hands. I lie on the bed and stare. Maybe I want attention. Maybe John will come and talk to me. I notice a little brown mouse is living in my room. That means I'll have to wear slippers. The farmers can make their own coffee. They can fight their own fights. It's too much for me.

After a while, after lunch hour I'm too bored to sit any longer. I amble down the path. I swing over by the rec house and look in the window. Nobody's there. As I go down the path to the main house Alfred walks out all excited. He stutters.
"M-Madonna a-a-and Obie are fighting, M-Madonna and Obie."
"Where?"
"By my room. In her room."
I race past him in the door and push past a crowd gathered by the stairs. Run up the stairs. Mark and Laura Lee are out in the hall, wringing their hands. Screams come from the room. I run in. Madonna and Obie are on the floor. Jesus. Obie weighs about 250 pounds.

"Madonna! Stop fighting!"

Her eyes have panicked. Obie is trying to hold her down and she scrambles away fast to the window. She raises her fist and hits the window pane. Two times. Smash. Glass all over.

Obie yells at me, "She's going to kill herself and me!"

Blood starts pouring down her arm and she grabs a foot-long triangular jagged pane of glass.

"Don't come near me. Stay away. Fucking God damned shit. Get away." Madonna means it. She doesn't care about her body. She doesn't care if it gets hurt. I stand there, just stand there, and I get a little light-headed. Madonna has painted her new room all red— even the door. Even the light bulb is red. And so when I see her bleeding I have this momentary flash that of course she has to bleed, it goes with the room. Everything is all red. Except Obie. He's black. And Madonna's eyes are white. And her teeth. It all makes me dizzy. She won't hurt me. I know this in my chicken bones so I talk to her.

"Oh, Madonna, you're such a pretty girl, it hurts me to see you so sad, oh please, put down the glass. Please."

Her eyes soften just a second from the hatred and they look just afraid but it doesn't last.

"Don't let them get you. Don't let them get you. They'll kill us all," Obie screams at her.

"We're the same. Hand over the glass. Hand it over." Obie and Madonna knew each other in the city and there is a bond between them. Obie then starts to get off the floor and as he's doing that John runs in and runs right past Obie and me and right over to Madonna. He grabs her left hand and pulls it behind her. The glass drops and makes an awful noise. Madonna puts up a deter-mined struggle. Then all of a sudden she gets tired and gives up. I go over and hold her and Obie comes over and John lets go of her arm. Three of us stand holding her. She doesn't cry. We all stand there. Madonna asks me, "Can I come to your room?"

"Yeah. Yeah."

"I'll clean the glass up, Carol, can you give a little first aid?" John's face now looks so white in the red room.

"I'll come with you," says Obie.

Obie and I keep hold of Madonna and walk slowly up the woods to Spruce Cottage. Obie instructs the gathering farmers to get the fuck out of the way or he'll kill them.

We tip the chair under the doorknob so Frieda can't walk in. Obie goes back. Madonna has a cut on her thumb but it isn't too bad. I put some Band-Aids on it.

Madonna repeats over and over, "Did you see how John twisted my arm? Did you see how he twisted my arm? I'm a minor, you know. He could get in trouble. He shouldn't of done that. I think he broke my arm. I could report him, you know. I never figured him to be so strong. You think my arm is broken?"

I look at her elbow. She has quite a wicked looking bruise but she's moving it all over to see if she can see it. I don't think it's broken. I go quietly to the kitchen and get ice and put it on the swelling. I rub her back now, and she lies on the bed and talks.

"It doesn't bother me when I get wild. I don't care about myself. I always start banging and throwing things around and then I can't stop it. I'll kill myself one day because I won't be able to stop. I have to feel the pain, you see. The fucking pain. That's why I do it. If I bust myself up every once in a while, then I can keep going. See these scars?"

She bares her arm.

"Well, I have lots more."

"Sometimes I hit things too, Madonna. I'm like you."

"You? No way."

"I can't stop sometimes either. I don't know why, though."

"I do. I hate my fucking self and I hate the fucking world and I get God damned Jesus fucking Christ mad."

"Mad? At what?"

"Jesus fucking mad at everything. That's what. And I don't care. I just don't care."

"When I do things like that, I care. I mean, I feel real bad." I confide in her.

"Not me. And I never will."

"You want to stay here tonight? I could sleep in your room."

"Yeah. I'm too tired to move. It's okay, huh?"

"Sure."

"I wish'd I could be like you, Carol."

"Why, Madonna?"

"Because you care. That's why. You Jesus fucking *care*. And I never will."

I pack a few things together and wend my way down to the main house to Madonna's red room. I can't bring myself to sleep there. As if I'd catch something in the room. So I put my parka over me on the couch in the living room nearest the fireplace. I put another log on the fire. John walks by, sees me in the flickering light and sits by me. I hold up my hand and he takes it. He is trembling.

"Is Madonna all right? I didn't mean to hurt her. My God. Obie said her arm is broken."

"Oh, John, I don't think so. You had to do it. There was nothing else you could do. You had to."

"I really feel pretty bad. Boy, I hate this kind of thing!"

"Hey, John, you're a very nice person. It's all right. You're a very nice man."

Before I sleep, I throw a prayer to that elusive Jesus out there who we cry out to in our pain. The one we swear at and curse, the one we blame. A prayer of thanks, because I care.

Thursday, November 6, 1969

I'm working on the large sewer drain at the back of the main house. It starts way across the road by the compost heap and continues along the whole length of the house right up to the summer kitchen. The long trenches have been dug and most of the pipes laid. We have an impressive crew working. It's raining. Our crew is up by the road. We all have shovels. Steve checks over the pipes to make sure they're in properly. He calls to us, and we shovel piles of dirt and stones on top. We all grumble and mumble and wonder why the tractors aren't doing this. Why should we be out in the rain? At ten-thirty we have a break and I sit with Maurice and Laura Lee on a wet rock. We vote not to go in for our break because nobody would want to come back out. Miguel has a small kitchen crew bring us hot chocolate and doughnuts. We can see the progress on our work, and we compete with the other crews to get as much done as we can. It's so muddy we get to a point where it doesn't matter anymore because we really can't get wetter. That's when we really work. When there's a boulder that's too large, John drives over with the tractor and either pushes it away or in. I light a cigarette and watch the rain pelt the paper. I throw it away. I look around and see nearly everyone on the whole farm working. Obscenities and groans and complaints. I can't help smiling. I guess none of us really knows what the hell we are digging this sewer line for, or even how we got *here*. But *here* we are. It's shared. And it's work. I think the sewer line has been my best job yet.

I take a shower and clean all the mud and cold off me. I sit naked on my bed. It's a special day, as it always is on Thursday. Don day and my appointment with Cove. This is hard for me. Don has to leave work early and get a sitter for the kids and he has to come to the farm and take me to Cove's. He doesn't complain about this. He just does it. And I work on sewer ditches. How can I smile working on the sewer when Don does everything at home? I think how beautiful he is. I think he's too good for me. How can he love me? I am a mess. I start to get dressed and go to the closet and stand. Maybe I should wear a dress. No! I'm not part of that world anymore. I put on clean dungarees. I'm no good. I deserve nothing. Dresses mean that other world where wives go out to dinner and take care of their children and drive to Agway for potting soil and talk on the phone about Cub Scouts. The good people who don't say shit and fuck. And they can love, too, can accept love. And they go to the Heart Fund luncheon and make zucchini casseroles for Saturday night dinners. Cove is one of the good ones. Don and Cove. I put them in this category. Their world is apart now. I deserve to be here. What is this farm anyway? A place for us moral degenerates? Criminally insane? A place for the very, very rich to put away their black sheep? I don't know. I'm all mixed up. And I get a little angry at Don and Cove. How come they're so good?

So when Don comes and he touches me, my insides freeze. He is too good for me. I can't love him. And Cove too. I talk to him, but I keep things away from him. I don't tell him I freeze when Don touches me. I don't tell him about the stairs. Cove hates me anyhow. Cove and Don both hate me. Cove has a different look in his eyes. I can tell. I tell him about Maurice and how I want Maurice to hold me, love me. See? Now Cove hates me because he's one of the good ones. Cove says maybe I'm looking for new ways to hurt myself. What do you know anyway, Cove? Now that you and Don are in a separate category, it makes me very lonely. And so as not to be lonely, I have Maurice. How the hell can that hurt me? But I keep both of you in a special place in my mind. That place reserved for beautiful things, beautiful thoughts. The love place. That feeling I have for Don when he rubs my foot and looks at me; the feeling I have for Cove that cuts through me—I put that good love in the special place. It hurts too much to have it floating around in the open. Because I am such a failure. So I have to lock it away. The comparison is too much. I sit on the bed and I look at my knee. God, how I hate that knee. I hate my whole God damned body. Shit! I hate my foot. I want to hurt it all. It sickens me. So I clench my fists and grind my teeth and choke in my throat. I say goodbye, outside world. Go away, leave me alone. I can't be a part. I don't deserve you. I see my mouse and he makes me mad. I go to the small kitchen and get some bread and bring it to my room and I set a trap.

Friday, November 7, 1969

They took Skin to the hospital. He couldn't snap out of it. That was yesterday. I miss him. And now today there is a going-away party for Mark. Miguel made a cake. Mark is going back to college. He sure doesn't look sick. Madonna says he was a mess when he came. Now he's better. He has been here four months as a staff member. Before that a guest. I'm angry that he's leaving and I'm not. Lots of people feel this way. Do we go like Skin or like Mark?

Frieda has left a note for me in my mailbox to come see her. I leave the party, go back to Spruce and knock on her door.

"Carol, Madonna told me that you offered to go with her to the hospital to have her arm X-rayed."

"Yes, I did. It's giving her a lot of pain and John and I felt that maybe it should be X-rayed. I think she needs to have it done."

"I forbid it."

"Forbid it? Forbid what?"

"Madonna is manipulating you. She doesn't need a mother figure." Frieda is half smiling. I stand awkwardly. Her revelations seem to give her great satisfaction.

"I'm really amazed, Frieda." I'm really amazed how you don't miss much.

"You must stop being a mother."

"Madonna is my friend." I'll always be a mother.

"It isn't good for her."

"Okay." I've got to tell Madonna to keep her mouth shut.

Tuesday, November 11, 1969

I'm goofing off. I even skip out of farm meeting, which is required. I guess the reason I'm getting away with goofing off is because when Cove is here, things get wilder and looser. Staff have meetings and then people that want to see Cove get out of work, so it's hard to keep track of us. I'm not predictable. I change moods so fast even I have no idea what mood I'll be in even for the next hour. Especially when Cove's around. I just hate him so much for some little thing, like maybe locking his car doors. And then the next hour I love him. Damn these Tuesdays anyway. But I look forward to them all week. So, it's hard for me to make an appointment to see him because I just might hate him when that appointment is due.

I decide to eat supper in the dining room. I'm at a long table facing the fireplace. I see Cove out of the corner of my eye. I've left the chair to my left free. I want him to sit next to me. My stomach is all fluttery. Cove is coming this way. He pulls out the chair, sits down.

"Hello. Can I sit here?" Smiles, warm eyes, nice man.

"Sure. Hi." Appetite gone. Cove is willing to sit next to me. Cove doesn't hate. Can't eat. Have to force-feed schoolgirl so as not to frighten off movie star. Take one bite and chew and then smile and act cool. Above all, act cool. His voice low and confidential.

"Are you all right? You weren't at the farm meeting."

"Ah . . ."

"You were nominated for council president and elected to allowance committee."

"Me? Doesn't that figure. If you miss a meeting you get elected." Schoolgirl forces out words to appear normal. She can only sneak looks at his face. She can watch his boots right next to her boots. But he insists on being recognized. He makes it personal. He looks at her. After all. It is Cove. Cove knows her. And he likes her because here he is sitting next to her. And he seems so dependable and stable. She swallows and looks right at him, into his face. And he looks at her. Not movie star, not schoolgirl. Cove and Carol.

"Would you like to join group therapy?"

"Yes. Can I? I want to."

Cove talks about group. I feel excited because I'll be a part of the exclusive group. Now I'll know what's going on.

Cove gets up to leave and puts his hand on my back. The way he acts always makes me feel a little more dependable myself. And a little more stable. It might not last very long but it's there now and it's something that hasn't been with me. Ever. I think about my new responsibilities. I was nominated for council president. I'm thrilled. It could present problems if I was elected. I'm afraid of crowds, so half the time I'm forced to leave the room during council meetings. Everybody knows this but still I was nominated. I wonder if it was John. Then again, if I was elected, I could get a glass of water, two Juicy Fruits and cigarettes all ready. Props. Maybe I could do it. I might even do a good job.

Now, allowance committee—that should be easy. It's time I took on some jobs myself. Anybody that wants to can work before and after work hours—before eight and after four for extra money. Allowance committee gets together and decides how much each job is worth by the hour. Say phone duty. If I sign up for phone duty and work eight hours a week, I'd earn eight dollars. That's a coveted job because you sit down. There's cleaning the game room, offices, store. Store is a good one. After lunch and dinner, the store opens up and sells cigarettes and candy bars and gum. There's also the dishes list. Organizing everybody's time for dishes. Skin had that, now Jud has it. I'm going to apply for a job soon. It will make me feel a little independent, financially. I'll be able to buy my own cigarettes.

Group therapy, seven-thirty. Nervous. Jake Healy and Cove are co-leaders. It's in the library. The fire is crackling. The door is shut. I am introduced to the two people who come from town. Jane and Jay. I look at Jay. He's the guy that had the ruckus with Skin. Jane is kind of pretty. Has long hair. Also included in the group are Hugh Wheeling, a former guest but now a staffer, Eden Smith, a guest, Rachel, guest, Benson, guest, and me.

Cove is across from me in a chair. I have decided that I won't talk. Much safer. Everybody just looks around at everybody else. Sure as hell isn't going to be me. Jay starts. "Well, I'm doing very well as you all know, except you, Carol." Jay talks a long time but rambles. He has no friends. He says he's better.

His eyes are ice eyes. Intense. They frighten me. He fastens them on me when he talks. Then they rove from one face to another. His eyes don't match his body or his voice. His body is slight, maybe even somehow crippled. His voice is high and shrill. But his eyes chill me.

JANE: "I've left the farm but I still have problems. I make friends all right. I opened up a lot and sometimes maybe too much because now I don't know about a woman's place in the world. I like to sleep with men but is it fair to bring a baby into the world without a father?"

BENSON: "I want to live on an island."

HUGH: "Let her finish."

JANE: "It's okay—go ahead, Benson. Speak up, we can't hear you. Raise your head up; don't mumble."

Benson flushes and his mumbles get louder. "I want to live on an island and be a hermit, away from people. I hate dirty people."

JANE: "Are you implying that I am dirty?"

BENSON: "Well, it seems to me that your kind . . ."

JANE: "My kind?" She stands up and points her finger. "Are you any better? Are you? Escaping off to an island. That's really stupid."

I'm getting a little nervous. I look at Cove.

COVE: "Let's see, now. Jane, maybe you could tell us in another way what's bothering you."

Everyone relaxes a little.

JANE: "I guess I get confused about women's place, or rather my place, out there in the world. I don't think I believe in sin, but sometimes I feel guilty about—sometimes I wonder if men take advantage of me."

RACHEL: "I–have–that–problem–too." Halting voice, dreamy eyes.

HUGH: "Ha! You jump at any man that will take his pants off."

RACHEL: "I–wish–I–didn't sometimes."

BENSON: "That's why I want to be a hermit. I hate dirty people. I hate them, they make me sick."

HUGH: "Women will get you every time, Benson. They're fuckers, all of them."

JAKE: "Follow your thought, Rachel. Why do you say you have a similar problem as Jane's?"

As they're talking I begin to feel a little sick. This is dangerous business going on here. My hand starts moving up and down, up and down. I don't want to call attention to myself. But I can't help my hand. Nervous. Don't want to talk about sex. Not now. Don't want to be here. Don't like it. I look at Cove. He'll protect me if anything happens. I guess he won't let anything happen to me. I see him put a Gelusil in his mouth.

RACHEL: "I think that men take advantage of me because I want to sleep with them. I wish I didn't." Voice falters, eyes look far away. I want to help her, say something to her, but I'm too afraid to join in.

2

81

HUGH: "All you women would cut off our balls if we gave you a chance. Jesus. You're all mixed up because your place is in the home, the kitchen, with the children where you belong. This God damned fem lib pisses me off."

JAY: "I say there, Hugh. I say. There are women present. Watch your language." Jay irritates us, the way his talk is stilted.

COVE: "What do you think about women's place, Eden?" So far Eden and I haven't talked. Eden has a soft, black beard. He has a quiet voice. I have seen him on phone duty strumming his guitar. Smiles easily.

Eden looks up, smiles. "I like women, I like them in dresses, I like them in pants. Makes no difference to me. I like to work with them, too. Good workers."

HUGH: "Doesn't it bug the hell out of you that they try to work like men?"

EDEN: "Not really."

JANE: "Are you afraid, Hugh, that women might do a better job than you? Is that why you have all this hatred?"

HUGH: "Go to hell."

Jakes steps in. "Do you hate women?"

EDEN: "You afraid you're not a real man?"

HUGH: "You can't tell me you like to see these God damned women walking around in their dungarees pretending to work. I say keep them in the kitchen."

My heart races. Takes lots of energy not to jump in. But this area is too much for me. I wonder about dungarees myself. And if he doubts his manhood, then I doubt my womanhood. My hand goes back and forth. I have a lump in my throat. I feel like crying. I don't know why. I see Cove look at me. Don't ask me anything. Cove, don't.

JANE: "I guess maybe something happened to you, Hugh, to make you so mad."

HUGH: "I've seen the world. I've been around. I know the score."

RACHEL: "I'd like to have babies." She looks at me. I'm incapable of answering.

HUGH: "That's all you're good for."

JAY: "My mother is a wonderful woman. Someday I'm going to visit her. She took very good care of me. I think mothers are the only ones that love you. If your mother doesn't, then nobody does. I don't know any girls."

I have to cry and I don't know why. I have to cry. So I leave. I make myself get up and leave. It's all right when I get outside. My nervousness leaves. Tricky business. I copped out. Damn it, I copped out. That will call attention to me next time. How stupid. Scary, tricky group.

I walk over to Cove's car. I just lean on the fender. I'll wait here and say good night to him before he leaves. I want him to know I'm all right.

Thursday, November 13, 1969

John is near me playing volleyball. I love to watch him. He has so much energy and is nice to so many people. Hugh is pretty nice too but bitter. I don't trust him either. Not after group. Maurice is looking very dejected these last days. His shoulders are stooped and he moves very slowly.

Eden is standing by the door chatting with me when Maurice slouches by. I run to catch up to him.

"Hey, Maurice. You okay? You look a little down."

"Leave me the fuck alone." He hasn't shaved. My face flames. I back up and walk away. I sit on a rock and pat John's little puppy dog. I feel I have done something wrong. I am a whore. I am bad. I'll have to avoid Maurice. I want to tell Cove about these things. Maybe he can help me. I'm glad I go tonight.

They have given us the afternoon off and are taking us to town for bowling. I sit in the front of the bus. Queenie sits next to me. I've panicked. I hold on to the metal bar with both hands.

"Why you scared? Why you scared?" Queenie stares at me.

"Don't know."

"Want me to stop the bus? Want me to tell Howie to take you home?"

"No. Damn it."

"You scared the bus will crash?"

"No!"

"Well, what the hell are you scared of?"

"Don't know." I go in my pocket. Let one hand go, and get my gum. I pull out two pieces. Helps the anxiety. Queenie looks scared for me. I start to laugh.

"It's s-s-s-tupid. S-stupid. See, I can't even talk. I'm sorry. It's so s-s-stupid."

"Sure is. Gives me the creeps. Never saw you like this before."

"What'd you think, I'm at the farm for my health?"

"Why sure. Didn't you know it's a health farm?"

"Oh, ha, ha, funny."

"What you need is some pot."

"Oh come on, Queenie. That's all I need. Another habit. That's perfect. Another habit to be dependent on. That'd be really smart of me."

"I see what you mean."

I've relaxed my hand on the bar. Both hands. The anxiety is leaving. I've made it. I turned off an attack. I took out its fury.

I say, "Be my partner, bowling, okay? I'll treat you to a sundae after." Queenie is so young and so old. I'm glad I beat the attack for her sake too. I didn't want to scare her or disappoint her.

Everybody leaves the bus but me. I'm just so delighted with myself I want to savor a minute alone.

I jump fast. Warm breath behind me. Jesus. Jud. Jud is still on the bus. He stands up and crouches over me whispering, "You make it with your father? You make it with your father?"

Sound goes off in my head and hits an alarm. His words hurt. Why is he doing this to me? I strangle a scream but it comes out. "Get away from me!"

Jud looks hurt. After all, these are just about all the words he says and he says them to everyone. I put my hand to my breast and take a couple of deep breaths. "Okay, Jud, here, take my hand. Let's go bowling."

But his words are buried alive inside me. Churning around.

. . .

When I was little Dad would polish his shoes and he would wear his suit and his tie and vest. He had a briefcase and would go off to work. When he came home he had his briefcase and the *Herald Tribune*. When I saw him, then I felt safe. Things were back in their place. As it should be. Secure. His white shirt and tie all in place. Then I would take his hand and sit on his lap.

Now I come from the farm to Cove's office. Don has driven me. Cove comes out of his office to the waiting room. I'm getting my green cup from his cupboard and I turn around to say hello. Cove has on a brown coat with tan slacks. He has a white shirt and a horizontal-striped green tie. My throat catches. The feelings come out again like they did in the kitchen at the farm. I love him. I want to run to him. Now, I am safe. I want to tell him all these things happening to me. Most of all, I want him to hold me and protect me. I am not all grown up anymore. I'm a child and I'm just starting out. I'm starting all over again.

I have trouble speaking and Cove sees that.

"I want to talk to you so much. I have to talk. I'm mixed up. I want to talk." I edge past him, so close. We go into his office.

I sit in the chair right across from him.

"Oh, Cove. I'm so mixed up. I get so scared. I have to figure things out. It's the touching and the involvements. And I get too scared. I don't know. I mean, all the touching and then Maurice, and I don't know what to do. And I can't talk to you at the farm because I'm scared for the same reason. Somehow, I want to, but I stop myself and then things get worse. And I harden myself to Don when I don't want to and not to the others and it makes me feel cheap, like a whore, and then John wants to help me by rubbing my back and I'm scared. I'm bad. I'm wrong, I've got things all mixed up and then there's Jud and what he said to me on the bus that hurts me. And stupid Frieda, and Maurice telling me to fuck off. This morning Timothy puts his arm around me and it scares me and Terry scares me in the ditch and group therapy scares me and Hugh does and the talk about sex makes me doubt myself and I get so involved and why is this touching business such a problem anyhow? I just don't know about anything." I put my head down and cry because it's all too much to think about. Cove comes around the desk and puts his hand on my back and I cry all the more, feeling sorry for myself. When I stop I feel safer and better. This is the office. Cove doesn't hurt. I blow my nose.

"Why don't we slow down a little and go through things one at a time? Maybe we can make a little sense out of it all." Cove smiles.

"Let's see. Well, it's just everything gets me so, well, for example, today. I got myself to go on the bus for bowling and I conquered my panic on the bus and then Jud says to me, Jud says, well, an awful thing, and I keep thinking about it. And I don't know why it hurts me so much. You know Jud. Oh, it's too much." I shudder and put my hands to the sides of my head.

"Jud said something that bothered you. Can you share it with me?"

"He said, 'Did you do it with your father?' It makes me . . . Well, then, that awful remark makes me think of Dad and it's all mixed up and I think of how safe, I mean I love my Dad, and everything was all right when I saw him when I was little, he looked so nice and safe and then when I saw you, you looked the same way and that's how come I could talk to you when I came in because you looked so nice and safe."

"Jud's remark made you think of your father as nice and safe. Why did it bother you?"

"I don't know! I don't know why it bothered me. Well, of course, the words, I mean, I don't want to talk about it. I mean that was just an example of how I get things mixed up. I mean, it's everything. Just everything. Like the touching business. I mean, that's all the time, with everybody."

"The women too?"

"Oh no. Just the men."

"The strong men or all the men?"

"Just the strong ones."

"Carol, I think you have trouble recognizing the difference between affectionate gestures and sexual advances. What do you think?"

"I don't know. Well, maybe it's because—like when John wants to rub my back I know intellectually that he truly is being friendly and kind. But I freeze. *Freeze* right up and get scared."

"If you know it, why are you so scared?"

"I don't know why! I don't know. That's the problem."

"Has this happened to you before?"

"Oh, Cove. You, I mean I feel so . . ."

Scared feeling coming. Not safe.

"It's all right, Carol. Go ahead."

"Well, when I was a teenager, you know my Dad and I . . . Oh please, I can't."

"The strong nice men, Carol. You're afraid for a reason. You *want* to straighten this out, don't you? You are asking to."

"I don't know, I-I don't know."

"What happened when you were a teenager?"

"Scared, I always got scared."

"Who were you scared of?"

"Scared always, scared before. It always happened. Always."

"When was that? Who were you scared of?"

"Scared of *him*. Scared of him when I was a girl." I strangle. Cove love, Cove hate. Father-Cove hurts me. Make him stop because it hurts, so embarrassed, sex coming out, I scrunch my eyes, cover my face with my hands to keep out his sounds.

"What happened when you were a girl?"

"No. Help me, no, help me, no, he touched me." Technicolor man is sitting in the living room and nobody is there but me and we are watching Sid Caesar and as we laugh together he watches me, watching me like there's a bond between us, only I don't like it, and I don't know why and he stands up from his chair and my insides freeze and he comes over to me and sits next to me, he is lonely, wants daughter to have a bond with the laughter, only she doesn't know this and gets mixed up, flaming face, and he puts his hand on her back and starts to rub her back, only she wants to scream, awful father, lovely father, and swallows scream and jumps up wooden-legged, makes jokes, jokes, hide feelings in jokes, hide scream, desire in jokes, eyes on her and she knows shame, shame, and she looks at Cove and she sees him and his eyes and she feels awful shame and she hurts and she wants to get away from Cove, touch her back, touch her back, might touch her, might touch her, and his eyes don't leave her.

"No! No! No! Leave me alone! No, don't do this to me, get away from me!" Voice rising, voice loud, jump up wooden-legged, fist raised, kill him.

"What was it you said to your father?"

"No! No! No! Nothing." Sounds so loud to block out bursting heart, see his eyes and he does something strange, awful, Cove does something he never did before, eyes never leaving mine, awful bond. I don't want awful shameful bond between us, but Cove says so loud, eyes through me, "Tell me!"

"*No!*" Scream. "*No!*"

"What would you like to say to your father? Say it to *me*. Out loud. Say it to me!"

Dizzy. Falling. Room fades. Where is she? No woman—a girl, funny girl with jokes. Cove eyes, can't escape eyes, shame, dead people on his shoulders, father, Cove, awful, awful. Get away, get away, and he keeps on and on.

"Tell *me!*"

He won't let her go, trapped her so she can't help herself any longer, so the fear rises out in a paroxysm of noise and she hears the noise as if she's far, far away. Tremendous noise shrieking in the air. Shrieking and shrieking so loud, piercing at him and the shrieks form into words to her dead father. Hateful, awful, awful, hateful words filling the room. Hate, hate, hate. And then the shrieks of love for you, love you and you left me, screams, shrieks so loud it mutes the pain. Pain being shrieked at him, lungs bursting. On and on, into a final last push of energy, body pushing out the pain. And then the release. The final push. Like having a baby. And she falls to the floor and there is no more pain left. Her mind comes back and she thinks so clearly it's like having a baby because then there's no more pain. And the office comes back as the office and Cove comes back as Cove. And like birth there is no more fear. A sense of calm. And exhaustion.

Friday, November 14, 1969

Sitting at the table by the fireplace in the dining room. Six of us. Poetry time. Maurice is the leader. A pretty guitar is being played in the other room. We are here for the fun of it. The day is done. Tired, so tired. I slept all day. Not troubled or even thinking. John came to see me. I told him something happened to me last night and would he please let me sleep. He sat on the bed and he held my hand and he let me sleep. Don talked to Cove and Don talked to John. They care about me. I am ready to start over. Another beginning. Sometimes I amaze myself at how many times I just bounce back ready to start again. So here I am doing it. I'm going to write some poetry. Maurice is the leader. We have five minutes per poem. Then we turn it over to him. There are six of us, Maurice, Frieda, Alfred, Jud, Eden and me. Maurice picks a topic and we write on that topic. We have to read it out loud and then we vote on whose is the best. The topic is *fear*. We write write write. Oh I think this is so much fun. I love to write. *Time*. We go around the circle. Maurice's is about the dead past and very gothic. Frieda really enjoys reading hers. I don't know what it's about. Jud has written something about Rasputin and women. Got to hand it to Jud. I'm next. I read:

Fear

Fear is when a
    Daddy-Long-Legs
Climbs between
    your breasts
And you kill it fast
    with your fist
but the
    legs
    keep
    moving.

Eden cracks up. Jud loves the image, Maurice says I'm not being serious and Frieda wants to analyze why I chose daddy-long-legs and not black widow. It's significant. Alfred says it would make him scared. I think it's a very good poem. So I vote for myself and Eden votes for me. I win the prize. The winner chooses the next topic. Let's see. I choose "snakes." Jud will have fun with that.

Tuesday, November 18, 1969

I'm making a list to be ready for my appointment with Cove. I'm scared thinking of last Thursday night and I want to make sure Cove thinks I'll be all right. I think a lot about my Dad and how I'm so scared of thinking about him. I don't want to scream like that anymore but I sure want to settle things. I'm all mixed up with this men-sex business and I'm determined to get it straightened out.

I ask Hugh for a time to see Cove. He says he doesn't think there's any time left, he's too busy to see me. This makes me uneasy because I don't know if he won't see me or doesn't have the time. I'm afraid of Cove again. I bet he'll get rid of me because of Thursday. He'll say he just can't put up with that kind of thing. Then I'll have to stay at this farm forever.

Cove's car drives in. His car, not his bus. S671. All of a sudden it's too much for me. I get up and go up the front main stairs to the bathroom and close the door.

I feel trapped. I don't want to think. I don't want to talk. I don't want to get so involved. I want to go home. But I can't go home. I'm all mixed up, jumbled. I go down the stairs, out the door and up the path to Spruce. I rummage around in a back hall and find a cardboard box. I tear off one side and bring it in my room and shut the door. I take my scissors and cut a neat rectangular piece about ten by twenty-five inches. I get embroidery yarn and braid a nice long piece. I punch two holes in the cardboard and thread the braid in the holes and tie it. I get out a black Magic Marker and write in big letters. I put my sign on my neck and head for work. There. I feel much better. No one can get to me now. I'm protected. My sign reads: "Deaf Mute." I feel insulated with my sign, like I won't have to respond to anyone. I don't want to. Timothy sees me coming down the path and walks toward me laughing. He gives me a big kiss.

"You're beautiful and that sign is wonderful! I'm going out of town for a few days. Have a good week and keep up the good work." Off he goes. I don't have to answer. How nice. My job is to make cakes. I only have Laura Lee with me. I get an intense satisfaction out of these cakes. Twenty-six eggs. I get to break twenty-six eggs. How wonderful.

"Carol, have you noticed how withdrawn Maurice is? Do you have any idea what's causing it?" Laura asks.

I point to my sign. I refuse to talk.

"Don't be ridiculous. Don't be stupid." I pretend I can't hear.

"Oh, all right. I guess it's all right." She smiles. I smile.

At lunchtime I sit with Queenie, Madonna, Eden and Glory. They don't expect me to answer them. They trust my sign and don't ask questions. We sit in the living room and just laugh and laugh. Glory has spotted Alfred's shoes and keeps staring at them and groaning. They're a soft black leather with designs tooled on them. Maybe she thinks they're socks. Glory goes, "Uhh uhh." We can't help laughing, so Glory laughs too. It's wrong of me. But I can't help it. I roll on the floor laughing. None of us can stop. Alfred can't put his shoes on to stop Glory because he already *has* his shoes on.

"Eeeee uhhhh," Glory groans. I take off my diamond and hand it to her. She stops her paroxysms and repeats over and over.

"Thank—you—thank—you—I—will—take—care—of—it. I—will—polish—it. Thank—you." She goes to her room where she has her polish. She will spend a long time staring at the diamond. She will polish it and take care of it.

John walks in the room, looks at us relaxing and walks over. He has a red and green plaid shirt. He sees my sign. I look at my feet. I'm a little embarrassed. He taps me on the shoulder so I look up at him. He exaggerates his lips and says, "Can you hear me?"

I blush much to everyone's delight. But I still won't talk. He goes over to the piano and gets a piece of paper and writes me a note and hands it to me.

Hi in there. Could you take a new guest for a tour around
the farm after lunch hour? Also Dr. Ashley would like to
see you after farm meeting. 4:30 O.K.? Hope you can come
back to us soon.

John

I read it and shake my head yes, then put the note in my pocket.
The rest want to see what it says but I can't talk. I store my sign
down in the game room, for later. Then I meet the new guest,
who's waiting for me on the front steps. Wouldn't want to scare
him.

His name is George Tent. He's my age. I show him all over,
telling how it really is on the farm. I tell him he can't commit
suicide and he can't steal. I tell him that people care about each
other here, but it is a very wild place. I tell him we have to work
hard but sometimes sneak out of it. I ask if he has any questions.

"Do you live here? Are you a member of the staff?" He has
straight, nice teeth.

"No. I'm a guest. I live here though."

"I think I might come stay. I have to go back to Philadelphia
and get my things."

"I hope you stay."

"Why?"

"I think we'd get along."

"I think we would too."

When the tour is finished I go back to the game room and get
my sign. I think about George. Was I making a play for him? Was
it because I feel so bad about Maurice? Why am I doing this?
Was I doing anything? I put my sign back on.

Main farm meeting. I have been elected the moderator. I put
my sign in the kitchen. Queenie sits next to me at the main table.
She's secretary. She also doesn't want me to freak out. I go to
the bathroom. Nerves. I get a big glass of water, gum, cigarettes,
Lifesavers, coffee, pen and paper. My back is to the kitchen door
so I can escape if I have to. The door is open.

As I see it, my job is to keep topics moving and to gracefully get the talkers to sit down without hard feelings. Also to break up fights. Meeting please come to order.

We discuss somebody stealing money from the rooms, unreported long-distance calls and upcoming volleyball games with the local jail. I do a pretty good job, even making Glory sit down when she is upset.

The meeting is over, and it was all right. I realize that I didn't have to leave. I had no time to panic. I was too busy.

I put my sign back on and head for the library. I have twenty minutes before I see Cove and I want to think.

Frieda follows me in and shuts the door. I stand there. She stands there.

"That sign! I want you to explain yourself." Frieda gets so mad at me, she almost stamps her foot.

I shake my head back and forth and cup my hand to my ear. I can't help it. It's so tempting, I can't help it.

"You are running away from problems. You can't run away from yourself. You must analyze your sign with me. It is a sick thing. A distorted thing. I shall have to report you."

I take my meeting notes, turn them over, take out my pen and start to write her a note.

Frieda screams at me. "I'm going to report you immediately!" She stomps out of the room. I watch the red patch on her crotch as it moves out the door. I'm really sorry, Frieda. I really am but I couldn't stop myself. It was too much fun. I take the sign over to the fireplace and put it in the fire. I wonder a little bit about who Frieda can report me to. All the staff have already seen the sign. Cove? Maybe to Cove?

I head back out the door to find Glory. I think she wants to talk a little more about the stealing discussed at farm meeting.

The fear comes back. The fear of Cove. She walks slowly up the stairs but she doesn't turn right into the fear room. She goes instead into the bathroom. Carol goes to the sink and touches the soap in the soap dish. Cove has used this soap. This is the bathroom he uses. Maybe soap will make her clean like Cove. Washes, washes, washes. Dirty. She still feels dirty. Whore. Talk about sex with this man. Awful inside feelings of sex. And last week it hurt so much because Father was brought in. The hurt went away and was forgotten. But walking upstairs, big barrier started coming between her and Cove. Iron wall tacked onto her body so Cove won't make her think anymore. She raps at the door. Heart pounding on the metal armor, obliterating other noise. She won't talk about sex again. Ever. She walks in, head bowed. Won't look at him. She sits on a corner of the couch, Cove across the room at a table and chair. Cove talking soft words.

"It must have been a difficult week for you. I know you must be concerned. You're going to be all right, Carol. You're strong enough."

She pricks up her ears. Cove says she's going to be all right. That's what she wanted to hear. If Cove says it, it must be true. She pulls off a little bit of the armor and glances at him.

He has that face that is kind again. She loves to see it. It's all right to talk.

Low voice, hesitant, faltering, getting stronger.

"I'm sorry. I'm sorry. You think I'll be all right? You think so?"

Cove must be thinking; has he failed her? Why is she taking so long? Why is she taking so long?

"You'll be all right. You are facing your problems and it's very difficult and takes a lot of courage." Cove strengthens her.

"It's this physical business that gets me, Cove. It makes me choke and scream. I think about it all the time. All the time."

"Maybe you shouldn't think so much."

"I can't help it. It comes down to physical with—everyone. Maurice in particular. I'm afraid I'm going to get into trouble with men."

"Do you want to get into trouble?"

"No. No! Don't say that. No." I get braver when I argue with Cove. Stronger.

"Nothing happens unless you let it happen. You have a choice."

"It doesn't seem like I have one. I let them, I mean Maurice, touch me and I don't want him to. It makes me feel dirty."

"And when Don touches you?"

"I can't, can't let him. I love him, you see? I mean, he's the one I love, so I can't let him love me. I'm not good enough for him." I can almost look at Cove now. I want to understand this.

"It sounds like you put Don on a pedestal. You make him untouchable."

I think about this. It seems to fit. Don is too good for me. I don't deserve him.

"You have choices. It doesn't have to be this way." Cove acts a little stern. He doesn't want me to be weak and to accept these lusts of mine as they are. I am encouraged by his caring. I don't want to accept them either.

"I'm really going to work on this. I really am. It bothers me a lot. It makes me feel so awful." My armor has dropped on the floor.

"You can do it if you want to." Cove smiles.

"Was it all right last week, I mean, in our session? Are you mad? I mean, I couldn't do anything else and I couldn't help it, I mean, I didn't scare your family, did I? You don't think I cracked up, do you? It was so awful and so loud."

"My family didn't hear it, Carol. It was all right. It takes a long time to accept your feelings. Do you think you would like to talk about it?"

"Maybe Thursday, huh? I have a list of things I made out but I . . . Maybe Thursday?"

"Of course. What have you got there?"

"Well. I wake up so early I write down everything. How I think. I wondered if maybe you'd like to, um, have it?"

"Yes. Very much."

"It's awful."

"It takes a lot of courage to give it to me."

"You think?"

"Yes. But it's very important to say what you really think. You must trust me."

"I know. I know. It's hard. But I'm getting better, don't you think? I can trust you more now than before. Thank you, Cove."

"Be kind to yourself, Carol. Be gentle with yourself."

I go downstairs and I get out my embroidery. It's coming along so well. Cove is going to be surprised at me for doing it. It's almost done so I can send it home with Don to get it professionally blocked and framed. I can pay for it myself now too. That's very important. My chore money. My gift to him.

I go to my mailbox and take out two letters. I put them in my parka pocket. I go down the cellar past the laundry room into the summer kitchen. I sit on a barrel of whole-wheat flour.

                                                              Mon.

Hi Mom,

I learned this in art. They showed us how to make a figrur. (I think I spelled that right) Hear I will make a little one now. Jimmy made me cry only twice. Today me and Jimmy wher whaching the Hollywood Squares and Jimmy said if you anser a question right I'm going to hit you and I ansered a question right and he hit me as hard as he could The second time he hit me was when he cut out a top a bucket and maed a basketball hoop and I nocked it off the wall and he slaped me as hard as he could and Jimmy wants to say hi mom. I want you to come home now. How are you. Are you feeling well. And don't tell dad about Jimmy today. OK.

                                                      Love
                                                      Tom

I very carefully fold the letter. I put it to my face. I have to tighten my inside muscles so I won't feel too much. Sometimes I wait a whole day before I can open them.

Dear Mommy

I love you. I hope you feel beder. When will you get home? Do they give you good food. I miss you. Will you send me a letter. I can make a dog face. Look down there.

Love
Peter

I walk over to the outside door. I put my hands up high on the door. "Ohhhh, Oh, Oh." I have a desperate feeling of wanting to run, escape. But there's nowhere to go. Like on a rack. Pulled two ways at the same time. The cellar door opens and someone starts up. I pull back and stand awkwardly. I'm ashamed I made the noise. Eden walks over to me.

"Hi."

"Hi."

"You okay?"

"Yeah."

"I thought I heard something."

"It was me. I get upset when I get letters from my kids. I feel like a failure."

"Kids? You got kids?"

"Yeah. Five."

"You got five kids?"

"Yeah."

"God. That's beautiful. Oh my God. That's really nice. Oh wow. Are you ever lucky!"

"Oh yeah. You think so, huh?"

"Oh wow."

"I am pretty lucky. But I feel I deserted them. Makes me feel so awful."

"Is someone nice taking care of them?"

"Oh yes."

"Is your husband a good father?"

"Yes."

"Do they hate you because you're here?"

"No, I don't think so. They say they love me."

"Do you love them?"

"Oh yes."

"Are you good to them?"

"Yes."

"Those kids will be all right. Kids are amazing. I think you're just sad because you miss them."

"I think you're right."

"You probably miss them more than they miss you."

"Probably."

"You know what I think?"

"What?"

"I think you're a winner."

"A winner? You do?"

"Yup."

"Why?"

"Jesus. Look at all of us. All of us farmers. Most of us are even scared to get married. Me. Me. I'm scared to make a commitment."

"Yeah, but that's because you're all so much younger."

"Not really. I mean, you figure you started having kids when you were how old?"

"Well, twenty-one. I had David when I was twenty-one. And I had Ki when I was twenty-two and I had Jimmy when I was twenty-three and Tommy when I was twenty-six and Peter when I was twenty-nine."

"I'm twenty-nine. God! You're a winner!"

"Hey, you make me feel pretty good, Eden. You know that? I feel good now. Thanks a lot."

Saturday, November 22, 1969

Carol's coming home for her first visit. She is excited, too excited
when she holds the beautiful children. Her face is flushed and she
talks with them about the teacher appointments and the library
books and church school and Girl Scout cookies and piano lessons.
Ki is not practicing because Mother's not here. Carol is too excited
and her hands are trembling. And Don. Don's doing everything.
Friends feel sorry for Don so they bring casseroles and sitters,
but sickness is very frightening and it might be catching and Carol
has been gone over a month. And now her sickness is rather boring,
don't you know. So Don doesn't get casseroles anymore and he
doesn't get help and his patience is wearing thin. But he is strong.
He can do it but he is weary. He'll have his wife for a weekend
and take her to the dance and make love and maybe she'll be able
to stay home.

But it's not working out somehow. Her hands are trembling
and she is afraid of the dance. What people will say about her,
who cares, Don doesn't care. He is strong. She shivers when she
puts on her gown and says she doesn't deserve to wear a dress. He
says that's stupid, what is she talking about? They go to the dinner
party. She drinks too fast. He gets his eyes on her and says with
his eyes, don't drink any more. She takes another. She's afraid
when she dances with him; that makes him angry. He's embarrassed
she said shit to Dr. Ashley as he went by, why is she doing this?
Where has his Carol gone? She should be back there until she's better. He can't take her, here. She is not strong. He would hold her
and love her but she pushes him away and doesn't want him, her
husband, and it makes him angry. He doesn't understand why she
doesn't want him. He wonders about this Maurice character. He
wants her to get better but not here. He can't take her here. He
can do it himself. It's lonely but he has peace from her. Take her
back to the farm where she isn't afraid.

Tuesday, November 25, 1969

Bitch. Hate. Shit. No good. Hate everybody. Can't even have one weekend without lousing up. Creep me. Don thinks I don't love him. Because of my insides all cold. Hate myself. Hate my body. Hate Cove. Shouldn't have given him my notebook. Who does he think he is anyway?

Volleyball. Skeleton team. People who can, go home for the holiday. Faces grim. Not much fun. Hugh comes down hard on my calf with his boot. Big bruise forming. Don't care. Glad it's there. I hate my body.

Cove comes today. Don't care. Hate him. A soft, white snow has fallen and the snow makes me angry. The snow covers all the dead leaves and pretends to make everything clean. But it's a trick. It doesn't do that at all. Everything underneath is still all ugly and dirty. The same thing happens with my showers. They trick me into thinking I am clean. We all know the dirt under there that won't ever come off.

Before farm meeting Timothy comes up to me. I don't smile. I say, "It was a big mistake to go home!"

"At least you learned something."

"What's that?"

"You learned it was a mistake to go home." Such pearls of wisdom. He thinks he's clever.

I walk through the living room. Cove comes after me. I see him coming but I pretend I don't. That way he won't know if I'm deliberately snubbing him or not. He catches up.

"I'd like to talk to you."

I plant two feet firmly. I'm defiant. Armor all in place. "When?" as if I have other things to do.

"Now."

No time to prepare myself. No time. We turn around and walk up the stairs to the room. I decide I won't sit down.

"Your weekend didn't go very well, did it?"

"No."

"Don called me. He's worried and . . ."

"I don't want to hear it! I mean, I don't want to talk about it." Cold.

"I think maybe we'd better." Cold.

Heart beating. Don't like the two of them talking. What do they say about me? I bet Don asked Cove about Maurice. Shit. Defiant. I glare at him straight in the eyes. Silence.

"Do you know why the weekend didn't work?" His eyes don't flinch.

"No!" I say it loud like that because it helps stop the feelings, a diversion.

"I don't want to talk. I hate it here. I can't hack it at home. I have no place."

"You can hack it. In fact, I think you can take a lot more than you have been. No more running away." Stern, cold. Bastard. I don't want to hear him talk. But I don't move. My feet took roots right through the rug.

"I want you to talk. You can do much more by talking than by putting up those walls around you."

"*All right! All right!*" loud at him. "*It was lousy.* I don't know what's the matter. I couldn't take it. I don't know what the problem is."

"Want me to tell you?"

"No. I can just imagine. No. I don't want to talk. I'm angry. I . . ."

"Sex is an important . . ."

"I don't want you to say that. I told you."

"I think we've ducked around the issue long enough, don't you? Let's get to the core, huh?"

"I don't want to talk about sex. I don't want to."

"I read your notes."

"No!" I forgot about the notes. Why did I give them to him. He has the upper hand. What did I put in them? Want to sleep with men? Horny thoughts about men. Awful Cove knows.

"I want you to talk to me the way you write in your note-book."

"Can't—don't—want. . . ."

"Do you think sex is dirty?"

"No! Get away, no. That's stupid. No. I don't think sex is dirty. No! That's a stupid thing to say."

Mother looks sideways at me out of her eyes. Mother knows I love Jimmy, my boyfriend. She looks sideways at me with a funny look like I'm doing something wrong. Looks sideways at me when my Dad rubs my back. Feel so guilty, so strange. No words to me about the horrors I commit so they lie hidden. The dirty, ugly things that have to do with pushing on my belly. Flaming face. Sideways, eyes darting, telling me I'm dirty. What I do is dirty. Unspoken so loud, unspoken, unclean girl who washes, washes unclean body but it doesn't work. Penance. Carry the load. I am heartily sorry—no forgiveness. Makes me feel so bad. Flashes through my mind, fast, dirty, dirty sex.

Legs waver, throat closes, eyes downward. Shame. Blushing shame and embarrassment. Cove making me ashamed. Sit down. Cover my head so he won't look at me sideways with his eyes.

"Carol?" Cove knows I lost my armor. It fell off so I'm naked. "Can you tell me?" Cove soft. Look at his green-brown eyes, not sideways, at me, so it's all right to be naked in front of him.

"I feel so ashamed talking about sex. I don't know why. It mixes me up most of all. Because I'm so cold inside to Don and it shouldn't be that way because I love him."

"No, it shouldn't be that way. Do you know why you feel sex is dirty?"

"I—my mother thinks I'm dirty—she, she . . ."

"What did she say?"

"Nothing."

"Well, *something* happened to you, Carol!"

"She told me that Dad wanted to, um. She confided in me that men have to prove themselves by you know what. I mean, that's what she said. And even then I wasn't sure what it was, but she said it funny like it wasn't good. I didn't want to hear. She was talking about my father. I didn't want to hear it. She had no right telling me and making it dirty. That's what she did. Made it dirty. I wanted to protect my Dad from her. I didn't want to be a conspirator with her. It made it dirty—I'm dirty. I'm no good."

"You can change this."

I'm ashamed to talk about it with Cove. So ashamed.

"I can't help how I am. I want the bad men and I can't help it."

"You can help it. Wouldn't it be nice if you felt the right way for Don? It would be the most wonderful thing in the world."

"Don't talk! Don't say that!" I pulled my armor back on. Cove makes me mad saying that because it's the thing I want most in the world. He's tantalizing me. Hurting me. Making me realize how awful I am. Who does he think he is, hurting me?

"You can't live your life shutting out problems. They won't just disappear. You must talk about them, then do something about them."

"Shit! I'm a shithead. I can't help how I act."

"But you can."

"No!"

Cove is exasperated with me. I'm mad. I don't like him saying that I can change. Makes me uneasy. Makes me think I won't be able to blame my sickness if I do something wrong. I don't want to hear any more of this. I close my ears.

Cove gives up. Stands up and opens the door. I stomp my feet. *"Have a stupid damned Thanksgiving!"*

I scream at him as if he didn't know I was mad. I won't see him until next week and that makes me mad.

"Are you coming to group therapy?"

"Maybe! Maybe not!"

I go out the door and turn around and grab it with both hands and slam it hard as I can.

That'll show him. He has a hell of a nerve, telling me I have a choice.

I bang downstairs and stomp over to the living room and pick up the tapestry and work on it furiously.

I have these memories of vacations, especially of Thanksgiving and Christmas, and they are all good, like the turkey cooking and the wind blowing cold and the fun in the living room with the fire and the grapes and the family. Such wonderful times with Dad at the head of the table—then his fork caught the edge of the placemat and the plate tipped over and Dad's ears were ringing with the cancer and his eyes were bleary with the martini and the tears rolled down and he looked at me and I walked away, we all walked away, left him, walked away.

And the time he pulled my mother on his lap because he felt so good because it was Thanksgiving and she looked so awful at him and she got off and his face was so hurt by her, so hurt.

I don't want to think anymore. I don't want to have anything to do with thinking. I've had it with thinking. I look at the tapestry. I love the feel of it. As I'm near to finishing I feel pride. I'm amazed I have some pride left buried down there. I'm amazed to think that I'm actually finishing something. I'm a great starter but not a finisher. I like this. I also get an intense joy out of holding the linen, the coarse tapestry yarn and the needle. I get pleasure from the pressure of the thimble. I had this kind of feeling a long time ago. And it makes my skin feel good. Now I have it again. My tantrum subsides. Those mad feelings toward Cove modify to just confusion. Because I love him and want him to have a good vacation and I will miss him. I forgive him this time. I let him off easy. But he'd better *be careful*.

I go into the library for group therapy. Jake and Cove are already seated. Cove is by the fireplace. He has a clipboard on his lap and is writing. I don't look at him because I don't know yet whether I want him to know I've forgiven him. Has he suffered enough?

The group is slightly changed. Rachel has gone home for Thanksgiving and "woods crew" Voss is there instead. Obie is here too. I don't know how they got him to join. Madonna and Obie are the only ones on scholarship. The rest of us pay. Don and I can't pay the whole price so I guess you could say I'm on scholarship too. Everyone else has a family that can afford the farm. Money doesn't mean anything here. I mean, we have to earn our own. So if Maurice's family has eleven million dollars and Maurice has a dirty T-shirt, all we see is the dirty T-shirt. And if Rachel's family owns a chain of stores, we only see her wanting to sleep with men. So that's how it works.

A big discussion starts and then an argument and then everyone sits quietly for a while. I get out a piece of gum and look at Cove. I feel very safe with him in the room.

Jane looks at me.

"Why are you here, Carol?"

"What?" I'm caught up short. She's talking to me. Hey, Cove!

JANE: "We don't know anything about you. You seem together, so why are you here?"

I look around and they're all looking at me. I look at Cove. He's looking at me too. I want him to answer for me and he doesn't. He's just sitting there looking at me.

"Well, I'm here because, well—I don't know."

And now I'm embarrassed and can't hide. I don't look at anybody now, just at my socks. They are those gray, black and white speckled ski socks. If I wear them with my hiking boots, my feet still seem to get cold.

JANE: "That's a cop-out."

HUGH: "Jesus, yeah, you've got to know why you're here."

EDEN: "I know you miss your family so there's got to be a good reason."

Cove, where are you? Am I supposed to tell them I have trouble with men and sex and how I tremble when I hear "Father" and how I can't stand my body and want to hurt it and am afraid? I look at Cove. He's still looking at me. Bastard.

"Well. It's hard because it isn't any one thing. I mean it's a lot of things and . . ."

HUGH: "It's a lot of things with everyone. We know that. We just can't figure out why you're here."

ME: "Well, I still panic. I panic. When I was home I couldn't do anything. *Anything!* Because I was always panicked."

HUGH: "What do you mean, 'panic'? I don't see you panic here."

ME: "But I do. When I walk out on farm meetings. I do that because I panic in crowds. And I don't go on Friday night bus trips because I panic."

HUGH: "What happens when you panic?"

ME: "Well, it feels like my throat's closing. It feels like I'm choking and my skin jumps and my insides feel like I'm going to scream."

JANE: "Anywhere else you panic?"

ME: "All over the place. I mean, I'd really like to go with woods crew into the forest but I panic when I go out of sight of the main house. And I'd really like to be able to walk down the hill but, the same thing happens."

JANE: "Does it always happen?"

ME: "Sometimes it doesn't. That's the hard part. Like I can walk up the road to the lake and I don't panic. If someone is with me. But I can't walk down the hill. And I don't panic on the paths alone. But I do off the paths if I can't see the main house."

I get all jumpy inside talking about it. Skin feels funny. As if someone might make me go into the woods alone. I mean, now I'm telling them. And especially Voss, the woodsman. Will they hurt me? Make me do it? My throat is funny. My hand goes to my throat.

EDEN: "So sometimes you do and sometimes you don't?"

ME: "Um, yes. And it stops me from doing things because I can never be sure I won't panic and then it'll be too late."

EDEN: "What happens if 'it's too late'?"

ME: "No." I close my eyes. No. Can't think. Lights dart back and forth. "I-I d-d-d-don't kn-know."

I put my hand to my mouth. They're all looking at me. They haven't heard me stutter. I told them and now I want to put my hands over my head because I feel they're going to hurt me. I sit with my eyes closed.

EDEN: "I think we could help you with these things. Let's see. You know, I'd be really glad to help you walk down the hill. As far as you wanted. We could turn back before you panicked. Every night we'd go further."

HUGH: "Yeah, sure. Jesus. I could help you on the bus on Fridays. You know. We could hold your hands or whatever and make you laugh."

VOSS: "And as far as woods crew—I'd be glad to go with you. Put you on a job not so far from the main house. You know, up in

Thelma's woods. That's only past the garden and pastures. I could show you where the main house was on the map."

EDEN: "We'll recondition you. That's what they call it."

I hear them. I take my fist away from my mouth and look up. They're looking at me expectantly. I smile.

ME: "You'd do that?"

HUGH: "Sure, my God. Of course. What did you think?"

ME: "Well, I'd really appreciate that. I mean, yes. But, well, woods crew, that is. . . ."

VOSS: "Well, when you feel like you can handle the woods put your name in the book and come see me. I won't bug you until then."

ME: "Okay. Thanks. Thanks."

I'm scared but I'm excited. Cove looks pleased. They're not out to hurt me. My friends. Cove might've left me but he left me with friends.

Thanksgiving, November 27, 1969

I wake up in my new room. Madonna has left for a while. We don't know when she'll come back. Maybe never. A crew helped me to decorate her room and I moved in. I like being in the main house. I smell something good. I've overslept. It's almost six A.M. Miguel is already in the kitchen. Thanksgiving. Oh no. Don is coming with the kids. I must make things good for them. Take my shower, race down the stairs, follow my nose to the kitchen. All of it is there. The Thanksgivings all over the country are right here. Nothing is missing. The linens and the crystal and the pies. Oh, so many pies and the families with all their children. With candy and fooling around. And then later my family and my children and Carol in a dress, a regular mother with regular children. I see them watch me. The other guests watch me, the Carol they don't know, Carol the mother and wife who sits with the staff and their families. The Carol who has such nice kids—not bratty—who laugh a lot. Carol whose husband talks to Timothy and John and Miguel the cook, who talks to Eden and Queenie and Hugh and

Jake. A different person. Carol who doesn't stutter, who wears a dress. Carol who is different somehow because she has all these people who care for her and they've come for Thanksgiving. But she sees. They don't know she sees but she does.

She sees that nobody comes for Spike and he stands in a corner thinking he's a nest and she sees Jud and how Jud has tried to dress up but somehow has failed because his aunt couldn't come and there are so many different people. Are they watching? And she sees that Benson never comes out of his room and many others don't either. This is a holiday for people who are strong enough to stand it. She sees that she is only separated from the people in their rooms by a tiny piece of caring and being cared for lodged inside her. But she has it and she's having a good time. She will not be sick on this day. Day of the turkeys. It's so subtle, the staff look at her a shade differently. She's more like them than not. She marvels in her mind at the beauty of the day and of her family. And she marvels that nobody threw any chairs across the room and nobody put the bread knife to his throat and nobody but nobody said fuck.

Monday, December 1, 1969

Oh, they've gone and I'm here and what am I going to do? They've left me up on the hill because I can't go home. Oh my. Put one foot ahead of the other. Go to the kitchen. Squeeze four oranges. Feel a little better. Allowing myself, my fingers the pleasure of the motion. Alfred is sick so I will bring him the juice. Lots of people are feeling lousy. Guests are subdued like a pack of wolves licking their wounds after a fight. I don't quite know how to nurse myself. I can help Alfred, but don't have the energy to help myself.

Work program. John looks disgustingly cheerful and energetic. Plan to stay away from him, but he puts me on his crew. He puts his arm around me and I back away. I back away and he takes my hand and leads me outside. Queenie and Eden, Benson, Hugh, Glory, Obie and even Ronnie are waiting. We trudge a little way up the hill to the buildings on the right that have the equipment in them. Marv gives us picks and shovels. It's a cold day and the sun isn't out. The mud has turned to hard ruts and the ground isn't frozen yet. Glory has lost her gloves so John sends Glory and Eden back to the main house to find her spares. Our gloves are very warm. The under glove is a black and white stripped mitten, wool, and the outer glove is tan leather. On the outside in black Magic Marker we have our names. The reason we have them all alike is because they seem to be the warmest. I've grown very attached to mine. They're work gloves and I somehow like the feeling that I'm able to work. I don't care if they get dirty.

We are moving dirt and stones around a dug-up septic tank. John and a crew have repaired the tank and we are moving the boulders and dirt to even it all out before spring. Another crew is working nearby, smoothing out a roadway which is a complete mess. I team up with Eden. We pull and tug at large stones, we shovel and move the dirt. I'm sweating and suddenly have energy. I don't know where it came from. John works so hard himself, it's infectious. He leaps from the bulldozer and grabs me by the arm. He says, "Come on." I jump up next to him. Well, more like climb, carefully. Both of us sit on the same seat and he does a ninety-degree turn and heads for the road crew. There are huge mounds of dirt. He has me steer while he works the levers. I have an instant, complete high. "Yahoo!" Nobody can hear. John is smiling and me too. I never felt this way before. It makes me feel religious. We work this way awhile and he yells for me to park it down the hill. He jumps off and walks away. I turn the thing around and head down the hill. This is so much fun—so much fun I can't believe it— it is so much better than amphetamines—so much better. Maybe Don can buy me a bulldozer. I keep going down the hill into a clearing and instead of parking it I go around in circles. Around and around. John's dog is following me barking. John comes over from the hill and stands near my circle. He just stands there and looks at me so I turn off the key, climb down and the two of us go back and work on the septic tank for the rest of the day.

Nighttime. Listening to the guitars in the living room. Soft, peaceful. I am slightly lost because I have finished my tapestry. I gave it to Don on Thanksgiving and he will have it blocked and framed for me. I gave him thirty-seven dollars that I earned. I've taken on two jobs, phone duty and cleaning the game room. Two hours each day, fourteen dollars per week plus five dollars allowance. Everyone gets five dollars free. When it is done he will bring it back to the farm so I can give it to Cove for Christmas. The music stops. Eden comes over to me.

"Would you like to take a short walk down the hill?"

"Down?"

"Yeah, sure."

"Well, all right."

We get our parkas and meet Laura Lee at the door. She comes with us. We start to saunter down the hill. I stop.

"You know, it's very nice of you, but I really don't care to, you know, walk down."

EDEN: "Yeah, we know."

ME: "But I might panic."

LAURA LEE: "That's okay."

We start again.

We get engrossed in talking. Laura Lee's flashlight dances back and forth. About fifteen minutes of walking and my body stops. I turn around. There are no lights, no main house. The fear is under the surface.

ME: "No more. Let's go back. Can't go any further. No more."

EDEN: "What's to be afraid of?"

ME: "D-d-don't know." I hunch up shoulders. Skin creepy. Creepy. I gasp.

LAURA LEE: "It's okay. We'll turn around."

ME: "Ooh." They each take a hand, one on each side. "Ooh." Insides flip, throat closing.

EDEN: "Hold it a second." He lets go and takes something out of his pocket and goes to the side of the road. He comes back and grabs my hand and we start to walk faster, me going faster, back toward the lights, up to the surface. Can't drown now.

Lights in sight. There they are. Tension eases, dissolves with the lights.

ME: "What did you do at the side of the road?"

EDEN: "I marked with a ribbon, a yellow ribbon. A yellow ribbon for the lady fair."

ME: "Marked what?"

EDEN: "Marked how far you got. Tomorrow the long hill. The next day further and the next day, *the world*. Ta da."

The accomplishments of the day give me a buzz. I head for the kitchen and have a glass of milk. I head up the stairs. I open my door and turn on the light. I jump, my heart beating fast. Maurice is on the bed.

ME: "Jeez—you scared me! What are you doing? You okay?"

MAURICE: "I came because I thought you'd need me." He rolls from his stomach to his back and puts his arms under his head. He wears dungarees and a navy-blue wool shirt. He has kicked off his shoes. He looks at me. His eyes are steady. My stomach lurches a little. I don't know anymore how to think of Maurice. There's something very seductive in his appearance which increases my uneasiness. I don't know if I imagine this or if it's because of my men problems. I gulp.

MAURICE: "Come sit down." He pats the bed.

ME: "I had a really good day today. You know, I really had fun working on the . . ."

MAURICE: "I know. I saw you. I think you had too much fun. I think you have to be more careful."

ME: "You mean, because I drove the bulldozer?"

MAURICE: "Yes, that and all the joking at supper. You'll have to make yourself pay." I sit on the bed next to him and he pulls me next to him. I open my mouth to kiss him. I want to kiss him. He shoves me away.

"Don't do that!"

I'm confused. I'm ashamed. I sit up and turn the other way. Oh, I am such a whore. But why is he on my bed anyway? I don't understand anything. Why did I try to do that? Cheap bitch. Shit. I blush. Embarrassed.

"Please go away, please." Even my voice is uncertain. I am mindless.

"Rub my back," he orders. "I want you to rub my back." He rolls on his stomach and I climb over him and sit on him. The bed is very small. I have no will of my own. I do what he says— I want him and he doesn't want me and I feel cheap. It reminds me of something that happened to me before. The priest. That's it. The priest who wouldn't kiss me and who ordered me around. The one who taught me I was a sinner. Maurice is like Father Anthony. And he talks to me the same way. I will have to pay for my sins. And Maurice says again and again, I will have to pay for my fun. And I think of Cove and of Don and I'm deeply ashamed. And I keep on rubbing his back.

Tuesday, December 2, 1969

Lena Mae and I are working on bread. Thinking over and over how *mad* I am. At myself. I don't want to express it anyway. Because then I might smash myself. I take the bread out for the first rising. I slam it on the table and pound the hell out of it. I flip it over and do the same thing on the other side. I am so damned stupid, bang pound pound. The bread will have a very fine, rich texture.

LENA MAE: "You sure are taking something out on the bread."

ME: "Sure am!"

LENA MAE: "Anything to do with Maurice?"

ME, startled: "No! It's me. I'm the one. *Me!*" Pound, pound.

LENA MAE: "What's the matter?"

ME: "Oh, it's the stupid men. I'm afraid of them. I'm so afraid of them I act crazy. I don't know what it is."

LENA MAE: "I think you should take the bull by the horns and make yourself talk to them."

ME: "It's not that so much as, well, my thinking is mixed up."

LENA MAE: "Dr. Ashley have anything to say about it?"

ME: "No! He has nothing to do with it. No."

LENA MAE: "Have you told him about it?"

ME: "No." I lie. I don't want to talk to Cove today. He'll think I'm a whore. He says I have choices and I've failed him.

LENA MAE: "Come on, Carol. Let's go to lunch. Let's talk about it."

Lena Mae is very small and petite. I trust her but not to talk about Cove. Her hair sweeps out in a flip and is a very natural black. She looks so healthy, so alive. She might have some answers for me.

We settle with our lunches at the table by the fireplace.

LENA MAE: "I want to see if I can understand, Carol. Tell me again."

ME: "Oh gee. See if I can figure it out." Terry walks by. "I'm afraid of the strong men like Terry there. I'm afraid to talk to them and I . . ."

LENA MAE: "Terry, Terry!" she yells out at Terry, who is just beginning to sit down.

Jesus! What is she doing?

"Terry! Carol is afraid to talk to you." As she's saying this so loud, my body flexes and I hit her arm with my arm.

"Stop!" I yell. The dining room suddenly is quiet. They are looking at us. My face is flaming red. Lena Mae looks at me with a look of astonishment.

ME: "Why did you do that? I mean, how could you do that?" The eating and noise has resumed.

LENA MAE: "It was for your own good. I think your reaction is very disturbing."

I feel cheated. Lena Mae cheated me. I pick up my tray, bring it to the kitchen and throw away the food. I feel sick. Head down, I go up the stairs to my room. On the stairs I meet Cove coming down. He has Hugh with him. I keep going, not talking, not looking. Can't look at him, have to get to my room. He stops for a second and turns around but I can't look at him. I'm not going to leave my room today. Jesus help me. I feel like smashing myself. I curl in a ball and lie on the bed.

I don't lie on the bed long. My legs are twitching. I pace back and forth in the room. I put the rocking chair way over in the corner so I have an extra step before turning around. I'm not going to talk to Lena Mae again. What I tell her is private. She had no right. Terry heard her. Everybody heard her. Shit! I won't talk to anyone again. I'm not going to talk to Cove either. I take out my new notebook and I write it all down. Big, bold, horrible letters that no one will ever see. I have a lot of different pens. I pick out the pen that fits my mood. This time I use a big fat ballpoint so I can attack the paper with it. The writing makes my tensions ease almost like the tapestry did. I get touch-pleasure from writing.

I skip supper. Queenie and Eden come in and bring me four brownies. They sit down and relax.

ME: "What's the latest?"

QUEENIE: "What happened anyway? You got yourself into trouble. Everyone's talking about it."

ME: "What trouble?" My thoughts go to Maurice on the bed last night. I suppose Maurice told Frieda he was in my room on my bed and now staff meeting has discussed it. Oh Jesus.

QUEENIE: "Lena Mae and Helen told Dr. Ashley that you hit Lena Mae. They had a big discussion."

ME: "*Hit Lena Mae!*"

QUEENIE: "Yeah, Jesus, Carol, what happened?"

ME: "Oh God, is that all? Nothing. I didn't really hit her. I mean, is she serious?"

QUEENIE: "They sounded serious to me."

ME: "Oh, wow. I can't believe it. I can't believe it." I feel embarrassed. I feel that all of *them* out there think I hit Lena Mae. Oh my God. I did hit her. I think back carefully to what happened. I did hit her a little. My arm came back and I hit her shoulder just as she was yelling to Terry. But not hard, Jesus, it was a tap, not a hit. I am on the defensive. Defending myself in my mind.

ME: "I only tapped her. What are they saying? Who's talking? I mean, holy cow. I feel like a mugger."

EDEN: "Don't worry about it. If you didn't hit her."

ME: "I did. I mean I tapped her. *Shit!*"

I begin to pace again. They leave. Oh shit, shit, shit. Cove will believe her. I know he will. He'll think I hit her deliberately because I hit him. But I only tapped her and Cove will think I attacked her like I've attacked him. That's what he thinks. Oh Cove, I wouldn't do that. How can you think that? Well, I sure as hell won't go near Lena Mae again. I'll never talk to her. I'll wait for Cove to leave before I come out. What a mess. And I was worried about Maurice on the bed. Maybe I always worry about the wrong things. Maybe that's my trouble.

I sit in the dark rocking in my chair. Tap on the door.

Cove opens the door.

I shoot out of the chair and stand up and get over in the back of it away from him.

COVE: "Can I come in?" He takes a few steps and stands inside the door. He leaves it open. I see him look around. "May I borrow your flashlight?"

ME: "Sure." I rummage around in my desk and hand him the flashlight.

COVE: "I hear you had trouble today."

ME: "Well. So they say. I didn't hit her hard, though, in fact, in fact it was only a tap and I was only kidding." What am I saying? Why am I so defensive?

COVE: "Maybe you weren't kidding."

ME: "You don't know what happened."

COVE: "Lena Mae and Helen told me."

He believes them, not me. He isn't going to listen to me. Of course, I am the one that's wrong. I am the patient, the guest, the crazy one, the looney, the murderer. And they can go to staff meeting and discuss me and I'm not there and he believes them. I'm not going to talk to *him* anymore.

ME: "I won't talk to Lena Mae again. That's the last time. Ever."

COVE: "Maybe you should talk to her. Maybe even more than before."

Silence. I won't discuss it. She hurt me so how can *he* understand.

COVE: "Maybe you really meant to hit her because you felt so deeply what she was doing. An instinctive reaction."

Silence. Cove won't listen to me anyway. I want to cry. Get away from me, Cove, get away. My feelings toward you are too much and they make me hurt so get away. I go over and sit on the bed and turn away my face.

COVE: "Will you come to group therapy?"

ME: "No!"

COVE: "It's up to you, you have to decide what's best for you."

ME: "Shit!" He leaves. I am in a rage.

A while later another knock on the door. Madonna is back.

ME: "Oh, I'm so glad to see you. Are you all right? Are you going to stay?"

MADONNA: "Yeah. I'm back for a while. I'm in with Queenie."

My insides are churning around about Cove. I'm so mad but now I'm worried about what he thinks about me. I keep my eye on the clock. Madonna looks subdued. Half my mind is on her, and the other half on me.

MADONNA: "I've got troubles."

ME: "You want to talk?"

Madonna is smoking. She takes her cigarette and flicks the ashes in the cuff of her dungarees. The ashtray is next to her but she prefers her cuff.

MADONNA: "I don't think I like men."

ME: "I don't either. I hate men. I get all mixed up over men."

MADONNA: "I like women."

ME: "I don't like women. I don't get along with anyone."

MADONNA: "I'm a lesbian."

I'm thinking that this stupid day hasn't been good for me. Maybe Maurice is right. Maybe I had too good a time running the bulldozer and working on the septic tank. Maybe I'm paying for my pleasure.

Madonna repeats, "I think I'm a lesbian."

I look at her. What is she saying?

ME: "What? You don't know what you're saying—of course you're not a lesbian." My mind isn't grasping, isn't working. I have my own troubles.

MADONNA: "I like to make love to women."

ME: "No, you don't. You don't really. You're just mad at men, like me."

MADONNA: "I had an affair with a girl this last week when I was gone."

ME: "No, you didn't."

My mind refuses to assimilate her words. She takes her cigarette butt and grinds it into the top of her dungarees by her knee. I look at her, fascinated. That must hurt. Why is she talking to me like this?

MADONNA: "I think I've known a long time."

ME: "Oh Madonna, no. You're too young. You couldn't possibly know. You're going to be all right. Men have used you, that's all. You'll be all right." I dismiss her. It's too much for me. Overwhelmed with my own self. She must be kidding me. I see it's close to ten. It's so important that I see Cove.

ME: "I'll talk about it later. I've got to be somewhere."

Madonna looks hurt. Looks lost. She's mistaken. I don't want to hear any more about it. Nothing. Go away.

I race down the stairs. Group is over. Maybe too late? I go through the kitchen down the back stairs and out the cellar by the summer kitchen. I race across the road to the tennis courts. I go across the courts into the trees by the road. I hide in the trees and wait. I picture Jay and Jane gathered around Cove. I hate him. I want to get even with him for believing Lena Mae. It's cold. I'm not frightened. I have this rage that powers my batteries. I see his lights coming down the hill and as he passes I mouth a silent obscenity and raise my fist. He doesn't see. I slump at the bottom of the tree. There, Cove, you horrible man. I showed you. I got even. I lie there and I don't feel better. Something bad happens. Something bad happens inside different from before. I feel something strange. A nothing feeling. I know it is bad for me. My eyes just stare at the leaves. The caring inside is gone. I lost it.

Thursday, December 4, 1969

Don brings me back from Cove's. I put my head in his lap and he strokes my hair. I tell Don that I love Cove again, not hate him. He laughs. He never knows which one it will be. He likes it that my wrath isn't directed at him. The snow is almost a blizzard. I'm concerned about the ride up the mountain. Don isn't. The darkened car is like a capsule. Warm and comfortable. We share a bottle of Cold Duck. Cove seemed to understand that I didn't hit Lena Mae very hard. I probably hurt her feelings. I can't understand. The three of us will get together and discuss the whole thing. I close my eyes as Don shifts gears. The long hill is slippery. We have to back down to the beginning. Don loves the challenge of the hill. He would never call to the top for the four-wheel-drive to pick us up. A matter of pride. In the main house it is dark and quiet. We sit in the living room by the fireplace and hold hands. Christmas is coming and it scares us both. Cove seemed so kind tonight, like an oasis. And so does Don. That part of me that took over, the not caring part, has receded. It made me very tired and very quiet. Like I didn't have the energy to fight anymore. I don't really want to fight Cove and Don.

Someone has brought a stereo into the dining room and it is playing this incredibly beautiful music, in the dark. It is a folk song. The popular one, "Help me through the night." It touches us deeply. The voice is a man's, bell clear and resonant. It fits our mood. We stand up. We are going to my room. As we walk through the dining room we look for the stereo. There is none. We look again. In the corner by the phone is a figure with a guitar. It is the new guest, Eric. He is the one with the beautiful voice. We go over and ask if we can listen. We put another log on the fire while he charms and soothes us. The music comes from his soul. We look at each other. It's amazing. Don goes to the phone and dials. He turns his back to us and talks quietly. Eric asks me my name. I say Carol. He sings a little louder. "The night don't seem so lonely—Sweet Carol-ine. . . ." I feel a lump inside. Don and I listen a little more, then go upstairs. He props a chair under the doorknob. He'll spend the night.

Friday, December 5, 1969

A happy kind of excitement fills the air.

Sauna night. The sauna is to the right of the main house across a brook. A dark wooden building. One whole section of woods crew cuts the logs to sauna length. Heat builds up and up, steam pouring on the bodies. They stand it only so long, then they run out of the building and jump in the brook. Screaming. My excitement grows too. There's so much snow. It's daring. And it feels good. The senior staff has taken their turn and they tell us it's our turn. Towels are whipped around bodies; running feet; excited laughter. Guests go naked.

That's part of the excitement. A legitimate, legal, staff-approved and socially sanctioned chance to go bare.

I look out my window, which faces the woods toward the sauna. I can hear them shrieking and laughing. I am pulled by the noise. I slip on my coat and head down the path. I stop before the bridge and watch. Big brown shape comes barreling out, shining and glistening. A naked Obie followed by a white Rachel, a white Madonna. They jump in the creek screaming.

"Come on, Carol! Take off your clothes. Come join us." They run barefoot, bare-bodied in the snow. I'm caught up in the excitement. They are like children in the ocean waves. Delightful, beautiful. They are like my children.

I turn around and go back to my room. I'm happy for them. But I just can't. I can't take off my clothes in front of my children. I'm sorry, I can't.

I laugh out loud, thinking of them out there. Jesus, they're cute.

Tuesday, December 9, 1969

I have stayed away from Lena Mae as much as I could. I don't trust her. I'm uneasy today. Our "talk" is scheduled. John has told me that when two people have disagreements they get together with Dr. Ashley to settle it. Queenie says the meeting is shit because it's two staff against one guest. These talks are something special, out of the ordinary. Everybody knows when one is scheduled. Eden and Madonna give me pats on the back. I'm scared. I got along all right with Cove on Thursday. I mean, he was nice again. I don't want to spoil it by talking to him with Lena Mae. I don't want to talk to her about anything. It's scheduled for after lunch. I go up to my room. I can't eat. I wish I was back in Spruce Cottage. I can't hide here. Maybe they'll forget. I'd rather not do this, Cove. I cover

my head with my pillow to stop my thinking. It doesn't work.
Knock on the door. Cove there, says it's time. Green sweater with a
turtle neck and old gray pants and L. L. Bean hiking boots. Old
friend, nice man, kind eyes won't hurt me. I stand up and go to the
fear room with him. My room, bathroom, then fear room. She's
there on the chair next to the window and Cove sits on the chair
by the table and I can't figure out where to sit because, in fact, I
don't even want to be there. I go over to the fireplace. The fire is
warm. I'm so cold. I sit on the floor and I look up at them.

This isn't fair because Cove certainly isn't scared and Lena
Mae doesn't look scared sitting there all neat and composed. She
probably found out that Cove is a regular person and so she's not
even scared of him, doesn't love him or even hate him, and so I
look at the floor and she talks at me. Her arm was so sore where I
hit her that she had to soak it in ice that night. I can't believe her.
Why is she making this up? Is she lying, why is she saying I did
this? My insides feel like jelly. It's a good thing I didn't eat because
my arms are wrapped around my legs and if I had eaten, all the cottage cheese would come spilling out of my mouth. And so she must
have a reason for saying these things. I look at her and she doesn't
seem to be lying so I have no defense against her. They won't believe that I only tapped her shoulder, so I won't talk to her and she
asks me questions about why I hit her, that she didn't do anything
to me, and I just say I'm sorry, and she says that isn't enough, that I
should explain my side of the story, and I just say I only tapped
her and she stiffens in her chair and her eyes are furious and she
switches topics right in midstream, her voice louder and more shrill.
You are a bad mother, you should be home with your children.
Why are you at the farm anyway, you shouldn't be here. As she
says this my jelly stomach coagulates and goes into the freezer like
a pan of white bread. Harder and harder until nothing can get out,
trapped by my throat. The hair on the back of my neck bristles like
Hennessey when she sees a cow. I will submit to her because she has
all the weapons. I lie down and show my throat. Yes, I am a bad
mother. I am a bad person. Yes, I shouldn't be here, you are right,
you are right. I only see Lena Mae. I don't see Cove. Only Lena Mae
who has to hurt me. She surprises me because when I agree with her

she gets madder. She wants my side of the story. I have no side. I am bad so I have no side. Maybe if I agree with her she'll go away. She won't have to kill me but she keeps on and I hold onto the floor with my arms. I hug the floor. My hands flat, then into fists, and as I say to her I am a bad mother it strikes me. I am. I am bad. I hear Cove in the background saying some words but it is too late because I can't hear what his words are. I raise my fist and I start on the floor and then on myself. I hear my fist hitting and I hear the noise but I feel nothing and Lena Mae jumps down on the floor next to me. Will she hit me too? I am a bad mother, mother, mother. She grabs my left hand and holds it down but I am so strong. I am so much stronger than she. I want to get out of the room, to punish myself. And then Cove has jumped to the floor on my right side and grabbed my right arm. But I am stronger even than he. I see his green sweater close to my eye. I pull my hand free of Lena Mae and I hit myself, bad person, but I can't get my right arm free of green sweater and I'll fight them so I can kill myself and I am so strong but I am tipped back a little and feel maybe I might lose my balance and it makes me weaker, that's when I hear the sound from him, the words spoken to me, I hear the sound then and it's not so much the words but the sounds. It gets into my head and once it's there I am helpless. The tonal quality, the rich soft sound of his voice, the sound of lovers in the nuptial bed. The sound of father nurturing the small child, the deep earth sound of my name, Carol, puts me in quicksand where the more I fight the more I am sucked in, so I give in to it and don't fight it anymore, my body goes for the comfort of the sound and dissolves into the green sweater and the clenched fists give way to tears.

Lena Mae releases my arm, I don't see her, she moves away maybe to the corner, she hurt me and she attacked me about the only thing that hurts me the most, my children, she isn't a part of me anymore, she doesn't play by the rules, when I gave her my throat she killed me so she means nothing to me and my feelings of hatred for myself are replaced with feelings of wanting to be held so long, protected and held. And the voice says again my name and my throat catches and turns to new wails. He holds me there on the floor by the fire until my body stops trembling and wailing, until it gets all calm and tired and the tears and water on the sweater begin to dry, until my body gets peaceful. I have never been safe, really safe, never been really ever safe out there but now I am. I am now so safe maybe I can leave the arms, go out and be safe out there. Maybe be safe without him.

Thursday, December 11, 1969

John puts me on shoveling. I can't handle the woods. George Tent is also on it. He came from Philadelphia last night. He's nice though and I don't see any harm in talking to him. Maurice has finally left. I'm glad he's gone. He's living with a friend until he gets settled.

George, Benson and I shovel snow from the front paths. George and I talk all the time. He says he has a really strong girlfriend, that he doesn't like to go out at night unless she's along. They walk down the middle of the street and his girlfriend knows judo. I think it's funny. George is letting his beard grow. He looks like a bum.

We both look over at the same time and see Benson lying on the ground, half on the snowbank and half on the path. My heart leaps. He's subject to seizures. We go to him. His arm covers his face as if he's sleeping. I peek through his arms and look at one eye. He's awake.

"Benson—hey, you all right?"

He looks rather dazed. George and I grab his shoulders. He is awake because he gets to his feet easily. We help him to the couch in the library. I run around and find Helen, who gives me some aspirin for him. He has a splitting headache. He can stay on the couch for as long as he wants to recover. The snow shoveling is hard and Benson gets out of a lot of work that way.

George and I go back out. We glance around, then walk the path across the snow-covered lawn. We stand upright and at the count of three let ourselves fall. We lie in the nice snow until John comes by. Our seizures don't convince John.

Friday, December 12, 1969

George and I sit together at supper and eat our fried fish fillets. I feel the excitement because I'm finally going to town on my own. We pay our fifty-cent bus fare to Hugh and board the bus. It leaves at six-thirty sharp and will bring us home at eleven. And I have a real date for town trip and we sit toward the back and hold hands like going to a high school basketball game. Hats are stolen from heads and thrown around and everyone giggles. We'll follow the crowd, I don't tell him I might panic, he wants me to protect him so I am calm. We follow the crowd, it's so strange going into bars for beer, I don't even like beer but I have a date with big strong George. We buy Vantage cigarettes for him and Juicy Fruit gum for me. I don't know how old I am or if I look old or not. It all goes so nicely—me and my friends sitting in a restaurant bar with candles. But I stop as if struck. A couple from home have seen me. They come to the table and say hello and my voice is gone. Where am I? Am I really here with my boyfriend? Hugh and Obie and Eden and Queenie and George and me. What am I doing here, oh they heard I had "nerves" and was away, and now I'm sitting with George. My head gets very dizzy, and I see them staring at the table. They stare and then they walk away. I'm not part of their world anymore. I'm part of this world. What is the real world? In which world am I living? I look down at the table and I see what they were looking at. Oh what fools we are, what fools to think we are regular people just out for a night on the town. Do we forget so easily who we are? On the table all stretched out for the city to see, among the drinks, our leather gloves, our warm working gloves. With our names in black Magic Marker.

Tuesday, December 16, 1969

It hasn't been too bad actually. Eden has taken me for walks down
the hill. Further and further each time. We pick up different people
and so it's more like a social event. George goes with me everywhere. The hill downward has lost its terror. I wonder why I made
such a fuss. This is Cove day but Cove isn't coming. He has a stupid
meeting somewhere. I didn't know about it and I wish he'd cleared
it with me first. I'll get back at him, he'll be sorry. If I die I'll be
able to say I told you so. I've made up my mind to go on woods
crew. I signal to Voss at breakfast and at morning meeting when
they call the work programs, it's just casually read off that I'll go to
the woods. All my friends look at me but I act cool. I won't let
them know that my insides are massacred. George probably won't
be going with me. He has overslept again. He'll be in a lot of trouble if he oversleeps much more. I'm glad my close friends aren't on
the crew. I wouldn't want them to see me fail. I skip volleyball and
go up to the bathroom. I spend a long time there. I don't want to
get caught in the woods having to go. Gregory and Voss are the
leaders. Glory, Alfred, Rachel, Hugh and four other guys are on the
crew. We start out on the path going past Spruce Cottage. Nothing
is said to me so I'm not special. Just a member of the crew. I decide to lag behind. If I can't make it, I'll just turn around and run
back. We trudge along with our saws. I keep my eyes on the footsteps made by the person in front of me. I'm afraid they'll absorb
me. I'm scared, so scared. I think of Cove saying what can happen
to me? I have a one-second urge to run away from the trail, into the
woods, and lie under the snow and be covered up forever. But the
feeling goes away. Maybe that's why I'm scared of the woods.
Really, I'm just scared of myself and what *I* might do. I see Rachel
disappear ahead. I'm alone. Oh, such a big beautiful forest, good
Lord, it's beautiful. I run over to a big white birch off the path and
hold onto it. It anchors me. I amaze myself. I like it out here. My
Jesus, it's pretty. And I like being alone too. It's so cold, must be
below zero. I just keep hold of that tree and then I see a figure up

by the road, watching me. It's Gregory. So I am missed after all. I wave at him and pick up my saw and get back on the path. I catch up to the group. We walk a long time across brooks and pastures and different woods. When we get to a clearing I see that the crew has been working hard in this area. They mostly work on dead trees, but also cut down trees that need to be thinned out. Gregory and Voss do the felling. The rest of us do the sawing. We work in pairs. Rachel works with me. We put a large limb, maybe eight or ten inches in diameter, on a sawhorse and mark off the lengths. We have yellow poles for measuring. Rachel doesn't seem to have a good rhythm for sawing and when she wanders off to get warm by the fire, I'm glad. Hugh takes her place. He doesn't expect me to work hard because I'm a girl, so I put everything I have into that saw. I learn not to push down and what to do when you hit a knot. It's not long before I'm sweating. Brush is burned in a big fire. I decide not to go near the fire. I won't want to come back and work. Glory's job is carrying the cut logs to the stacking piles and neatly stacking them. She takes huge loads and works very hard. I wonder what she would be like if she didn't have this work she loves.

My legs hurt. My back hurts and my feet are frozen. My hiking boots just aren't warm enough. I don't like Glory taking our pile away so fast because I like to see all the wood we've cut. I will be so lame. But I love it. I love it out here. I smile and I laugh and they are amazed to see the old lady work so hard. And I *do* have to go to the bathroom. I *do*. But I can hold it and if I can't hold it, I can go behind a tree. I'm a big girl now.

Friday, December 19, 1969

There is excitement about Christmas next week. It makes me awful nervous and mad. I'm mad because I feel helpless. I'm not going home for Christmas. I'd wreck everything. But I haven't done anything for Don and the kids. I hate Christmas. Hate it! I pace around in my room. I saunter downstairs. I kick the table leg. I sit by myself. We're supposed to make a huge garland in the summer kitchen for the wooden posts in the dining room. We cut boughs a certain size and tie them to the rope base. I throw the scissors onto a barrel and walk out the back door. Tantrum. Only it doesn't work because it's freezing outside, and I don't have my parka. I walk back in. Hugh looks at me and I growl. Everyone looks disgusting to me. And I head the list. I walk upstairs and get a cup of coffee. I think about my appointment last night with stupid dumb Cove. We talked about Lena Mae and all that. I guess maybe she worries about being a good mother too. I don't know. It's all dumb, dumb, dumb. And that stupid Cove getting me to talk about stupid fantasies. And dumb me telling him! Sexual fantasies where I want the hero hurt. Cove says that's my harmless way of getting even with men that have hurt me. He says the sexual part is natural. That it means I want to be loved and accepted as myself. What does he know anyway? I go into the living room and slouch onto a couch. Jud ambles by and grumbles his usual gross talk and I look at him.

How could I ever have liked him? How could I ever like anybody around here? Misfits, all of us. Misfits. And ugly. Gross.

John walks in and sits next to me. He puts his arm around me and smiles. I wrench away and bark at him. "This whole place is stupid! I hate it! I hate everybody! It all makes me sick, I'm not staying."

JOHN: "Let's go to town. I'll take you to lunch. We can get you some warm boots. And wouldn't you like to do Christmas shopping for your family?"

ME: "I hate this place, I can't do anything right, I hate Christmas and I can't go home. Stupid people."

John looks at me. He's so skinny and almost bald and I love him.

"Except you. You aren't stupid and dumb. But I can't go shopping because I'll get scared with the stupid anxiety and freak out in the lines and you'll be embarrassed and I'm no good."

"I'll give you one half-hour to get ready. Jake is in the library. He can give you the money you need."

ME: "Well, oh, well, all right, I guess. At least I'll get out of this stupid place."

John smiles at me. He isn't afraid of me and I appreciate that. He jumps up and strides away. He always does things quick like that.

We have lunch in a small café. It is a café that some of the farmers once wrecked. We're not allowed here, but here I am. I have pea soup. My spirits are soaring. I have just bought Don a Zero-King coat. It's heavy corduroy with a fleece lining. He'll love it. I feel so good about this present. I don't feel like such a creep. Then I bought the kids ski sweaters. Mostly I feel good about Don's present.

I feel almost good to be who I am and where I am. And driving back to the farm John says what a pleasure it was to take me to town, and I have that feeling, that funny feeling, creep up—that feeling I won't admit to anyone, even myself. The feeling of being happy.

Saturday, December 20, 1969

GEORGE: "But, what should I do? I don't know what to *do* with my life."

ME: "What do you mean *do?* I mean, can't you get a job?"

GEORGE: "What kind of job? I can't direct my energies on a job now."

ME: "Is that why you always sleep late?"

GEORGE: "I guess so. You see, my girlfriend takes care of me. Now she wants me to do something. So does my guardian."

ME: "Your guardian?"

GEORGE: "Yeah. I hate her. She administers my trust fund. She will cut out my allowance if I don't shape up. She thinks I'm incompetent."

ME: "Allowance? You get an allowance? How come you get an allowance? You're almost my age."

GEORGE: "Don't lecture me! I have to figure what I want to do. I wrote my girlfriend about you."

ME: "Me? What did you say?"

GEORGE: "That we're always together."

ME: "Won't she be jealous?"
GEORGE: "Sure."
ME: "You going home for Christmas?"
GEORGE: "You?"
ME: "No."
GEORGE: "Me either."

We put on our warm clothes and head over to George's cottage. We talk like this all the time. I listen to him as he talks. I'm glad to have someone to be with. I'm flattered too. It's like I have a boyfriend. He sits with me when I eat and gets on my crews with me. Me and George. My boyfriend. I mean, this is my world now and the other world has faded away, doing their Christmas things. George and I aren't good enough for Christmas. We walk into his room. It's a mess. All his clothes dumped into a heap. I sit on the bed and we talk about his trust fund. It's like he's made the fund into a living person. I borrow phrases that I remember from Cove, like "What do *you* think?" and things like, "Do you want to get better?" I'm being therapeutic. George seems to like it when I do this, that's why I keep on. Only thing is, I don't know what I'm talking about. I feel like Frieda. I want to say to George, "I have problems too." But I don't. I separate my family from George. I don't talk about them. He's the first person I don't discuss my family with. I distance myself from the outside world this way. What do they care anyway? They're to blame I'm in this place. They're the ones that got rid of me. Now they don't have to put up with me. Don and Cove and their good lives. So now, I have George for myself.

Hugh knocks on the door and opens it and stands and looks at us. George is putting a record on the stereo. Hugh gives me one of those looks that say I know what you're doing. I sneer at him. What is he to me? George likes the innuendoes. Not me. When Hugh leaves I decide we should get out of his room. It's too early for bed and nothing's going on in the main house. And it's Saturday night. We decide this is a good time to break out the bottle of wine that we bought in town. It's hidden under the pile of clothes. He puts it under his coat and we head for the rec house. The rec house is a large building at the end of the center path from the main house.

It has a sink and toilet, a large fireplace and tables and chairs. It has an open ceiling and a ladder leading to a loft. There are mattresses in the loft. I think they're for visitors if no beds are available. The rec house door is open about three inches. There's a hose attached to the sink and leading out the door. John is making a skating rink and that's what the hose is for. It is a clear and cold night. Someone is already in the rec house. He is a guest I don't know very well named Sparrow. He's not very tall and has straight, dirty, long hair. I don't know why people don't wash their hair. George doesn't wash his either. Sparrow's eyes light up as we come in and he says real loud and fast, "Gladtoseeyoujoinmypartyscrew-themotherfuckersscrewtheworld."

George and I look at each other. Sparrow is on some kind of dope. George and I scrounge around and find glasses, actually pottery. Somebody's making pottery. I drink a large cup of wine fast like it was water. Pour another and another. There. Now I don't have to worry so much about that other world that always bothers my mind.

I push a lot of newspaper and scraps of wood together in the fireplace and get a little fire going. It's cold in the rec house. Sparrow and George are arguing about something and loneliness hits me like a kick in the stomach. I want someone to care for me, to love me, I want to be cared for and the other world is far away. Sparrow and George get louder and then Sparrow starts leaping over the chairs and benches. It scares me. He jumps onto a table and reaches up his arms and grabs a rafter. He swings back and forth like a monkey. What scares me is that George is caught up in the action so he leaps on the table too. And he starts swinging. I get up and climb the wooden ladder to the loft. I pull over a mattress to the railing and lie on my stomach there looking down at the monkeys.

SPARROW: "Do it!"

GEORGE: "Naw."

"Do it."

"Naw."

"Do it."

They scream at each other and laugh. Then they look around and they miss me. When George looks up and sees me in the loft, he becomes quieter and grabs the wine and tumblers and comes up the ladder. Sparrow jumps off the table, scrambles up another, jumps down and climbs the ladder. His eyes white and wild. My heart's pounding but I don't move. He steps next to me, balances on the railing, leaps out and catches a rafter and falls to the floor. My God, somebody's going to get hurt. George is lying next to me on the mattress and we watch Sparrow pick himself off the floor and weave out the door. He gives the door a mighty fling but it doesn't bang. It hits the hose and springs back open. In my relief I start laughing and I can't stop laughing, so funny, and George puts his hands on me and turns me over and says Sparrow wanted to watch us, oh ha ha, so funny, as my parka comes off. And the other world fades away; after all, all I want is to be held, other world leaves me, want to be loved because then I am safe, just be safe, and George wants to be safe too, and he takes my breasts out of my clothes and puts his lips to them; I think of the monkeys swinging on the rafters and there's nothing more than the feelings and they stay forever when nothing else does and the other world has gone. We can't hack the other world and we don't care about it. And we won't ever again.

I hear footsteps below and I freeze into a rigid ball. Outside world has me in its clutches after all. John has walked into the rec house. Jesus help me, John mustn't know how bad I am, John's my friend, I mustn't let him see me. George doesn't care and sits up. I crawl over to a back corner and cover my head with my parka. Maybe he won't see me. John looks around and stands still. I stop breathing. Then he goes to the sink and turns on the water for the ice rink. And then he walks out the door.

What John thinks of me is suddenly the most important thing in the world. He won't like me now, he'll hate me and so will Cove and Don. George doesn't know what the fuss is about. My body is so stone cold that I think a cross section could be done of my heart and it wouldn't bleed or anything. It would just slice away frozen solid and fall on the floor. I know now that I am a bad person and I will have to pay for my sins, atone. And George just talks regular at me and he explains how his girlfriend has long hairy legs.

Sunday, December 21, 1969

I see John coming over to me out of the corner of my eye. Oh God help me, I avoided him yesterday and now I can't anymore. My piece of toast sticks in my throat. It won't go up or down. I grab for my coffee and gulp it and start coughing. John has a serious expression on his face, he wants to talk to me after lunch. Sure, okay, John, okay, and then he goes away. Oh, I am out of control, I'm not in charge of myself, oh, what will I ever say to him? I put myself on woods crew for the morning. My new boots are so nice and warm. John tried to get me in the Christmas spirit and it only lasted a little while and now I've wrecked things. I work very carefully in the woods, very deliberately. My control is slipping and if I work too fast I might just fling myself on some blade and go berserk in the woods or start flying or I don't know what, so I concentrate on the log. Very careful, precise. Saw saw saw. Look at the snow. See the specks of dirt. See the solid, brown log with the cream insides. Smell the cut wood. Look at the designs in the wood. Don't look at the sky, keep eyes down only on the things right by my head. Draw all the world inward, downward. Push it all together and concentrate on the wood chip. It is shaped like New Hampshire. In this way I keep control. But it slips. It's elusive. So all morning it slips away and I grab it back. Like a black eel I catch on Enfield Pond. Fearful and slippery.

As we pack things up for lunch my fear escalates and is unbearable. We trudge down the path. I hold back and I get to the end of the line. I let them get ahead. I concentrate on where my next step will be, but I'm not looking ahead or up. I come to a frozen stream with snow mounds hiding most of the water. I hear it under there. I tighten myself up so I won't throw myself into the stream. It's an overwhelming desire. I make it across. I must punish myself, and I don't want to. I don't want to face John, I'm a bad person. That's why the control is gone. That's why I have to hurt myself. But I'm afraid to. It's so hard to do it. They have gone ahead without me. I grab a tree and I hold onto the tree. I open my eyes and look at it up close, so close. The white and black. A timeless tree. It gives me strength and I think as I continue on that maybe I will make it after all. I might do it. I might! I go probably a whole mile and I get to the path above Spruce, and my hope is I can catch them before I give way. I start to run. I see them way ahead, yellow sticks, saws glistening in the sun. I run faster and I come to a boulder at the side of the path. It's too late. My control leaves me. I throw myself on the boulder and throw myself over the other side. I shouldn't have started running. That was my mistake. I opened up too much of the world with the running. I land in a heap at the foot of the boulder. I have wrenched my shoulder. Oh Jesus, I really am crazy. I look ahead and see them way ahead, they don't see me. I am so crazy. Why did I do that? I had no choice because they don't punish me. I have to do it myself.

I pick myself up and brush off the snow. I feel ashamed. I'm so sorry. But I can lift my eyes again. I don't feel like I will fly in all directions. My loss of control wasn't fatal. That's the big fear. That when it comes, I will die. I'll be able to talk to John now. He'll want to talk about my involvement with George. I did some penance. Flinging myself over the boulder is equal to ten Hail Marys, the stone-altar sacrifice to the gods. It probably isn't enough, probably not near enough. But now I can look ahead. I don't have to keep my eyes down, magnifying the dirt. I can look straight ahead and walk down the path and can walk right, not all held tight. I clench my jaw and head for lunch. I can't look upward at the sky. That's too blinding. And that would mean, too, that I forgive myself.

Monday, December 22, 1969

Don brought Cove's tapestry to me last Thursday. It's wrapped in plain brown paper. I stuck it in the corner, against the wall. Cove is here early because it's Christmas week. This is the day I should give it to Cove. I'm scared to. I carefully undo the brown paper and look at it. They pressed it and blocked it and framed it and it's really beautiful. The frame is walnut. This is going to be one holy damn trick of a day. I'm mad at everyone. All the staff. A while ago I went and found George. I was going to tell him we should be careful and all that, but before I had a chance, he said that he had a talk with Timothy and Timothy thinks he should cool it with me. I didn't get a chance to decide on my own. George rejects me first.

So I'm mad. Nobody better tangle with me. They better stay away from me. Cove's thrown in among all these feelings too. I'm afraid to talk to him. And I don't want to see his eyes look at me. But I have to give him his Christmas present. I'll have to plan how. There are two things going here. One: I'm not going on work program, I'm sticking in my room, I won't see Cove. Two: I have to give him the tapestry.

I sit on my bed and try to figure it all out. Nobody is bothering me. That's the trouble. I get madder than ever at them. They've all left me alone. They've taken away my friend George and now they're all at staff meeting talking about how awful I am. I sneak downstairs through the kitchen, past the cooks and into the cellar. I go into the unlocked cage and get supplies. I steal a box of raisins, a box of apricots and a box of brown sugar. Maybe they won't talk to me for weeks and I won't be able to leave my room. I race back up fast, faces a blur, slam my door, lean against it.

Time goes by and still nobody comes for me. It's about supper time. I can hear noise and confusion downstairs. I break open the apricots. I can't figure why I took the brown sugar. Is this a game I'm playing? Why is my heart beating so fast? Why am I not smiling? It doesn't feel like a game. I have no strategy or plan. And I'm scared. It must be the tapestry more than the other. He won't like it. He'll throw it away. He won't know I made it, it looks too good for me to have made it. Maybe he won't like me even though I made him a nice present. Maybe he won't like me because I made it. Maybe he'll think I'm trying to buy him. Oh what a fix. There's a knock and I freeze. Jay's been sent to get me for group. "Sorry, Jay. I'm not coming. I can't go tonight." He leaves. There's no way I could go to group tonight. As he leaves I think maybe I'm burning all these bridges behind me, how will I get back? But I am so stubborn. Knock again at the door. This time it's Eden.

"I can't go tonight, Eden, but will you wait a minute?" I go to the desk and tear a page out of my notebook and write a note for him to give to Cove.

Cove, will you please come to my room after group therapy is over?

Thank you
Carol Ferland

Eden says he doesn't mind. He takes the note and goes.

And I sit on my bed and wait. Whatever happens, at least I will give him the present. I would never sleep if I didn't do that.

Sit on the bed. Take brown paper off. Put it back on. World-shattering decision has left me weak as a baby. Almost hysterical with this decision. I can't decide. I drop the paper over the tapestry, loose.

What will I say to him? I must plan.

Knock. Paralyzed.

The door opens. I back up toward the bed as Cove comes in. He has on a brown belt, corduroy pants and hiking boots. That's as far as my eyes can look, his bottom half. My hysteria is at such a pitch that looking him in the eyes would mean disintegration. So I look at his knee and squeeze out croaking sounds from myself.

"I made you a stupid, dumb, Christmas present." As I say this I run to the wall and grab the tapestry and lunge toward him and throw it in his arms.

"You can throw it away if you hate it!" I yell at him.

And this is too much for me. The strain of it all. I fly out the door and down the stairs and race through the house. Such grace. I am pleased with myself though. Really pleased. I sure hope Cove likes it. I actually finished a project and am proud of it. I think of Cove up there standing in my room and I also think that giving gifts is not one of my strong points.

Tuesday, December 23, 1969

At Cove's. Scared again. Go up the stairs and it is different from before because Cove is smiling. He asks Carol into the house to see
his tapestry. She feels awkward, but so pleased to see the Christmas
tree and his wife, a regular wife, and to see the tapestry hung so
nicely on the wall. A strange, nice house with halls coming and
going and leading to the living room. Seeing him with his wife
makes her feel secure and safe and because it is Christmas, hope
leaps up in her for her own regular husband and her own tree. She
can't very well *not* talk to this man who is helping her along the
way, so when she gets to the office the cold steel barriers drop for
a while and a flash of spirit moves in her and it makes her smile.
Cove could say to her, "Jump out that window," and she would just
go over to the window and jump. The flash that came across her
was trust and at the same time a realization that Cove wasn't going
to ask her to jump. That's how come she could trust.

And so she tells him about George and the grip of her sexual
confusions and they talk about her pattern of hurting herself in this
way with these men and he doesn't condemn her and gives her
some alternatives to total sex like friendly affection and she wonders why Cove and Don don't reject her like the others and she
knows then it's because they aren't playing games with her and
they are strong men. And they love her.

Back in the car, she positions her head in Don's lap. He keeps his
fingers stationary and she just moves her head under the fingers
where she wants him to rub. It soothes her and she is content. The
drive from Cove's to the farm is like a reprieve. They talk about
the kids and he sees the true Carol peeking through. And in that
short hour she doesn't feel that he's better than her or that she's
better than him. They are lovers, after all. And they again do the
silly things they did when they were first lovers. He sneaks a label
into her pocket. Woolrich, off his old shirt. They did this long ago,
surprising each other with a label, back and forth, never knowing
where it would turn up. One time she found it in her bag of cheese

popcorn. Her head is on his lap and she takes her hand out of her pocket with the label in it and puts her hand down and massages his leg slightly, his foot on the accelerator. In this way she can slip the label into his sock.

They are beginning to talk of being together and the excitement is brand new. They talk about the gift that has been returned to them. The one that got lost along the way. They clasp hands, tighten their belts and say a prayer. Neither of them will give up.

They know their peace is very short-lived. As they step out of the car the blackness envelops her and shrouds her soul. She walks through the darkened farmhouse and sees alone there in the corner the red glow of a cigarette, George. They are waiting for her. The devils inside her are waiting for their chance. They hear the bell and, like fighters, they stagger into the ring for another round. Pounding and pounding, each determined to win. And getting bloodied along the way.

Wednesday, December 24, 1969

Christmas descends on the farm. The staff make Herculean efforts to drive the gloom of total failure out of the farmers' minds. They decorate and they cook and they sing and they pray and they plead with us and we don't hear them. And they light candles and we blow them out. We are listless and agitated and we feel the bitter wind of isolation. And the staff step up their efforts and they invite strangers into our midst in pretty clothes and with gifts. And we reject their gifts and we reject *them*. We are suspicious of foreign eyes on us, those do-gooders who force us to our rooms. And the more they try, the more we retreat. Our pain is too great. Too great.

I am sitting at the table nearest the kitchen door, facing the windows. Voss is serving the roast beef and as he passes it to Rachel he looks at Obie and he says oh so quiet, "Nigger."

Oh so softly the word shatters the fragile peace into jagged particles of desolation. Obie in one smooth motion grabs his water glass and throws it full force at Voss, who is grinning. The glass just misses me and it misses Voss, he ducks, and it hits the chair at the next table and smashes. It is Jud's chair and Jud gets wet and splattered with glass and Jud stands up and starts to shout because it is Christmas and the obscenity hits us, Christ has no penis, and it hurts Jud to say this in his pain because somewhere along the line Jud thinks he's Christ. And Rachel looks dazed and begins to open her blouse and take it off. I am transfixed, fused to my chair. Madonna who never could resist a good fight picks up her glass and joins Jud in his chant, "Jesus fuckin' Christ is a Nazi," and turns and smashes the glass through the window facing me, and Frieda says, "We must not act this way." I can hear her voice coming through the obscenities. And by now Voss and Obie have moved to center ring and are poised to kill each other as Queenie has joined Madonna and picks up the glasses on either side of her and hurls them on the floor. Coward George scoots out to the kitchen to watch as Alfred runs to his room for his doll.

The other tables are involved and the chant picks up speed and rhythm. "Jesus is a Nazi, Jesus is a Nazi." As if from deep inside we can't think of anything worse, we've dredged the pain out and thrown it into the air. The very worst part of us there is. Obie stretches back and picks up a chair and raises it above his head to kill the bastard enemy. As if he knows who his enemy is. The rest of us don't. I leap out of my chair and move to center ring and stand before black Obie and smell the fear in him as he towers over me.

"Give it to me!" I scream.

He looks at me and he sees a way of escaping the totality of murder. The disparity in our sizes makes the battle short-lived for his code of honor does not allow him to hit a girl. He very softly puts down the chair and as he does this I see John race in with Timothy and Gregory. The sweet faces of the riot-control police. And they sure look sweet to me because it restores a little order, with cardboard in the broken window and glass swept into barrels and food taken away, eyes down, feelings once again submerged, as Frieda stays and makes an announcement—I can't believe my ears, absolutely the worst timing in the history of Christmas announcements: "You are all invited to the annual burning of the yule log with all the little children."

Blasphemy and murder and violence and fear and hopelessness and isolation and little children and yule logs.

Okay, Christmas. Here we come!

Saturday, December 27, 1969

I got through Christmas. I'm glad it's over. Don and the kids did all right. Now what? I'm here. Here I am! What's going to happen to me? I sit at the back table for morning meeting. I feel nothing whatsoever. Numbed. John makes an announcement that work is canceled for the day. Whoever wants to can go cross-country skiing. I go to my room and lie on my bed, oh shit. Can't do anything. Heart starts beating. Can't go? Questions form: Can't go? Can't I? Can I? Hey, Carol, you shit, why can't you go? Heart pounding. So what if you flip? So what? What can happen if you flip? You do anyway.

Okaaay. Carol, let's go. Excited. Race to room. Get long underwear, get Kleenex, get a couple of hidden pills, in case, get gum and cigarettes. Okaay, I'm prepared to meet you, world.

Get on bus, people stare at me. Yeh, Carol! Sit in front and hold on to railing. No panic. Beautiful day. Cumberland Hill. Have Englishman fit us with boots and skis. Me laughing, laughing. Glory saying in her loud voice, "Diamonds sparkle, diamonds sparkle," and Jud says, "It's Mao Tse-tung's birthday." Well, hot shit! Man puzzled, oh funny, so funny. Man, didn't you know we're all crazy? Oh funny. Cumberland Hill. Just ten miles over the mountain to Sugar Hollow where my kids are skiing. Hey kids, Ma's skiing again. Have a good day, okay? Don't know how to cross-country.

We all start out together. Jud and Glory have trouble moving, they are too slow—can't wait, see you later. Can't wait. Get down first hill and go toward a trail. All alone. All alone. Maybe you should be scared, Carol? Time later to be scared. Tree's marked, trail good. Lots of snow. I'm coming around a turn going easy and I'm in a deep wood. There's a hollow dead log and I stop. Nobody is around me for miles and on my right is a little ledge and an under-snow stream. The sun filters through and I look down and see a tiny track going around in circles. I think maybe a mole or other silly little thing. I just stay there for about ten minutes and the blinders come off my eyes and I wonder where have I been not to see such beauty, dear Jesus, is this real? And I start to laugh right out loud because I can see the beauty, oh thank you God, I can see the beauty and I just then at that moment see the world beautiful. And I was sweating and my sweat was drying and I was getting cold. Got to keep moving, you beautiful woods. Also don't want the men to catch up. Too nice alone. I love you so very much, you cross-country skiing. You are so beautiful.

Monday, December 29, 1969

Morning work is different because we're putting on an auction after lunch. Work crews are small because so many guests have gone for the holidays. These different things perk us up. Leftover clothes, unwanted Christmas presents and junk are auctioned. I buy an incredibly ugly mumu just for the fun of it. I go to my room and put it on and return. It's black with pink flowers. When I put my arms to the side I look like a vile, fleshy mammal. It gets a lot of laughs. I bid on a dinner for two at John's. I get it. I ask Eric to go with me. I tell him it's a payment for his music soothing the savage beast.

I get ready for dinner and put on a pretty brown and white polka-dotted silk dress. Strange wearing a dress. Reluctant to leave my room. Embarrassed. No one has seen me in a dress. No one. Actually I haven't seen them in dresses either, for that matter.

Eric knocks on the door to take me to John's. I'm glad for my dress. He looks fantastic. My God, we look like nice people. His suit has a western cut but it must be expensive. Take off our dungarees, ta-daaaa!

As we come down the stairs a crowd of the jealous are waiting for us. We bow and they applaud. George is toward the back. He pulls me aside and says he hopes I'll have a lousy time. He's mad I didn't ask him.

The dinner is very nice. There are two other couples plus John and his wife and Eric and me. Eric and I are the only farmers. I am a little scared but I forget to be shy or awkward. I have a nice time. They have a big kettle on the fireplace hearth. A metal rod heats in the fire and is placed in the kettle to warm the cider. A regular dinner. Something is happening to me. It happened at woods crew. And it happened cross-country skiing and now at John's dinner. What's happening to me is that I'm feeling good a lot of the time. And then I think maybe oh maybe I might be getting better.

Tuesday, December 30, 1969

We trudge up to the horse barn, six of us brave ones, with our sleds. John is stationed at the bottom of the hill with his truck to stop any cars that might come up. Starting at the barn the hill is maybe two miles long. I am the last one to go. I push off slow, then go down fast, screaming, fast around the turn, past the audience, faster and faster, screaming and dragging my feet. Screams of joy and fear disappear into the wind. Oh fun, fun, so much fun, down the hill winding and steep, on toward the bottom. Down and down forever, thrilled by the excitement of letting everything go, roar to the bottom, no more dragging feet, letting it all go. As the dark descends we scoop out little hollows in the snow about every 20 feet or so and stick in little votive candles. The snow protects the candles from the wind. We pat down the snow so sledders can see the flames in the dark, whizzing by those little candles—past one, check to see how to steer to the next. Pass the next fast, faster. We sledders are the hardy ones, the fearless conquerors. We are envied, we have let it go, we are a group. We know we are going to make it. It is unspoken.

Don meets me and my sled at the bottom of the hill. He sees my fun and laughs. He has come to drive me to my appointment.

. . .

Now I must run up the stairs to tell Cove.

"Cove! Guess what? Guess what happened? Oh Cove, I had fun. I can't believe it. I went to dinner at John's and I went cross-country skiing and today I sledded down the hill. Things are different. It's different."

So I am pleased to present Cove with something nice. Now, he'll really love me because I'm all better and he won't hate me. Oh Cove, Cove, I love you, you are beautiful, I can never tell you that, but there you are. I think you are beautiful and maybe now you'll be my lover. Since I'm nice. Whoa! Halt! Stop! Look! Listen! Oh dear, oh dear, wait a minute, hold on here, stomach doing flip-flops, better be careful with these thoughts, get back to the farm to think things over.

I see Cove's warm body behind the desk and I want the body and I hear his words blurring through, something about going easy and taking my time and things like that, and then I hear some words clear as a bell, have I thought about leaving the farm, and the knot in my stomach grows. My smile fades and as I leave his office I am very quiet, the stomach knot growing larger. I glance over my shoulder at his so nice bushy blondish-brown hair and I don't see how come I can't make love to him and the knot in my stomach grows and grows and on the way up the hill the knot turns to fear. If I get better, then I'll never see him again.

Wednesday, December 31, 1969

I shouldn't have told Cove those things, I shouldn't have! Oh what was I thinking? I wasn't thinking. I was happy. That's what tricked me. The happiness. It was impulsive to tell him good things. And foolish. And now my stomach is tied up. I'm not getting better. Who the hell am I kidding? Momentary lapses into health. Flukes. Mistakes. The real thing is the knot in the stomach and the fear. They tricked me again into thinking I could be like them. And I fell for it. To build me up like that knowing all the time I'd fall down and break into shameful, despicable, ugly parts. My stomach wrenches in spasms of hate. George, where are you? It's New Year's Eve,

let's go to town and celebrate. We *are* good for each other. You
and me. What are you saying? You like women with hair under
their arms? Oh, how nice, George, how thrilling. You said that
you're schizoid? Oh, great, George, now you know what you are.
At least your doctor told you that. Mine never did. He never told
me what I am. Oh George, put your arms around me and tell me
your problems. You say you take the trust fund money even though
you hate it? Don't you worry your handsome little head about it.
Maybe that's what makes you so stingy yourself, always worrying
about every penny. And the fund has millions. Oh poor George.
Let's go to town, okay? Back of bus, touching, laughing. "My doctor asked me what I planned for the New Year. But I see through
him. I catch on to him. He wants to get rid of me. Let's drink and
celebrate." You suit me just fine, George, you creep.

I'll get even with them for making me feel good. Show them
they can have their world. I got a guy, see? He can hurt me good
and I'll like it because he's mine. Let's drink, George, okay? Fiddle
with the matches and tear them up with the cover into tiny little
pieces and play with the candle wax. The other world is going fast.
No one exists now but me and George. What do they know anyway? Those holy, saintly and good people are driving me crazy. I
hate them. You Coves and Dons of the world, leave me alone. You
have fooled me long enough. You tricked me into thinking I be-
longed and that I was good. You are liars! Liars! My stomach is a
solid knotted pulse of tumor. I want to take a knife to that tumor,
sitting there in the bar. Cut it away. No knife. Let's go back to the
farm, all right? To my room, George? Okay.

Fast. In room, no lock. What do you want to do? Drink? Okay.
Past the bathroom into the fear room. Hugh's room. He's away.
Can lock door. See how we stagger. In room, lock door. No one's
around. Oh Jesus, this is the fear room. Cove's conference room.
I hate it here. I hate it here. My stomach. Scared of this room.
Look around. George doesn't know about this room. Go over by
the fireplace. Lie down. Cove gone. Where's Cove? Knot in my
stomach convulsing. Want a knife. Want a knife. The pain won't go
away. The pain, lots of pain, it won't 'go away. Holding stomach,
rolling on the floor, George excited, George doesn't know, getting

rough, hurting. She'll fight him, fight them all, but he is bigger and he pushes her down and all she thinks of is to cut out the tumor. The knife. She stops fighting, stops fighting, knife is there punishing her, slicing into her, way into her inside stomach by the fireplace, go ahead, go ahead, go ahead, knife going into the tumor and slicing her up good, so good, so good, she gets even with them, feels so good as she tells him to keep on forever until the pain is gone, world gone, Carol gone.

Thursday, January 1, 1970

Waking up, stomach hurts. Knots. Knots in her heart. Body won't move, doesn't want to move. Mind confused, hurts. Can't forgive herself for committing crimes so stomach has to knot itself up. Body can't work. Body can't eat. Body groans and clutches itself and turns into a ball and puts knees up to chin and head down and gets close to the wall and groans. Body can't seem to detach itself from the brain so it doesn't get any reprieve. Brain is very, very cruel, very, very mean to this body. Won't forgive it, won't give it comfort, won't let it cry. Brain thinks in its hardness that this body should be destroyed. Such an ugly betrayed useless stump should be stomped on like a reptile. Put out of its misery like a broken-legged horse. Mind says, how can I do it, get rid of this stupid body? I can heave it down the stairs, but it's so dumb it won't get killed. I could knife it in the stomach, but it would just get peritonitis. Or I could pill it to death, but there are not enough stashed away and it would just get sick. How? How?

Okay. I think I know how. Okay. It might work. Brain will get body way way far in the woods, way far in the snow. Mind will bury the body under the snow where it belongs with the dead winter decay. Mind says, you stupid body, won't have gum or cigarettes or pills so you'd never have a chance of surviving. Body just lying there gripping arms around the stomach. Mind says, "Get up, be on with it! Out, far out in the woods with you. Go ahead. Hurry up!" But the body can't move. That lumped-up mess wants

to obey but doesn't have the energy. Tries to get up. Can't. A long
time struggling. But strength is all gone, used up.

Body stays on bed for the day, just looking at the wall. Mind
frustrated and mad but gives it up as a lost cause. The lump just
can't move. Body has won that day. But mind says, "You really
better watch it, turkey, you better watch it. Someday I might
creep up on you when you have more energy and *zap!* You've
had it!"

A hand is put on the shoulder. Outside hand, warm hand. Hand
of a friend. John. And the hand unleashes the floodgates and breaks
down the cruel mind and allows the body to cry. She cries and
sleeps and when she wakes a truce has been called. The brain isn't
so cruel and the body has more energy.

Monday, January 5, 1970

Well, I happen to think it's Cove that got me into all this mess. He's
got me loving him somehow and got me all mixed up with the men-
sexual business. And it's his fault because he's my problem. So I get
even with him and yet I still love him. I think of him always and I
want him as my lover. I go to him because I can't stay away. And
then I want to go out in the snow. I ordered wallpaper three weeks
ago and now it's come in. I pick myself up and collect my mind as
best I can. Damn Cove anyway. I'm going to paper the hallway
going up the stairs and the entire hall on the second floor. I'll stay
at this damn farm the rest of my life and never go home and never
see Cove again. Don and Cove would kick me out anyway so I'm
just saving them the trouble. If I could have Cove's baby, then I
could just forget the whole thing. I think that all the time. Is that
too much to ask? That is my fantasy and it's written into my notebook and Cove has my notebook, so he knows. If I could just have
his baby I'd never have to see him again. Shit on him. See what he
makes me think?

I'll work hard. That'll show them. I won't fail working. Not any
more. I can work.

And if I can't love the right people, then that's their fault, not mine. I just wish George didn't make me sick.

I made a bargain with John. If he put me completely in charge of the wallpaper crew, then it would get done right. First we scrubbed the woodwork and ceiling and then we painted it. White. I knew what I was doing. I liked it. After that I told the book table people I wouldn't need anyone else. I didn't want any clowns lousing me up. And now the paper has come and I can start the fun part. The old paper peels off really neat, like a sunburn. Lucky. Then I size the walls. I sit down by the vegetable table and wait for the sizing to dry. Being my own boss makes me light-hearted. I know I can do a good job. They look at me as if I am somebody. And in this job I respect myself, so people treat me with respect.

I'll work on wallpapering the rest of the week or until it's done. I set up a big table in Alfred's room where I measure, cut and paste. I get a string and tie a pencil to one end for a plumb line. I'll have to keep the lines straight because it's striped paper and old walls. Yellow and orange stripes.

When I work real hard like this, all those problems go away, peel away, like the old wallpaper. A ladder, scissors, paste, brush, pencil, string, rags, paper, and a feeling of confidence. That's all I need to hang wallpaper. And I have peace and time. Time to think about Cove and his baby.

Thursday, January 8, 1970

It's with fear now that I talk to Cove. I feel I've done something so bad he really will kick me out. And I *have* to see him. I have to. Things are building up in me and I have to squash the feelings down so I won't lose him. I need more pills to keep them down. My pills have been regular every day. Morning, noon, night and bedtime. Thorazine and Librium each time, plus a sleeping pill at night. But for a while I haven't taken them at all. I go into the pill room and get my envelope with my pills in it and I go to my room. I decide if I really need them or not. If not, then I take the extras and put them in a little metal jar. A fancy little thing with black and white circles on it. I hide the jar in my desk. Cove would absolutely flip if he knew I was doing this. If there's one thing he's particular about, it's pills. He spends a lot of time explaining about each pill. I think the reason I'm doing it is because I have the feeling that he's going to get rid of me and I won't have any. So I save them this way. Before this appointment I take a couple extra. One of each. I'm much more afraid. It's hard to believe that I gave up the amphetamines. Sometimes I really crave the high. But never again. I psyched myself up to it and gave them up forever. Maybe someday these pills too.

Gregory drives Queenie and me into town for the bus. Queenie is so glad to be getting out of work. It's an adventure. I thought about it for a while and made a decision. I could save Don one whole round trip on Thursday if I take the bus home and have him meet me at the bus station and then drive me to Cove's. Then when Cove's done with me, all Don would have is the late night trip back to the farm. It would help Don. And also test me. John and Timothy are pleased that I'm taking this step. So is Eden. The world—ta-daa. Queenie is my friend and my companion against panic. We have no trouble on the bus.

My clothes are looking pretty bad lately. I feel half put together. I wear my red coat that I hate. It has a button missing and has shoulder pads. It fits my mood. When I walk up the stairs to Cove, it takes a real effort to make my boots go one ahead of the other. I watch them as if they are independent from me. Clomp clomp. Up they go.

I sit. He sits.

"Well, Carol, how are things going?"

"Oh, not very well. I'm not doing good at all. I'm doing awful." I'm certainly not going to talk about wallpapering.

"Did something happen?"

"Yes, it did, as a matter of fact. I got into trouble with George. And I guess I feel like hell about it."

"What kind of trouble?"

"You know."

"No. I don't know."

Cove's going to make me spell out the whole thing. Damn him.

"Um—um—um." Hard to say the words. No nice way for me to get out of this. We sit quiet for a while.

"Well, well, sex, you know." I glance at him. He looks concerned.

"Well, I got scared for some reason and kind of desperate and mad, and my stomach. Well, I don't know why it happened, but it was bad."

"You've punished yourself in this way before." Cove so serious. We sit a long time.

Now it's harder for me to think. In fact, I go blank and stare at a little scratch on the front of his desk.

"Are you afraid of getting well?"

"That's stupid. I hate it when you say that."

"Last time you told me about your skiing and sledding, and about feeling happy. When good things have happened to you before, you have felt the need to hurt yourself. Is that why you're having a bad time of it now? You're punishing yourself for feeling good?"

"I don't know. I don't know."

"Are you afraid if you get better, I won't see you any more?"

I look in surprise.

"Maybe. Something like that."

"I want you to know I'll be here as long as you need me. To not see me would be your decision."

Fear comes again to my insides. He *is* dumping me. He is. He's the one that just brought it up. He did. I didn't. He wants to get rid of me, oh, he's had enough of me, oh, awful Cove hates me, I knew he would because I told him.

"I'm not better. I'm worse. I told you what I did. I'm worse. You hear me?"

I'm louder now. Cove waits until I calm down.

"You're pretty upset."

"It's because I'm worse and you don't believe me. Damn it. I don't tell you everything. I mean, I've wanted to go off and sleep in the snow. I wanted to kill myself. All those good things mean nothing! That isn't reality. The real thing is I'm bad. No good."

"You never have been able to take anything, *anything* good

about yourself. And you turn all the good things into something not real. I think the good things *are* real. And they *are* good."

"Well, when I feel this way, nothing seems good at all. Nothing."

"I know. I understand."

We sit quiet and then Cove turns to me, puts his hands on his chin. Looks at me close. Scares me. Cove's eyes looking at me close. Never like him that close. I push my chair back a little. The desk is between us but it doesn't seem big enough or heavy enough. Puny slip of a desk.

"You throw it all away, all your progress. Bam! As if it never happened. As if you were the same little girl. Well, you're not. Things have changed. The good things come and you turn against yourself—want to wipe them all out. I know the good things don't seem real. But they are. Maybe you slipped back a little. But nothing can take away your progress."

Silence.

"You are loved and respected. It's time to make use of your many talents. You're not a little girl anymore."

"Well, I can't help it. All the good things slip away and I can't fight things when I feel this way."

"You can fight it. Now is the time to fight it. You have to make these decisions yourself. It's something you must decide."

That's it. He's leaving me. My insides converge and band against him. He doesn't care about me. He thinks I don't have courage. I feel rage. It comes so suddenly, how can I leave the office with this rage? I look at his diplomas on the wall to the left of me. I want to smash the glass and flail around with the broken glass at myself, cutting, gouging. I hold my body tight.

"You're going to make me fight this all by myself. I mean nothing to you. You don't care for me, I can see that. You have no reaction to anything. You sit there and don't care about me at all. You're leaving me alone, you said I have to do it all myself, and that means you finally are getting rid of me." I stand up and grab my pocketbook.

"I do care."

"You do not! You feel nothing! Nothing!"

"I don't think you want to leave this way."

"Go to hell!"

He has the audacity to say it is up to me. He says I have to do it myself. Oh, don't worry, I won't hit you, Cove. Won't smash you! I'll smash myself. I'll smash your office with the jagged glass. I'll break your doors with my foot. I'll kick your house, I'll kick it down. I'll tear down your birch trees and smash your bird bath. I run outside with my rage and I go to the back and I try to break up that tree with my foot. One last heave of energy to let him know I don't care.

But the trees are too big.

And the snow is too deep.

And the woods are too tall.

And the bird bath is too hard.

And the world is too dark.

And I am too tired, too tired.

And Cove is too much for me.

Saturday, January 10, 1970

I'm not sleeping well at all. I think all the time about shameful things. I think about how I can fight the bad parts in me. Cove has made my mind speed up. It races ahead of my understanding. And now I think of Cove every minute. Cove and Dad somehow all mixed up. I want to go away someplace to get away from him. Never to think of him again. But I love him, so I can't. If I could just make love to him I'd be done with it. He could never forget me then. I get out of bed. It's only three-thirty A.M. but it's useless to try to sleep. I get my towels, shampoo, and soap and walk into the hall to take my shower. . . . There's blood on the floor. Damn that Queenie. She should be more careful. She must be having her period. I take my shower. Cove would like me now because at least I'm clean. I come out of the shower and there's more blood. Did Queenie go downstairs? Seems like too much blood. I look a little to the left toward the stairs. I flip on the light. More blood. I'm uneasy. I follow it. It's fresh, I mean, bright red and too much of it. I hurry along down the stairs—it's not hard to track—and across the dining room side toward the kitchen. The kitchen door is open and the light is on. It's usually closed at night. It's open and covered with blood. I get scared. I call out, "Anyone there?" Silence. I go in the kitchen door, past the milk machines and sinks and into the kitchen proper. Jesus! My breath goes inward. On the table is Miguel's butcher knife and it is covered with blood. I stand there for a second, stunned. Oh, oh. All the blood.

I realize then that I've been following the blood in the wrong direction. The blood started here, at the butcher knife, and then went *up* the stairs.

I start running now through the dining room and back up the stairs. The blood goes past my room and down the hall. I hesitate. Two rooms, Queenie's and the guest room. A new guest arrived yesterday and is in the guest room overnight. Don't know his name. I go to his door. That's where the blood is, not Queenie's at all. I knock on the door. No answer. I go in—and freeze. Then I see the horror, the massacre—not the pools of blood, not his naked body, the horror is his face. His frozen eyes, his white-green cheeks, his despair.

He's alive, lying there. I go toward his face and tell him he mustn't die, that he is safe. I won't let him die. His eyes are staring away. I put his face in my hands and beg him to help me. He has to look at me. I tell him I have to get him to the hospital fast. He moves his head and his lips move—his despairing eyes tell me he'll help. I pick up his right arm hanging off the bed. It isn't bleeding so much now, the slash marks across the wrist and up further, the cuts down to his bones neatly separating flesh all coagulated but still oozing and wet. I take my bath towel from around my neck and wrap it around his arm and stand over him pressing my fingers into the open flesh. I need help fast, I ask if he would help me please, please take your other arm and hold the towel in place while I get help. But he doesn't move and I lean across his body to the other side of the bed and pick up his other arm. Oh, your other arm, you've done that to your other arm, blood still flowing fast and bright. Poor arm. I tell him I'll be right back and put one arm on top of the towel and pull a blanket over his body and race down the hall to Hugh's door. Bang on the door, pound on the fear room door.

"Quick, keys to the jeep, quick, got to get the new guy to the hospital, can't let him die." I race back into my room and grab a box of Modess and back to him. Hugh stands there, he slips a little on the floor and goes back to his room to get dressed while I wrap and tie his arms in Modess up and down the slashes. When that's done I pick his pants off his chair and slide them on him like a large baby by grabbing his foot and pulling them through the leg that way, with two hands. He can't help, he's in shock. Hugh comes back for the second watch and I go to my room and pull on my clothes. I sure wish John or Timothy lived in the main house. There's no time to get them. Hugh gets Gregory and the three of us get him up and half drag him down the stairs out the front to the jeep. I sit in back with him, hold his body like a baby, blanket wrapped around him for warmth.

He talks now. His father. He did it to escape his father who doesn't love him. His father hurts him, terrified of his father, kill himself to get away from his father. . . .

Into the emergency room—we wait. And wait while the doctor puts him back together again. All whole. A new person. We wait. We go to see him, sit by his bed and say he'll be all right and shut out his words about his father.

He's clean and new, wrapped and helpless, fresh blood running into the sliced veins and we stay with him all day, phone calls, whispered conversations and connections and authorities.

I hold it into myself and I ignore his eyes, so pleading—as if we are sending him to his death. The next day his eyes look at us out of the window of the ambulance—taking him back home —back to his father.

Tuesday, January 13, 1970

I go out on the side porch and get an armful of wood and bring it in the library for the fireplace. I set up the fire and light it. We're getting ready for group therapy. The fire doesn't catch. People move in talking. Cove is all smiles. He walks over and does a few tricks with the logs and poker, and the fire catches. I want to talk to group tonight about the guy's suicide attempt. I was all right Sunday, but Monday and today I've been very jumpy. Cove sits by the fire and I sit on the floor on the other side of it. Maurice is visiting group. He has come up the hill from where he's staying.

ME: "I'd like to talk about that guy who tried to kill himself. It's made me pretty jumpy."

VOSS: "What's there to talk about?"

ME: "Well, I'm scared over it, I mean his face was so . . ."

MAURICE: "I don't think we should talk about it. What's done is done. Leave it alone."

BENSON: "I agree. That kind of person doesn't belong here. I think we should be glad he left."

ME: "But his face. It was so awful."

MAURICE: "You're trying to be sensational, Carol, trying to hog the spotlight."

I'm hurt. I put my head down.

VOSS: "I think you are stupid to bring it up."

COVE: "I'm sorry, I don't understand. What happened?"

ME: "This guy cut himself Saturday night pretty badly and . . ."

HUGH: "Let me tell it! A visitor cut his arms and went to the hospital and an ambulance took him back home. That's it. Nothing more."

ME: "But it bothers me. I mean, it scares me."

EDEN: "We probably should leave all this, Carol. No one wants to talk about it."

I feel a conspiracy of silence. I have felt it ever since it happened. I even feel a little like people have been avoiding me but can't be sure. Nobody wants to talk. Maybe I *am* being grisly about the whole thing. But I am troubled.

RACHEL: "I have been having trouble with a certain man at the farm. I can't understand if he's taking advantage of me or not. You see he . . ."

COVE: "Excuse me, Rachel, I'd like to have Carol's feelings about the suicide attempt cleared up a little more."

We sit quietly. I feel that Cove is on my side and I come out of my isolation.

ME: "Nobody will talk to me about him and it shook me up. I managed well enough when I found him and all that, but later, Sunday until now, it makes me so nervous thinking of his face and what he did."

COVE: "You found him?"

ME: "Yes." I look around. People won't look at me.

ME: "Nobody wants to talk to me about it."

COVE: "Tell us what you feel."

ME: "Well, his face had such despair it went inside me. It hurts me to see someone that feels so bad. Almost like, well, I want to do something for him and I don't know what."

ERIC: "I think he was stupid to do that. A bid for attention."

HUGH: "I don't think he should have been here in the first place. We should have better screening procedures."

ERIC: "It took a lot of people's time away from us that could use it."

MAURICE: "I think it's cruel for you to bring it up. You just want praise. Want to have people think you're great."

Cove leans forward, intent.

ME: "That's not true, Maurice. Not true. How that guy felt is what gets to me. I don't care about the other, I was the one that just happened to be there. It's the despair. I don't understand why you're all so reluctant to talk about him. Why?"

VOSS: "It doesn't concern us anymore."

Silence. They refuse to talk.

ME: "Well, I happen to think, maybe you're all scared just like I am. I think you saw yourselves in him just as I did. I think you're scared, too."

I sit back. I told them what I think and if they won't talk, then I can't make them. I feel frustrated but there's not much I can do. I wonder why the staff didn't tell Cove. He didn't even know about it. Maybe they don't talk about it either. Maybe they're scared too.

We then discuss Rachel and her problem with men. When group is over I go out the door past the crowd around Cove. I go in the kitchen and get some coffee. I go to my room and lie on the bed. Oh lonely world. It sure is hard to understand things.

Knock at the door.

"Come in." Cove stands there.

"I just wanted to tell you that you are on the right track. I was with you tonight."

"Really?"

"Yeah. You are thinking of other people and are concerned about the man that attempted suicide. The others are more into themselves. They can't give to anyone outside themselves. And I think you are right about their being scared."

"Well, it sure scared me!"

"You did a good job, Carol."

Oh that one hundred percent down-filled comforter, praise by Cove, warms my interior pockets and crevices, melting the ice chunks out of the Arctic seas.

Thursday, January 15, 1970

I take the bus home. I walk from the bus station to our house. I don't have Queenie with me because it would mean Don and I couldn't be close for the trip back. Oh, little children, please don't hate me for being crazy, I love you very much and Daddy too. Best, most wonderful children for me and best Daddy in the world, I can tell you now that maybe, just maybe, sometime soon, maybe I'll be coming home for good. My sickness has nothing to do with you and it's going. See, I can take the bus and cook our supper and my hands don't shake so and my heart doesn't beat so fast. And I can hold you in my arms and kiss your necks and love your cowlicks. And more and more, see my smile, hear my laugh, and more and more, Daddy and I go to the bedroom and I kiss his neck and love his cowlick and smile and laugh and so sometime soon maybe soon my craziness will go and I will work hard for your sakes. For you I work hard and that's why I have to leave now and go see Dr. Ashley, because I want to come home to you.

COVE: "It bothered you very much when we talked about your progress. It bothered you when we talked about making your own decisions."

ME: "It was because I thought you were getting rid of me. That I'd have to do everything alone, it's as if I have to prove to you I'm not better so you'll still see me. I have all this rage and hatred in me and I hate people and want to make sure you *know* this."

"It's very hard for you to talk about goodness in yourself, isn't it?"

"Well . . ."

"Why is it so hard to talk about kind feelings and warmth, the love inside you?"

"Because that doesn't seem real. Only the hate seems real."

"You love Don and the kids?"

"Yes, you know that. They're the best thing I have. All the other love is twisted, confused."

"What other love?"

I don't want to talk to Cove about any other love.

"You discuss George because you don't love George. Anyone else?"

Fear in me. Can't talk. We sit. I try to concentrate on the books in the bookcase. *Homosexuality in the Male, Summerhill.* I read the titles over and over. I wish I was done with all of this. If I could have his baby I'd just go away. I wouldn't need him anymore. He makes the problem. He is the problem. *Intimate Enemy.* That's an interesting title. I'll have to get that.

"You know, Carol, I think it's about time we tackled this problem once and for all. We must sit here face to face and discuss the subject. You want to and you are ready to." Cove stern.

"What? What problem?"

"You are playing a game with me. You put me in a position where you force me to bring out the issues. No games. I want *you* to talk about it. Now!"

Oh Jesus. What can I say?

Cove says, "We both know what the problem is. No more games." He's silent and I panic. I choke. He isn't paying attention to that. He continues, "You are able to write it in your notebook and give your book to me. Now I want you to *talk* to me about it. It's time it came out in the open."

I feel like crying. Silence.

"Do you remember what you wrote?"

"No. No. Can't remember."

And he swings his chair around and gets my file and gets my notebook.

"Let me read something you wrote."

"No, please no."

" 'And I hid behind the window and watched Cove walk up to John's house for the meeting. I love Cove so much I want him to love me so much. To hold me. If I had his baby then it could all be forgotten.' "

"Stop!" I want to leave. Too close. I stand up.

"Sit down! I want you to talk about this. About your loving me."

I sit. I'm afraid. I try to collect myself.

"I can't, can't. It's too hard for me." I'm hunched over head down so I don't have to see him.

"What are you afraid of?"

I think, think, think.

"Don't know. Nothing. Don't know. It's silly, silly. I don't know why I'm scared."

Blank mind.

"Do you think I will do something to you?" At this I look up. I glance at him.

"No. No. You wouldn't do anything. I know. No. Never. No."

"What if you didn't trust me?"

"What?"

THE LONG JOURNEY HOME

"What if you didn't trust me? What would you be afraid of then?"

"But I do trust you."

"If you didn't trust me, what would you be afraid of?"

Silence.

"What do you fantasize?"

"I wrote it in the notes."

"Talk to me about them."

"Oh. Ohh. I just am so sick of this whole thing. I just think, just think. Oh Jesus. If I could have. . . . Um, it's in the notes."

"I know it's in the notes. I want you to say it to me."

"Well to—to have your baby, you see, then, then I could—could be done with it all. Done with it."

"If you had my baby the whole thing would be solved?"

"Then I could be done with it. Done with it."

"Is that why you are afraid of me?"

"I don't know why. I don't know. The other, that other, is just thoughts, you know, not real. I don't really, really think that, not really. In fact it's not reality, it's just dreams, you know." I feel a little better because it's silly.

"Why do you love me?"

"Um, well, um—you see, the other is ridiculous really. I was only kidding. Heh, heh—joking I mean. I love you because you are a very nice person. You are very kind." I explain very precisely to him as if he were a child. "You are nice. I love you because you are nice." I feel self-satisfied and sit back.

"What about wanting my baby?"

"That isn't real, I told you. That isn't real. That's just a stupid thing I think once in a while, doesn't mean anything. I told you."

"Why do you watch me at the farm?"

"Oh well, I just like to."

"You love me when you watch me?"

"Yes. But I told you it's because you're nice."

"Now. In the office? What do you feel?"

"No—no. Well, no. I don't feel anything. Nothing! You aren't nice, you scare me."

"What are you afraid I'll do?"

"No—don't." I move back in my chair, head spinning. What's he getting at? Want to get away. I stand up. Cove stands. I shrink back, cover my head in my arms.

"*Don't touch me!*" And I give a strangled scream, surprised to peek through and find Cove still in his chair, never moved, watching me.

I sit frozen, cold slab, death cold.

Cove doesn't say anything for a long time. We sit. It's embarrassing. Shameful, awful. So awful, Cove. So shameful.

"It isn't me that you're afraid of, Carol." Cove's voice so nice. Like he's going to be nice.

"I, I'm confused."

"I know you are. But you haven't run away. I want you to substitute 'Father' for 'Cove.' "

"Oh no, Cove, don't do that. Oh please. Oh no. Don't drag Dad in here. Oh please. It has nothing to do with Dad. Nothing. You are you and Dad was Dad. Oh please don't drag him in."

I'm turning cold now. The bastard always making things evil. What does he take me for anyway? I stand up cold. I open the door cold. I take my cup carefully and put it in the cupboard, controlled. He's turning me out into the outside and has to throw in evil things. Now my mind won't be able to stop dwelling on all that evil Dad business. Cove doesn't understand. Cold.

"I—love—you—because—you—are—nice." I say this to him louder, as I leave, louder as if he were deaf or a foreigner. "Because —you—are—nice—but—now—I—don't—love—you—because—you—are —not—nice." I make it clear to him and I hold my head up and put on my boots very haughtily—which is not easy—and I go out the door, quietly shutting it. He is not very bright, that Cove.

Saturday, January 17, 1970

Tears well out of her eyes, she gasps and sobs. Why oh why? Her mind feels so sorry for the little girl she used to be. The images from the past, the lonely little girl in her antiseptic bedroom with the clean sheets and clean floor, so alone, and clean rug hanging out the window to air. The poor lonely little girl with the big gaping hole in her, so crippled without warmth, no arms to love the little girl and no arms to tell her she is nice, so the hole grows and she thinks she is bad. It's nobody's fault, nobody's fault, nobody is to blame but the hole is there permanently; forever. But then she found Cove and she talked to Cove and she thought the hole was closing up, his warmth filled it up, he was filling it up with steaming hot mud packs, handful by handful, and then she saw beauty and she could feel the love given her by everybody and now it feels like he has taken his foot and raised it and kicked out the filler, just smashed it out, and now the hole is there again only wider. And so she sobs and feels so sad because she can never love him again because he doesn't love her. He wants her to go away, this illegitimate love is no good, he has won, he has kicked her. The cosmic battle waged with him for his love. She has lost. The sadness wells in her and she thinks of her own children. She'll never let a hole grow in them, never let a hole hurt their insides, and she has an urgent wish to go home and make sure they know they are special, they are loved, and she will be free with her arms, the warmth not held back. She grapples with the rejection by her Cove and wonders why he is the one so important but she doesn't grasp it all, doesn't get the data down right. She'll have to test him. If he fails, then there wasn't any love at all. If he fails she'll have to run away. She loved her father in this way, she thinks of her father and how she wanted him to fill the emptiness. A baby in the hole, a baby? She doesn't know, but she knows he failed her, she counted on him and he wanted her to stay little in his arms and when she didn't stay little he couldn't accept her and left her with a hole and then she ran away.

She gets down from the bed and goes to John's house. They've asked her to babysit. A warm, nice house, two lovely children. As she reads a bedtime story, the little girl snuggles to her. Carol holds her gently, rubbing her little back, more determined than ever to go home soon to her own children. She'll stop the cycle. A beginning of a new clan, a dynasty, of children that are held warm and of children who are told they are good.

Tuesday, January 20, 1970

Queenie and Madonna come up to me this morning while I'm wallpapering. I'm almost done. I'm so wrapped up in myself lately I haven't spent much time with them. Queenie has quit school. She seems happier. She says she didn't fit. Madonna has been pretty quiet but I see her leg moving up and down. I wonder about her problems. I sure wish she'd talk to Cove. I'm going to test Cove today. See if he loves me or not. See if he's going to leave me.

Through the window I see Cove walking from his car. I remember he doesn't love me and I remember how I can't figure things out. I see him and want to wave and run to him and he doesn't want me so I can't. I return to my room. I shut the door and stay there. If he comes to see me, then he cares for me. If he doesn't, he hates me. I don't like doing this, feels dumb. But it's something I have to do.

I wait all day and I wait through supper. I'm getting scared. Knock. He knocks.

He comes in and leans on the door frame.

"Hello, hi. Is there a reason why you're avoiding me?"

I jump off the bed and stand looking at him. He cares, he cares. He came to me. It makes me so happy. I love him, and then I remember he's made the love weird.

"Well, the last session—you make me feel permanently—make me feel like, well, my feelings for you aren't real. You make me feel like a sicky. And it makes me mad and hurt." Cove listens to me. He puts his head down a little and thinks. I go on, "You somehow make it *psychological*, and it doesn't feel that way to me."

He looks up. "I think I may be wrong. I think maybe you're right. You understood me to imply that the love for me was not real, not genuine—only a carryover of the love for your father."

"Yeah. I know that's what you think. But it isn't fair because it isn't true."

"How about this? We both bend a little. I know that your feelings are not *all* displaced from your father and you admit that some might be. How about that?"

"Well, okay. Maybe I'll go along with that."

Cove passed the test and I feel easier inside. It is very important that he believe I love him because of him and not because of my father. It makes the love real and not so mixed up. I want to put my arms around him. I want him next to me. But I can't. He would reject me. Maybe if he were asleep. . . .

Oh fantasy land. I must be careful of you. You lure me with your promises of relief from the world. You lure me like the sirens of the Greeks. You promise a land away from reality where we hear voices not there and see visions not true? I must be very careful because you can rob me of control, I see it in Jud and Alfred. You will make Cove not real but sublime. And so I push you away though so tempting. I force my eyes on the real Cove. The Cove biting his thumb in concentration, the Cove that has bifocals and the Cove that wears the wedding ring.

Thursday, January 22, 1970

I decide to branch out in my activities. I sense uneasiness when I work. I have no trouble working but I'm restless. Even the expenditure of energy on woods crew doesn't satisfy my restlessness. I don't like thinking about how I love Cove. I try to fight it. It makes me angry. But it's something more than that and I can't put my finger on it. I make curtains for my room. Blue. I sit in the dining room and hem them. Then put them up. Such a pretty room now. That makes me uneasy too. Too much permanence in curtains. Much too homey. I go to the art building and sign up for ceramics. We can choose this as part of the work program. I start designs and drawings for a key chain for Don. I think about him. If I didn't have him I wouldn't bother going through all this. I think of George and I don't even think of a betrayal to my Don. There is no betrayal. Don is the one I'm working for. But what has all this got me? I'm itchy.

In the afternoon I ice skate. With my skate blade I hack a design on the side of the rink where all the bumps are. The ice chips fly. Suddenly I miss my friend Katy. And I miss Evelyn. I miss church. I miss our dumb dog. I miss home. I give the ice one last kick with my blade and take off my skates. I think I'll take the bus home early today and surprise the kids. I'll make supper and see how it goes. I hunt around for John and he drives me to the bus. I have no trouble with the bus. I wonder why I had all that trouble with the bus.

Don picks me up and takes me home. Fear descends on me. I have forgotten what to do. What do I do at home? When I left I wasn't doing anything. I look carefully at the kids to see if they are harmed by me. I can't tell. They want me home. I put out the bird food. I cut up the cheese for macaroni and cheese. I talk with Dave and Jim and put in a load of laundry. But the work is mostly done. Don is very organized. They know I'm not staying so they go on with their lives. I lie on the floor and talk to Ki who's brushing the dog. I can't do it. I'm not good enough. I can't. I forgot. They don't need me. I don't belong here anymore. I don't call Katy. I don't call Evelyn. I can't do these things expected of me. Call the plumber about the water softener, get a lube job on the car, wash the windows, listen to the lessons, iron, cook, shop, worry about the money, see the people, talk to the outside people. Shovel the walk, go to the library, can the vegetables, laugh. I can't. Mostly it's the people. I go to our room, I get under the covers, I can't see them. I hide. I can't take care of these kids with my sickness. Cove won't see me anymore if I come home. It'll be like before. I have no place. Cove hates me. I cover my head. Don comes in and finds me under the covers.

"You all right?"

"It's too much for me."

"I know. Better get ready to see Cove now."

"I'm sorry."

"I know."

"I'm sorry."

It would be better if somebody broke my knees. Then I'd have a reason. I don't have a reason and so they all look at me sideways.

At least it's familiar at Cove's.

"It's too overwhelming for me at home. I can't do it there. I'll never be able to go home. Never."

"Have you been thinking about going home? Is that why you left the farm early?"

"Well, maybe. But, it'll never work. I left because I'm uneasy at the work program. I have to fight the fantasies."

"Why are you uneasy?"

"I don't know. It doesn't matter."

"What do you mean, 'fight the fantasies'?"

"All the time I dream about you and it's all mixed with my father and it's your fault. And it makes me uneasy. I can't understand you. You! You always bring my father in and now that's all I think about."

"What do you think?"

"Just for once why don't you tell me what *you* think. What the hell do you think anyway? You're always harping on the similarities between the two of you. Why don't you give me one?" I glare at him. It's easier for me to be mad than scared.

Cove sits quiet a minute.

"Unattainable. You can't have either one of us."

I stare at him. I see him for the first time. How awful he looks. Awful. It hurts me, what he says. It means he hates me. It means I can't ever love him.

"You're cruel! You feel nothing!"

"I feel a lot. And I think you must deal with this."

"No! It has nothing to do with my father. There are no similarities!" I scream at Cove.

He sits forward, then sits back again and tilts his chair back. "Okay. There are none."

I'm surprised. "I was born a shithead and I'll always be one!"

"Okay. You are a shithead."

"I said, I am a shithead!" louder.

"I know."

I'm uneasy but I keep on. "You feel nothing for me."

"If you feel that I don't, all right."

I have to get louder now, I don't think he understands.

"You and Don get together and you both hate me."

"If you think that, it's probably so."

I don't know why Cove is doing this to me.

"I want my file. I'll throw it away!"

He swings to the cabinet, gets the file and puts it in front of me. I stare at it but leave it alone.

"If you keep after me like this, I'll do something rash, if you know what I mean."

"It's up to you. If you want to do something rash, it's your decision."

"You have no right to talk to me about my father. And you hurt me."

"I have no right."

"What are you doing to me? I think you're awful, awful. Why are you doing this?"

"Doing what?"

"Why are you agreeing with me? I think that's hateful of you."

"Probably is."

"I think it's just awful that you won't fight with me. Awful cruel!"

"I know."

Well, I just give up. There's nothing I can do with Cove when he's like this. I smother down the word, the awful word, as I clomp out, it's as if the sound will make it go away. I clomp my hardest down the stairs and slam the outside door twice. I wait for Don to take me away from this horrible man with his horrible vile word that gags me. He strapped me down and force fed the word and it gags me and makes me sick. Unattainable.

Tuesday, January 27, 1970

Well, I'm just not going to accept it, that's all there is to it. It takes away my purpose, my hope. So to hell with his word. Unattainable. I'll show him I don't need him. I don't need him. I won't think of him. But—all I do is think of him. Something has to be done. If Cove doesn't come to me today, give me some indication that he cares, I'll have to run away. I walk down from volleyball. I run a little and catch up with John.

"I'm all mixed up, John, I can't figure things out. And I'm feeling desperate, desperate. I feel like running away. I can't handle things."

John pulls me to the side. We walk down the path by his house slowly.

"What's all this about?"

"Well, my therapy with Dr. Ashley isn't going too good. I'm a failure and now I'm desperate. Please tell me what to do."

"Why don't you talk to Dr. Ashley today?"

"I can't."

"Why not? He's here."

"I hate him. He hates me. I can't crawl back to him. He's kicking me out anyway."

"I don't think it'd be a good idea for me to interfere in this."

"But I need somebody to tell me what to do."

"I can't. You've got to decide for yourself."

"Oh—I hate everybody being so therapeutic. Everybody has to do the 'right' thing." I stamp my foot and John laughs.

"Hey, I know something you can do today, Carol. How would you like to be Florence for the day. You'd sure save me a lot of trouble!"

"Florence?"

"Yeah. Nightingale. You know that lots of people have the high fevers. Stop in the med room and have Hugh give you supplies and tend the sick."

"Oh all right, John, you're no help."

"Find me if you need me."

I leave him and walk toward the main house. I see Cove's bus parked on the drive. I go over and try the door. It's locked, and this infuriates me. He doesn't even trust me. Locks his doors against me. I raise my foot and kick his tires with my hiking boot. Oh Cove, I want to hurt you like you hurt me. But I am nothing to you. Nothing. A patient among all the rest. You go through this with them all. I want to be special. You'll be sorry when I'm gone. But you won't be sorry when I'm gone. I'm not special. I'll make you sorry. I'll run away.

I go in the med room and gather aspirin, thermometer, rubbing alcohol, something like Kaopectate and the pills in the envelope for people who haven't picked them up. I plod through the snow up to the cottage on the hill. The path isn't plowed very well. It's so cold. Today I'm Florence. Two people sick here. Benson and Obie. I sit with Benson. I push his hair from his eyes. 104°. The room is a mess. I straighten it out a little. I sweep and put all the clothes in a spot in the corner. He's a boy really, and scared. I get that uneasiness again. I should be home. How come I can do all these things here and I panic at home? It's not fair. Must be Cove's fault. I see Obie next. He's raving, funny, out of his head, but his fever is only 101°. I sit with him until he falls asleep. His room is dirty too. I wonder why everyone has dirty sheets and dirty rooms. My room is clean. As I go around from cottage to cottage, I notice. I see their fear. I think maybe I'm a lucky one. Maybe the luckiest one at the farm. I find out that Obie was having LSD flashbacks. The fever brought them out.

Dirty sheets, clean sheets. Dirty room, clean room. That's how I rate them in my mind. On a scale from one to ten. I get a nine. George gets a zero. Oh, George. I'm sorry I used you. I won't anymore.

I don't see Cove at all. Not the whole day. I skip group therapy and hide in the rec house. If he really cared for me he'd find me. Then I get scared he won't find me so I run back to my room. He knows where my room is. Well, it's ten o'clock and now eleven o'clock. He never comes. Cove, if you only had come, I would be all right. Oh Cove, don't you see? Now I have to run away. I saw your coat today hanging in the common room. I saw it and I wanted to take it. Even if I just had your coat, then I wouldn't have to go. Oh, if I just had your coat. Oh Cove, was it too much to ask?

Thursday, January 29, 1970

It has to be a Thursday that I run away because if it isn't a Thursday, then Cove and Don won't miss me. And it won't do any good if they don't miss me. I have to get them to notice me. I have to make an impact on Cove. I don't feel I matter to them. All this confusion. I'm supposed to take the bus from town to home, where Don will meet me and take me to Cove's. They'll have to notice. Don will notice. Cove won't. He'll look at his appointment book and it'll be after nine and he'll say, "Well, that patient couldn't make it," and that'll be all. I'm not going to be on the bus. I'm running and so if he notices or not won't matter because I'll be gone.

Do I dare? I don't know. I pack my laundry in my red duffel bag as if I'm going home. But I won't get on the bus. I go to my desk and put the black and white jar of pills in the duffel bag. I have a lot of them saved. They give me a sense of freedom. Almost joy. I have enough now for anything.

Maybe I'll be saved at the last minute. John knows I'm upset. Maybe he'll be the one to drive me to the bus. Then I'll have to go home.

I pack my aspirin, cigarettes, gum, money and notebook along with the pills in my bag. Ned, the regular driver, drives me to the bus station in the jeep. Not John. I go in and sit at a booth with a cup of coffee and I watch the clock and I wait. The time is important. I don't know why. The whole world is going around doing things and their lives are ordered and their jobs and families are neat packages. The thing to do is to get on the bus and go home. The bus comes in and I watch it. It's so cold. Ice has frozen on the side of the bus; above the slushy snow I can see my reflection. I have on the horrible red coat and Glory's hat, dungarees, hiking boots and a purple scarf. I have on the farm gloves with my name. How appalling, how gross I look. A castoff, a refugee with her dirty laundry, looking for some benign country.

I can't get on the bus. I don't want to. I have a feeling of power and I am excited. To them, I don't exist. To them, I am only a distorted reflection in the muddy ice. I want to cry out to them, I am real, I am *real!* I move away and watch the bus as it pulls out. I feel strange. Nobody knows where I am at this minute. Nobody. I feel like a wanted person running from the law. I'm not where I'm supposed to be anymore. I feel weak and lost. Like a spelunker exploring a cave without a rope around his waist. I mustn't be seen. Have to get off the street. Across the street, down a bit, I see a hotel. I better check in. Before going in the door I take off my hat and scarf and straighten my hair. I wish I'd taken more care. I was confused at the farm. I take off the dumb gloves and I put them and the hat in the duffel bag. I wish I had a suitcase. I look at myself the way others will and I look weird. I stick out. Oh shit, get hold of myself. *Act cool.* Walk to the desk and ask for a room for the night. My tongue sticks and stutters—"N-n-n-ight." He looks at me strangely. He turns the book around for me to sign. I fumble and drop the pen. Where do I live? I don't know. I write Foxcroft Farm and he watches. I want to cross it out. How stupid of me. I get to the room fast. Close the door. I lean on it. Relief. No one can see me now. I fumble in the bag and get my jar of pills open and take two Thorazines and a Librium, hesitate, then another Thorazine. My heart's racing, got to slow down. Take off my coat and lie on the bed. Feel slightly dizzy. Cove and Don. I lie there for a while. Now what do I do? I go to the window and open the blind. It's getting dark. I see a restaurant across the way, past the parking lots. Maybe go have some food as if I were somebody.

I straighten myself up as best I can. I can't get over that I look like a castoff. I go down to the lobby. Cool. Smile. Whisk by. I make my way to the restaurant. I sit at the bar, order a martini. And another. A warm feeling comes over me with the drinks. I'd better have something to eat, so I order a hot turkey sandwich. But I can't eat. The drinks with the pills make me queasy. I want to get out of there. Things aren't working out right. I think people are watching me. I go back to my hotel room and lock the door. Safe. I'll call somebody to come talk to me. I'll call Jane from group. I dial and wait. It rings. My jar of pills is on the bureau and the reflection in the three mirrors makes a lot of jars—perhaps it's the drinks. The phone rings. No one answers. Why isn't she home? I look up Maurice's number. Won't hurt to talk to him. Have to talk to someone. They hate me now out there. I'm not where I'm supposed to be. Maurice answers. I tell him I'm upset and where I am. He says he'll be right over. Phew! I'm not alone anymore. Good old Maurice. My friend after all.

Maurice comes in and sits down. I tell him I've run away because I'm upset and I want to explain it all to him but he won't let me go on. He goes over to the bureau and picks up my jar of pills. I jump up and take them from him. They're mine. He asks about them and suddenly I can't talk anymore. Not about the pills. I want to talk about Cove, about people hating me. But he won't listen. Maurice says we should go to the bar downstairs and discuss it over drinks. I agree, I don't want him in my room. The desk people see us go into the bar. I have one drink but it has a bad effect. Dizzy, anxious, shaking, I decide not to have any more. I don't know why drink doesn't take away the fear. Maurice talks on and on. About himself. He still hasn't found a job. Wants to give riding lessons but can't get himself together enough to go out and do it. As he continues drinking, I am quiet. He has no intention of listening to me. I feel betrayed. He says for me to get my stuff and stay the night with him at Mrs. Castings'. I don't want them to see me leave with my stuff so I sneak up the stairs. I've already paid them for the room. I take another pill because I can't stop shaking. I go back to the bar and head for Maurice's car. I'm embarrassed about the shaking but no one sees us leave through the side door. The cold air clears my head some, though my shaking increases.

Maurice drives out of town. I don't know where we are. We're on a lonely road and he's driving too fast. I can't talk anymore because of my shaking. I'm way over on the passenger side, hugging the door. His driving is bad, back and forth across the road, fast. Maurice says he knows exactly what to do in situations like this. It crosses my mind that I don't know what "situations like this" are. I think of Cove. That's where I'm supposed to be. Nine o'clock. I think of safety.

We get to Mrs. Castings'. It's a big house. It looks so nice. I get out of the car fast. I want to see her and go to sleep. She is the widow that Maurice is staying with. Have to curl up somewhere to give my head a chance to stop ringing. Maurice is still in the car when I reach the kitchen door. It's open. I go in to find her. "Mrs. Castings—Mrs. Castings." No answer. Oh, please help me. Where are you?

From the car, Maurice says, "She's gone for the night."

I'm shaking, mostly my hands and then my head and then my insides. I feel like throwing up but I don't give into it. I sit on a couch in the living room. Maurice comes in with my duffel bag. He says I must cry or I'll never stop shaking. I say I don't have any tears anywhere, not to worry about me, I'll be all right, just let me sleep. I get my jar of pills out of my duffel bag and I take maybe three or four pills, because I have to sleep, have to stop shaking. Maurice stands over me but I don't look at him. Shadow on me—I don't want him near me—scared, makes me shake more. Leave me alone, shadow, leave me alone, but it stands there, I see his knees in front of me, I stand up and brush past him and go behind a piano in the corner and sit on the floor to get away, to be alone. Cove, Cove, I should be at Cove's, safe Cove's, safe, I should be at Cove's, it's Thursday, Thursday, it's Thursday, I should be safe at Cove's, they miss me, they have to miss me, they have to notice I'm gone, they will protect me, won't let Maurice near me anymore. I see the shadow over me in the corner and I scream, see the fists coming down on me, on my head, why on my head? please not my head, and I cover my head, he screams at me to cry, to cry, he reaches down, wrenches the jar of pills away from me, I see a different person, a strange person, Maurice's eyes so infuriated by something in me, eyes furious at my cowardice, my weakness, my submission to the blows. Makes him double his attack. Then he hits me on my body, in my ribs, it makes me roll over and then he kicks me in the back, new pain radiating, he's killing me, killing me, and I don't want to die. Right then the thoughts come. Where is your spirit, your will? Cove says it is easier to succumb, it takes guts to fight, guts, and with this I kick at him, kick out with my feet, no more cowering, no more wooly lamb bleating bah bah, offering red meat to the wolf; strong hoof, boot smashes into his kneecap, strange new energy mounting in cascades of adrenaline surging into bloodstream. As she rises, new strength in fists, the fear shadow diminishes, iron fists attack, pummeling iron on his body, he will not kill me, he will not kill me again, ever again. He folds like a bruised bully, surprised at the strength and daring of the victim, small child, and the fear and shaking drop down out of her and miraculously transfer to him as he curls on the floor, copiously weeping and wailing the tears she should have.

She stands over him and takes the pills from his pocket and she goes over to a straight side chair and sits motionless, her insides like a vault, secure, locked-away feelings nobody will ever see because she swallowed the key. She was almost killed, well, never again, never again will she allow this, no one will ever again kill her like this. She feels nothing. She focuses her eyes on the wall and part of the window and she doesn't blink, if she sits so quiet like this then nothing can ever happen to her again, she will be safe. Pretty soon because of the staring the rest of the room blurs and she can only see a section of the window, a little section. She thinks she is safe if she stays like this. She hears the background noises but she blocks them out. Time has no meaning anymore, she can sit there forever, dead cold sphinx.

She hears, later, voices in the background, different voices, but she won't acknowledge them, it isn't safe. They all hate her now, all of them. Cove and Don and all the others. If she sits still no one will bother her. A hand is on her shoulder, someone touches her; how can they touch her how dare they? It means she isn't safe after all. And the touch ground into her insides, stole the vault key; she jumps from the chair and runs through the house screaming screaming screaming and the hand reaches out for her again and pulls her to warmth. John, John, don't hate me, they hate me, they hurt me, hate me. Please don't hate me, please don't hate me. He took the jar of pills clenched in her fingers and held her, took her back to the farm as Mrs. Castings and Maurice and others watched— bruised girl thinking that all the world was looking at her sideways.

Friday, January 30, 1970

John comes in. I hear him from under my pillow. I won't come out. I am raw, my insides and my outsides. My back hurts and my head hurts. He talks to me under my pillow. They all worried, they all worried. The manager of the hotel saw me and called John; and Don called John; and Mrs. Castings called John and he came and got me. He came for me. I shit on them all, I did it and now they hate me, I pushed them too far, over the line. I can't face them so I have to stay forever under this pillow. I can't take their hatred now, my head hurts. John sits on the side of my bed, I hold the pillow tighter and tighter to my head.

I feel warm hands on my back. John is rubbing my back, soothing parent, injured child. Childlike my arms go to him, little girl cries and sobs and wonders why the parent doesn't spank, doesn't take the whip, doesn't hurt, and her fears come back with her feelings, they hate her, they hate her. She buries her head in him and sobs how they hate her; he makes soft sounds, wind whispering in the pines and she isn't afraid of him anymore because he isn't hurting her, taking advantages. And he doesn't hate her.

"John, I found out I don't want to die, I don't."

"We're all so worried. Please, when you're ready, tell me what happened."

So she tells him about Maurice and she tells him she ran away because she wanted to matter to them. Make them think she was real.

"But don't you know, Carol? Don't you know we all felt that? That you matter very much!"

"No. I can't feel it. I don't know what to do."

"Well, now you know you want to live, right?"

"Right."

"I think it's time you had something to eat. Come down to supper with me."

"People will stare at me, they know I ran. They know something happened."

"Of course they'll stare. They want to find out *details*. But they're your friends."

"I forgot."

"Now, about the pills, Carol, that's really serious. I don't know how you got so many but that scares me. I threw them away."

"I'm sorry about the pills, oh I'm sorry. I didn't plan to take them, I didn't plan to. But anyway, John, I don't want to die. I promise. It's inside me. I won't abuse pills. I promise."

We go downstairs together. My heart lifts in hope. John doesn't hate me. In my terrible need I let him touch me.

My friends gather around but I am quiet. They respect it.

He can rub my back, I let him, I let him, I don't pull away, I like the security, I let him touch me. Should I be more careful?

I go across the room. Madonna and I head for the game room for a game of pool. My back hurts a lot; I sit down a minute, she goes ahead. I think I hurt enough. I don't want to hurt this way. I'm not going to again. I've had it with myself. The disgust is different from before. I don't want to attack myself, hurt myself. This disgust is at myself for letting this go on so long. Jesus. I look at my knee, my foot. What's so God damned bad about my knee anyway? Why do I always have to pick on my knee? I look at my foot. Jesus! It's mine, isn't it? Why am I always kicking it around, maybe giving it arthritis or something? It's mine. I should take care of it. I get up and hobble downstairs. I go into the bathroom and walk over to the mirror. Jesus. It's my face, isn't it? Why am I always hating it? How come I never look in the mirror? I force myself to look. There are the eyes. Well, Christ, that isn't so bad. I mean, I never pretended to be pretty. But I mean, I'm not Quasimodo, after all. So don't go attacking your poor old face. I always felt that my body failed me. Well, it didn't. It's here now and it works. I failed my body. I punished it. Well, not anymore. Not now. I don't want the body to scrunch up and die. I need it.

I think about how they give people shock treatments. They zap them around with electricity and volts and miraculously the people get better. Sometimes, anyway. I think maybe that's what I did to myself. I gave myself shock therapy, hit the bottom. Now

I discover I want to live. The pain forces a decision. And so we get better. Well, I better start getting used to liking my body. I'm going to need it.

Sunday, February 8, 1970

Don visits her at the farm. His head is bent, worry increases his fear. He is desperate worrying about her. He says if Maurice has hurt her he'll kill him. He's afraid she will do something awful, something unpredictable. He knows she loves him, that keeps him going. He has a trial he must prepare for, yet she consumes his thoughts. He thought she was getting better and now this. He doesn't know how much more he can take. They go for a walk and he takes her hand. She is very quiet. They talk about the January thaw. She looks at him and tries to explain something. She wants him to understand. He looks at her carefully. He is frightened for her. He doesn't know whether she'll survive. It hurts him not to know anymore. Hurts inside. They go to her bedroom after the walk and she tells him a story. She wants him to understand something. It's hard for her to talk. She cries and he's glad. He hardly ever sees tears. She says when she was really little her mother read to her out of a large Mother Goose book. It had a black cover. It was a library book. Her mother liked it so much that she went and bought it from the library. The pictures were mostly in black and white. One was a picture of a scraggly old black and white witch being blown away and killed somehow. She doesn't remember the rhyme, only the picture. And the most important one that scared her the most was one that was always read. There was a picture of a vulture-like bird sitting on a perch watching over some children. The watchbird is watching you. No matter what you do, he always sees. You can never escape. The watchbird. She says that the nursery rhyme always makes her feel just that way, watched.

She sits on the floor by his feet and cries. This is the part he tries to understand. She says it's gone. Over and over says it's gone.

He must believe her. She's going to be all right. The watchbird is gone. He wonders if she has flipped.

"What are you saying, Carol? Plain language. Give me something to hold on to. Please."

"I've been released from something. Something from way back. Don't you see? Please see. No matter what I did I felt evil and sinful, you know that. Well, it's gone. Most of that feeling is gone. I don't have to hate myself so much. That watchbird isn't watching me anymore."

"I don't know if I can believe you. I don't know if I understand."

"I know."

"When did all this happen?"

"Well, I looked in the mirror and I wasn't revolted. I mean, that's something, isn't it? Please. I don't know but I feel something has changed. I'll start again. Please don't hate me or be mad. Please."

"I never hated you. I'm not mad. I'm sick with worry. So worried."

"I didn't know."

"You're dumb not to know."

"I know."

He holds her very close. He doesn't understand. But if that watchbird is gone, it's sure fine with him. He puts the chair under the doorknob because she isn't pulling away from him now. Such a long time since she hasn't pulled away. In fact, she comes to him and helps him in his fear. He doesn't know much about her mind, but if there's one thing he knows it's now, in his arms. Now he can believe her. She's giggling too, and stretches out tentative thoughts about coming home. He has been so hurt. He doesn't know whether to believe. But the truth is here. On the bed. She loves him. It has seemed forever, but here it is. Now he can believe her.

Monday, February 9, 1970

I may be wrong. I just may be wrong. If I'm wrong in this, maybe I'm wrong about a lot of things. John doesn't hate me. Don doesn't hate me. If I'm wrong about them, maybe I'm wrong about the others. But Cove doesn't love me. He must hate me. I have my Don. I will get better for him. But Cove is there. I love him in the bad way. It's too much for me. Oh Cove, I don't understand. How come I want you so badly? How come I want to break you down? hurt you? have your baby? So then I can wash my hands of you. I don't understand. I want to make an impact on you. How come it's so important?

I pull on my boots and get my parka and gloves. Timothy and John are taking a bunch of us to play volleyball at the armory. I'm not withdrawing to my room. It's too boring. I miss too much. That business with Maurice—I fell into a foul black pit. I grasp and struggle to climb back out. I see the sunlight at the top but I'm still pretty smelly. It's been precarious and dangerous. I hate thinking about the ways I have of killing myself. I don't want to kill myself. Ever. Especially now. My insides trick me into feeling the vast pleasures possible in a life with Don. That would be worth the pain in climbing back out.

Don is apart, not involved in this chaotic problem that goes way back. He doesn't hurt me. I wing a prayer thanking God that these primal disturbances were unknown when I loved and married him. Because of that we will always have each other.

So we go to the armory to play volleyball with the inmates of the correctional center. It's exciting. The police cars arrive with the prisoners. Stony-faced guards stand every fifteen feet, hands behind their backs. I look at our "guards." Sweet, skinny John and handsome Timothy, laughing, grabbing the ball, arms around us planning strategy. We surely will beat them. The doors are locked and the game starts. The inmates jump and they punch the ball, fight alone, hard, grim, isolated individuals. Alfred stands in one spot, he tries—he has made such good progress—he misses, his nervous hands grabbing at air, we console him, laugh, give him courage to try again. They win the game. But we don't feel defeated. We had fun. We band together with pride. Us farmers. We may be crazy but we aren't locked up and we love each other.

Tuesday, February 10, 1970

I'm on phone duty and I'm scared. Cove day. I hit bottom and it was all about him. *Him.* What if he really hates me? My face is flushed. Don't hate me, Cove, I'm going to be different. I am. I'm even planning on eating in the same room at supper time. See? That's good. I'm trying. Don't hate me.

There is a lively discussion going on at the phone table. Why can't you see the carbonation in the Coke before the cap is removed?

Too heavy for me. Eden takes over phone duty and I go outside. I take a walk around the main house, go over to the chicken coop and in back of it. The sun is warm. It's the first time I've felt warm all winter. The snow is dripping off the roof, cutting a huge snowbank away from the wooden wall. I see stones at the base of the wall and then I stop. I can't believe what I see. It's a little purple flower. I sit on the snowbank and face the wall and watch the flower. Unbelievable. My seat gets wet on the snow. I stand up and walk back to the house. A flower growing. Right in the middle of cold, bleak winter.

I go to my room. When the gong rings, I go downstairs for supper. I shrug off my friends' kind whispers that Cove is here. I know he is. I see him. I go right over to his table and sit down. I watch for hatred signs. Don't see any. I'm pretty subdued. I listen to the conversation. I join in.

I say to Cove, "Do you watch football games?"

"Oh, yeah. All the time. I go to the home games as often as I can."

I'm so amazed. That is so normal. All the men I know like football. Wow. He eats his supper and has a wife and watches football. Jesus.

Oh paradox, paradox
He is like two lines
Askew
Never meeting,
Infinite.
Greek God and human
inexplicable contradiction,
My mind too fogged
to make them
fuse.

We go up the stairs to Cove's room. There's a fire in the fireplace. We pull our chairs near it.

I put my head low. Quiet. Afraid about his love.

"I'm sorry. I'm sorry. I caused an awful fuss and I'm sorry. I could've been killed. I'm sorry." I can't look at him.

"Do you know why you ran?"

"Nobody cared for me. That's what I felt. I wanted somebody to notice me. I wanted to make an impact. I want to mean something to somebody."

"You want to mean something to me?"

"Yes. I don't—I mean nothing to you."

Cove stands up and walks to the couch and back. "I do care for you! I was worried about you. What kind of a person do you think I am?" His voice is stern. Mad.

"Well, I, I don't think I—I don't know."

"It hurts me very much for you to say this. I am a person. I care very much. You make me less than human by thinking I don't care. Just once it would be nice if you thought about me. My feelings." I look up.

"I didn't think that you would notice." I put my head down.

"Look at me, Carol. I am real. I feel. I care for you. I have feelings. I hurt. I wonder if I've failed you. I want the best thing for you."

I look at him. I love him. I don't want to hurt him. But how can I believe him when inside I'm so alone? He doesn't love me.

"I don't know if I can believe you. I mean, I understand, but I don't feel it, inside. I don't think you understand how I feel."

"I think I do understand, Carol. I know you better than anyone. I want the best for you. I care for you, like your *family*, I care."

A flash hits me. My family cares for me, loves me no matter what I do. I see Cove worry. I see him care. Does he feel like my family? Can he?

I look at Cove. Can I believe him? I don't know what to say. A good love? Pure? For always? The fear recedes. I hold it away as I watch him. It feels right, but I don't know if I can trust my feelings. I've been such a damn fool lately. Can I trust my reaction? I want it to be right. I want Cove to love me this way. My family loves me because I am part of them. Cove is a part of me. Cove loves me. Do I trust it? It's so new. It's too precious a thing to trust right away. I won't speak of it. I'll have to see.

We sit quiet for a long time. Watching the fire.

"I'm sorry, Cove. I was wrong about Don not caring. Also John. I thought they didn't care. I thought you didn't care. It's something I am never sure of. Now I am. I feel different. I want to live. I'm sure of that."

"I think there were other reasons why you ran, too. What do you think?"

"I think I wanted to hurt you. For some reason. That's the first appointment with you that I ever missed."

"Why would you want to hurt me?"

"I don't know. I mean, I don't really want to, but I do want to, too. I don't know. I just get so mad. I just get myself in a rage at you."

"What's the rage?"

"Well, it's anger and . . ."

"Impotence?"

"Yeah. Anger and impotence and helplessness. That's it."

"Why?"

"Why? Why? Why? I just do."

"I think you feel rage because of your dependence on me. When you ran away it was a bid for independence."

"But I *want* to see you. I *want* to. Well, maybe I resent *needing* to see you."

"I think you were testing me to see if I would seek you out. To see if I would reject you."

"But I didn't plan it. I didn't plan it to happen the way it did. I didn't plan to hurt everybody."

"Oh, I don't mean that you consciously did this. Inside, unconsciously, you did."

"It scares me. When I do these things, I just am awful scared. I don't know what I'm doing."

"I know, Carol. I'm not going to let you down. I'm not going to leave you or reject you. I'm not going to kick you out."

"How come it feels like you will? How come it always feels like you'll hurt me?"

"Because it always happened in the past. It always happened before. Father Anthony should have been safe. But he wasn't. You test me to see if it will happen with me as it did with the others. It will not happen. It will be up to you when you stop therapy. And you will make that decision when you don't feel it's necessary to come in any more."

"It scares me. I don't like talking about it."

"I know."

"I don't even like the thought of not seeing you on Tuesdays if I left the farm."

"I will always see you when you need me."

"Oh I know. Oh Cove. I'm going to make it, you know. I have confidence inside that I'm not such a shithead. I looked in the mirror and didn't see such a shithead. But it's all so hard."

"I know." We look at the fire for a while. Cove stretches his legs. I don't ever want to not see him. It makes me very sad.

"I think the word 'unattainable' had a pretty profound effect on you. I think that might have been a cause for your running away."

I glance at Cove.

"Yeah. I guess. I know. It scares me all over."

"I think that's what you have to work on. Your irrationality toward me and toward people who really care for you."

"Yeah, I guess. It scares me but I know."

We both stand up. My head is low. Cove comes over to me and puts his arms around me. I put my head on his shoulder. It makes me so very sad. I don't want to let go of Cove, my God. I don't want to. But he's leaving and that makes me sad. The arms aren't jabbing, horrible pokers, fear, or stone or arms of the lover. Just the arms of a warm friend. It makes me incredibly sad.

Wednesday, February 18, 1970

He put his arms around me and he held me. I pretend to myself that it's just regular. At the time it felt regular. It didn't hurt. Now I think of it. I dream of it. They were Cove's arms, charged with power. I want the arms, the body. It doesn't fit. Something isn't right. So now it hurts me. At the time it was all right. I conclude that it's me that makes it wrong. Makes it sexual. Me. There must be some way out of this mess. Some way. But it's hard because I like these thoughts I have. I like them. Cove mentioned Father Anthony. I think of the others. Must I reenact this same scene the rest of my life? Shit!

Morning meeting presents a problem. Lena Mae has assigned me the dishes list. It's before volleyball and we're all milling around. I go up to Jud and sit down.

"Hey there, Jud. How come they put me on dishes list?"

"They did. The Nazis. Nazis."

"Listen to me, Jud. Isn't dishes list your paid job? Isn't that what you get paid for?"

Jud mumbles. He's in distress. I put my ear near his mouth. He's close to tears.

"Jesus fuckin' Nazis took my job."

"Who, Jud?"

"Lena Mae took over. Nazis don't let me do the job. Nazis . . ."

"She helps you with the dishes list. Isn't that what you mean? Doesn't she just help you?"

"She took it over. Took the power. Took the penis away."

"Why did she put me on it? Do you know?"

"Because people, the masses, the Jews are complaining. Somebody wants Sabbath Saturday night pots and pans and somebody wants Day of Atonement Friday table setting. See? See the tags are all fucking mixed."

We go to the board. Little circles are on pegs. Our names on the circles. The chart beside it.

"You're right, Jud. It's all mixed up."

"She took away my power. She mixed it up. Now I have nothing to do but unclean vegetable table."

I go over to Lena Mae and I explain how hurt Jud is to have his job taken away. She looks at me and her face gets florid.

"Are you trying to get out of this job?"

"Why, hell, it isn't my job. I don't know why you put me there anyway. Jud feels horrible you taking over as it is."

"He messed up the whole thing."

"He says you did."

Something inside of Lena Mae breaks, she settles back, crosses her arms and yells at me.

"You are afraid of the job, aren't you? You can't take static from anyone, can you?"

"But it's wrong for me . . ."

"You are a big fat baby."

I look at her in amazement. I decide to keep quiet. She's got something on her mind.

"You need diapers and a bottle!"

A crowd gathers and watches us. I stand quiet. I wonder what I have done to her to make her so mad.

"I order you to take this job. I insist!"

I turn around and start walking out the door. I won't fight and I won't take Jud's job.

She yells at me as I leave the dining room.

"You shouldn't see Dr. Ashley *anymore!*"

I hear the words. I guess I know why she's mad now. She's jealous. I get a lot of attention here. I get pats on the back and I'm getting better. I think she's jealous of me. I am such a part of the farm. I'm all over the place. And I am comforted and consoled as well as liked and accepted. I stroll out the door up to volleyball.

I have a strange new confidence in myself. I know I could straighten out the dishes chart. But to do it would take away Jud's job. I know also that Lena Mae and I are on equal footing. No more putting myself down. No more guest against staff member. We are equal. I am not dependent on her for my self-esteem. Since I'm not dependent, her power to hurt me has disappeared. I think maybe she is having problems of her own that she can't figure out. She'll have to do something about it. She really should talk to Cove. She really should.

Hey. Something new here. I'm not jealous even thinking she should talk to Cove. If Cove really loves me, I can let him do things I couldn't let him do before.

Thursday, February 19, 1970

Nine o'clock. Time to see Cove. I tell Cove about the confidence I have and how I dealt with Lena Mae. I'm using my head more. It feels good because I make up my own mind. I even stand straighter. I can look at Cove—right in his face. I see his eyes. They are brown.

"Well, how did things go, Carol?"

"Sometimes good, sometimes not."

"I mean regarding the feeling you had that I cared about you?"

"Oh. Well, it stayed with me. It really did. I mean for a while." Then I sort of slump again. I remember my dreams and my insides stop being rational and turn back in uncertainty. I just want to tell Cove it's there, the pure kind of love, all the time. But it isn't.

"For a while?"

"Yeah. Yeah. Oh Cove, I get mixed up so easily. I sort of slip around."

"I think we should talk about the word *unattainable*."

"Oh, yeah, I guess." My heart drops. I'd rather not. I go on. "But, Cove, I know what you mean and you know I know and so, well, couldn't we just, you know, just as easily skip over this. I mean."

"We have to talk about it. If it isn't put into words, it won't be clear."

"Oh." I lower my head, no more meeting of the eyes.

"What do you think it means?"

"Oh, you know. It means that I never can, can, have you."

"What exactly do you mean by 'have you'?"

"Well, you know what I mean."

"It means you never can have sex with me."

I tighten up.

"I, I—it makes me so nervous when you say this! So nervous I don't want to talk about it."

"It has to be said."

I put my hands to my face.

"What would happen to you, Carol, if I made love to you? I'm serious. How would you feel?"

"I'd like it. I would. That's what I dream about."

"Think about it."

I press my hands to my cheeks. They are flaming. I close my eyes.

"It would be awful! Awful! It scares me. It would be the end of me. It would be the end of my hope. I would've broken you down and that's what I wanted but not really because it would mean I lost the whole thing. I'd lose you. Lose myself. It would be the end."

Cove silent.

"Oh"—I burst into tears—"Oh, I want you so much and it would kill me! It would kill me! I don't know why."

"It would be like the other men. You needed them and they took advantage of you. They thought of their own needs before your needs. Every man except Don. So very early you had anger and hatred for men. But you also needed them very much."

I hear him through my sobs. I hear him.

"Carol?"

I nod.

"There can be real caring and love without sex. There are many types of love."

I grab some Kleenex off his desk. I blow my nose.

"Is that why I was so afraid of you, so afraid all the time? I was afraid it might turn out like the rest?"

Cove silent.

"It was always so hard to talk to you. I was so scared to let you know. Like about the fantasies and stuff."

"I think you were afraid I'd use them against you."

We sit quiet. And then I remember wanting his baby.

"What about the ah—baby business? I felt with you like with the others that if I could have a baby, then I could be done with you."

"What do you think?"

"It's maybe to make an impact, so you'll never forget me, or maybe then you wouldn't leave me."

"Maybe it's a feeling that if you had my baby you'd have a part of me forever."

"Yeah. Immortality and all that."

"I think it's something more, too. Maybe to have a baby is a symbol of being completely fulfilled."

"I have the feeling a lot of times that I was born with a big hole inside me. Loneliness or whatever. You think maybe I thought you could fill that emptiness?"

"No person can be everything to you—can be responsible alone for filling the void. Your father couldn't. I can't."

"You know I think in absolutes all the time. I think if I can have your baby, I'd be all right forever or if you really loved me, everything would be solved. Is that what you mean? Do I put the whole thing so absolutely that there's no chance of fulfillment?"

"The possibility that one person can make everything right is a fantasy."

"Oh Cove, I know. But what happens to me? I'm still dependent. I still have needs. I'm still confused. I feel lonely now. I don't feel like you're dumping me, just lonely. It is different though."

Cove smiles, I smile.

"Whew! Wow! This is quite a business we're in here together, isn't it?"

"Sure is."

Sunday, March 1, 1970

A kind of relief has come over me. Like in college. The exams are almost done. If I can pass the French orals and the botany final, then I'm free. Free for summer vacation. Oh, the freedom. I'll have time to do things I like to do. It seeps into my pores, freedom sneaking into my cells and giving them new life. I've been sleeping so late in the morning. All the way to six-thirty and seven A.M. I hurry downstairs and everything is already in motion. The coffee has been perking for a while and Jud has been mumbling his obscenities. I missed it all by sleeping. I don't feel I have to write it all down. My notebook stays on my desk. The urgency is gone. The pencils and pens lie unused. The need to gouge the paper with injustices and fear is a sluggish need, not demanding attention. I say to myself, how come I don't get up early and write down all the good things? How come this new beginning is different, is somehow working? How come I don't write about my confidence and my feeling that Cove loves me no matter what? Because it sounds trite. And it's hard to do. When I feel bad I get relief from the pain by writing. When the pain is gone, the urgency to write is gone.

Tuesday, March 10, 1970

She walks into the room and sits next to him for lunch. She has figured out all the answers and thinks her smartness and bravery should be applauded. She doesn't know how to file Cove in her mind though. He isn't her lover or her friend or her husband or father or an associate or a member of her family. And he isn't a god. There is no name for him. He is telling Jake about flying a plane over the weekend and her smartness and bravery are dashed to the ground. Her mind darts warning signals and her body gets weak. She leaves the table and goes to her room. How can he take chances like that? He's going to be killed if he does that. Oh, how can he! He does it deliberately to hurt her. So in one sentence she remembers the devils inside her, lurking, waiting to attack. She can't get smug or think she's smart or has the answers. Because if she thinks that, they catch her. She straightens her back, combs her hair and returns to lunch. But caution accompanies her. She decides to be very careful in her optimism. She decides to let Cove fly if that's what he wants. She lets him have his plane. But she has to watch out for the devils. She feels guilty because she's afraid he'll be killed and she loves him. Is it all right to feel these things? Is it "sick behavior?"

She doesn't know. She puts the feelings in the "no name" box; reserved just especially for Cove.

Thursday, March 19, 1970

I walk fast up the stairs for my appointment. My head is spinning. Hands shake, slightly manic. Impossible thoughts have blanked my mind and made my body shake. I want to go home, leave the farm. But I forgot what to do there. Forgot. What will I do?

Will I drink? Will I take pills? What do I say? Will I go outside? Where will I go? Will I go to see Cove's car? Will I be strange? An embarrassment? Will I panic? Can I sit and help with Ki's piano? David's trumpet? Jimmy's cello? Peter, little Peter reading? Tom, so sweet, is he hurt? He has pinkeye. Can I cut his hair? Hold him? Will I finish wallpapering? Bake bread? Can I? Can I read? Will I iron? Do people iron anymore? Will I want to fish? Did I change? Will I put talcum powder on our sheets? Will the evening grosbeaks be at the feeder? Will the dog push her head at me? Remember me? Can I get supper? Breakfast? Lunch? Do I do laundry? Can I switch loads, put them on the kitchen table? Are things different? Coats on the bannister? Boots. Where do the boots go? Will I see Cove on Thursday night at nine? Put candles on the table? Still laugh? Wear a skirt? Will I wear the farm gloves? Can I look at a tree? Stuff a turkey? Make love? Where is the parka zipper I never put in Don's coat? Can I drive, can I create, do stiff shaking fingers know how to knit? Can I mend the torn leather chair? Will the socks, the hundreds and hundreds of socks with the blue and red and yellow stripes, turn me into a babbling idiot? Can I teach the kids to be kind? To cry? Can I never look at them sideways? Oh what will I do? What will I do?

I jump from the chair, I can't stop the thoughts running away, I pace over to his bookcase, back to the chair, over to the bookcase, back to the chair. Cove watches me.

I say, "I'm nervous," as I keep pacing.

"I noticed."

"I'm too nervous t-t-to t-talk."

"Let's play Ping Pong."

"Huh? Oh, sure. G-g-good idea."

We go out to the waiting room. Cove takes some stacked papers off the table and we play. We play hard and fast. Sweat dripping off me like the intense thoughts dripping out of my mind. All the nonstop fears pouring into my hands, feet and on out to the paddle. Two, three, four games. We stop. Gone shaking. No more. Cove and me, we're tired. He says, "Think we can talk now?"

"Yes. Thanks, Cove."

"Now, what's making you so tense?"

"Oh, Cove, I'm so terribly afraid that when I go home I won't remember how to do things. I'm so awful afraid I'll fail. And that things haven't changed and I won't be able to do anything. So afraid that I have forgotten how to act and what if everybody hates me and I won't be able to see you on Tuesdays at the farm?"

"Any change like this causes fear. It's all right to be afraid. It doesn't mean you're going to fail. You have a whole lot of courage. I know you can do it. I have a lot of faith in you."

"It scares me when you say you have faith in me. I don't know why."

"You are afraid I might think you are better. And I won't need to see you anymore."

"Yeah. I'm not all better yet. See? I'm not."

"Remember when we talked about loving and caring?"

"You mean the feeling inside me that you're not going to dump me? Yeah, I know. But it does come sneaking into my mind, you know. Now and then. Comes sneaking in."

"I know. It takes time. You've got to fight it though. When it creeps up on you."

"But, Cove, how can I be sure of anything? You, home, Don? Oh, Cove."

"You can't. I guess you just have to trust."

"But, what if I fail them, what if they hate me?"

"No one is going to hate you and I will still be here."

"You will? I have the feeling that when I leave the farm you'll think I'm all cured."

Quiet.

"Do you think I can make it? Do you think I'm nice? Do you think I'm a good person?"

"You have always been a good person. You just haven't always seen it. You should start thinking about leaving the farm. You'll have to fight off the shithead feelings but I think you can do it."

"Oh, it makes me feel so good to hear you say that. Thanks, Cove. I'll think about going home. I will. You think I'm nice?"

Cove smiles.

I've changed. I'm a good person. I'm nice. I'm likable. I'm nice if you get to know me. I'm good. Cove says so. I trust Cove. It must be true. Cove doesn't lie.

Tuesday, March 24, 1970

Group therapy time. Eric comes in with his camera. I bought him a roll of film. He's taking pictures of my friends for me. He takes one of Cove, too. Cove's sitting in the chair by the fireplace. He's looking at some papers on his clipboard. He wears his green sweater. He jumps at the flash. We settle down until it's quiet. Benson comes in late and sits in the corner on the floor.

I start off: "I'm thinking a lot about going home soon."

HUGH: "What will you do to your kids if you flip out?"

JAY: "Are you trying to prove something? It's cruel out there."

QUEENIE: "Do they want you at home?"

ME: "Wait, wait, I, I, don't think I'll do anything to *them*. I'm not trying to prove anything."

VOSS: "Does Don want you back? Even if you flip out again?"

ME: "Well, I think he does. Yes, he does."

ERIC: "How can you take care of all those kids?"

QUEENIE: "What if the kids don't like you?"

ME: "Don't know. I love them. I miss them. I have to try."

HUGH: "What if you have an attack and you pound your fist like you do? Will you pound your kids instead?"

ME: "No! No! Leave me alone. I'd never do that."

HUGH: "But what if you do? What if you don't fit into your home anymore? You said yourself that they are doing fine without you. If they are doing fine, shouldn't you leave it that way? Wouldn't it be better for them? Huh? How about that?"

My insides clutch in fear. Why isn't Cove helping me? Cove is just watching me. No rescue. He doesn't say anything, not a word.

VOSS: "Aren't you just dreaming when you think you can go home and take care of your kids?"

ME: "But, yes, yes, it's true. I don't know what I'm going to do. True that things are running smoothly without me. But, but, you're forgetting something. I'm their mother, they love me."

HUGH: "Doesn't mean they love you. Lots of people hate their mothers. What then?"

Mind goes blank. No thoughts. Too many thoughts. All the fear flooding back. Face flushing. Maybe selfish to go home. Can't talk. They're crowding her. She feels like a shithead again, monstrous for wanting to go home—go home to pound her kids—monstrous. Silence.

EDEN: "Do they love you?"

She hears the words. Think, think, fight off the shithead feelings —take a board and swing at the bad feelings about herself—knock them down before they destroy her faith.

ME: "Well, I, I, I, love them more than anything, and, and if they don't love me, it's, it's because I left them and I'll just have to, um, have to earn their love and trust again. That's it, I'll have to try. And I'll have to trust myself that I won't fail them."

HUGH: "That sounds all well and good, Carol, but face it, you're not being realistic. Cold facts don't have much to do with trust and love and all that. What if you fail? How about that?"

ME: "Oh please Hugh. Leave me alone a minute." I sit quiet thinking. "It sounds like you don't even want me to go home and try. Sounds like you want me to give up before I even start."

HUGH: "But you've been here for six whole months and . . ."

ME: "Listen to me. All of you. I'm scared to death I'm going to fail, scared I'll hurt my kids and Don, but what do you want me to do anyway? Sit around here forever? If I don't even try I'm a loser anyway. If I try and fail I'm not any worse off than I am now. If I try and win—God, I'll have the world."

HUGH: "I think you're making a mistake."

VOSS: "Have you thought it all out?"

ME: "I think that you are all afraid for me because *you* can't leave yet. I've made up my mind and you *haven't*. You're jealous."

EDEN: "I know I'm jealous. I wish I could make up my mind!"

ME: "Well, I'm going to try. And soon. I'm going to make it. You hear? I'm going to make it."

HUGH: "Who says?"

ME: "Me. I say so. I told myself I am, so I'm going to do it."

Group talks together, tension eases. Voices congratulating Carol, wishing her luck, silent envy of her decision. Wishing they were going with her.

Cove smiling, smiling. She passed a test.

Easter Sunday, March 29, 1970

I wake up early and I take a shower. Clean. Early and dark. The day belongs to me. I go downstairs through the kitchen to the cellar in my bathrobe. I have all my wrinkled and dirty clothes and all of the ripped ones. I fumble for the lights. I say out loud to the cellar, "Here I come." That gives the mice and bugs a chance to scurry and hide. I turn on the bulb over the tubs and get out the iron and ironing board. I pull out the washing machine and fiddle with the hoses and fill the machine for the first load. I sort the clothes into three piles on the floor. White, all my underwear and white blouses. Put them in the machine with Clorox. Want them all clean. I go upstairs while the machine works and get my boots, silicone and a needle and thread. I go back to the cellar with a cup of coffee and I clean and treat my boots. I mend a three-cornered tear in my parka. I sit on a high stool waiting for the machine. I drain the tub, put clothes through the wringer, refill for the rinse. When that is done, I use the dryer. As one load gets done, I put in another. I go over the clean clothes meticulously, careful to mend each rip or tear. One by one. I'm feeling some kind of elation welling up in me. I look around the cellar. I have an urge to clean it all up. But not this cellar here. The one at home. While waiting for the machines I go over and look in the cage and see all the food. It looks so good. Barrels of flour and boxes of condiments and fruit and fresh oranges and tomatoes and eggs from the chicken house. I feel like making apricot bread. But for my own family. I switch loads and fold clothes from the dryer. I iron a white blouse and use the spray starch. I iron the dungarees when they are done. I step out of my robe and get into the clean clothes. I'm not afraid because it's so early. Elation hits me full blast now. Bang. I feel great. I tie my boots and fasten my belt on my ironed dungarees. God, I feel good. What's making me feel so good? I must take after Dad. Oh he was always so clean, so meticulous in his clothes. Oh Dad, here I am, all clean. I feel so good I start to laugh. I'm the cleanest darn person in the whole world. I squeak. I start to sing. "Detour, there's a better road ahead, detour . . . ," terrible singing voice. I only sing when no one's around.

I hear the door open. I stop singing. Jud appears at the top of the stairs.

"Who's there? Anybody there?"

"Me, Carol."

"Watcha doin' down there, Carol, huh? Doing it with your father? Doing it with your father?"

"Right on, Jud. Right on. Been doing it with my father for years. How 'bout that, Jud, huh?"

"Can I come down and watch?"

"No good, Jud, father's dead."

I laugh. So funny. So funny and ridiculous.

"Is it better when they're dead?"

"Oh Jud, Jud, Jud, what am I going to do with you? You sure do have a way with words. You've always seen through to my soul. Hey, Jud, what makes you see my soul?"

"Make it with your father? Did you kill him?"

"Didn't kill him, Jud, just failed him like he failed me. Sorry, Jud. Can't make it anymore with him. Not anymore."

Jud disappointed.

"Does he have a long penis like the Nazis?"

"Not anymore. Not anymore. Don't be disappointed, Jud. I'm just singing down here. I'm a real live clean person. Come down, get your slippers on, you can see."

Jud comes down the stairs halfway.

"The Nazis like clean fucks."

"Okay, okay. Let's go back upstairs. I'll get your breakfast. I guess our minds have been fucked up for a long time. Let's get some toast and eggs. But not any more talk, all right Jud? All right? Not any more." I take Jud upstairs and I get our breakfast. We sit and eat quietly. I want to tell Jud about my father. How nice a man he was. About his laughing eyes. I take Jud by the shoulders and I shake him, just shake him slightly. I want to tell him. But his eyes don't see. His eyes have a wall that makes it hard to get inside. I pat his back and go down cellar again to switch clothes from the washer to the dryer. I've almost finished my cleaning.

Oh my Dad, my dear Dad, Dad with the laughing eyes. You didn't let me grow up. Dad, my Dad, I have to leave you now, I've got to catch up. They're waiting for me. Outside. Don and the kids and Cove too. If I don't catch up, they'll go on ahead. So you see? They'll go ahead without me. I can't be angry at the men anymore and I can't be hurting inside anymore. I love you. I always love you. But I have to go. I put you up here on the shelf next to the Clorox and detergent. All bleached out and clean, so clean. It wrenches me to leave you here but it's time now. Don't you see? It's time. Oh my Dad with the laughing eyes.

Tuesday, April 7, 1970

Morning work is a new one. I sit on a large lumber pile by the gym. The logs that they cut last year have been returned from the lumber mill. Clean-smelling boards. This one pile is two by fours. I unfasten the metal band that holds them and hand the boards to the next person down. It's Eden. He hands one to the next, Queenie. She takes it to the appropriate pile on the ground and starts a new pile according to length. I'm on the top. I look around. The snow is almost gone. The sun has turned the hard paths to mud. Yesterday we washed the sap buckets in preparation for sugaring. Everything is dripping, melting. There's that smell in the air, an unexpected smell of earth. We take a break. Instead of going to the main house for coffee I sit in a niche of boards still on the top. I watch Queenie and Eden walk down the path. They look different, like sweet strangers. I'm suddenly not a part of them any-more. I'm not a part of the lumber either, or the woods crew or the sugaring. I have a terrible urgency. I jump to my feet and climb down. I head for the main house in search of Cove. My heart's pounding like jungle drums, a village message of a new arrival. I go up the stairs to the fear room.

"Um, um. Hi, Cove. I, I want to go home. Now, um, today." I wipe my sleeve across my mouth to cover the mouth trembles. Cove smiles at me.

"Sounds like a good idea."

Hope leaps in me and carries me up on the crescent wave. No doubts in his mind, no questions or glances or dread interrogations of shameful promises not kept.

"Can I ride home with you? To save Don a trip? Tonight?"

He smiles again.

"Sure."

Oh boundless excitement of my soul, let loose, trapped no more, only by the skin covering, separating it from the outside.

Cove goes down the hill every Tuesday night at ten. This time, I'll go down with him. He gives me the key to his car. Queenie helps me load my stuff in. We go out the back fire escape so as not to have everybody make a big deal. Queenie loves being sneaky like this. I don't think she really thinks I'll be leaving for good. John comes by and hugs me. We load my skis and skates and clothes and records and boots; and the last thing, my notebook. A diary of the past, a reminder. A reminder.

Cove has group therapy but I don't go tonight. Ha! No more group. I'm out into the world. Good luck, Queenie, no more dope now. Good luck, Eden and John and old Jud and all of you. That's it for you, farm. It's been great. You've been good to me. But so long, goodbye—fare thee well, my friends. I can't stand you anymore.

So Cove is ready to leave. Down the hill, no glancing back.

"All set, Carol?"

"Yup."

"The weather is getting so much warmer now. It's like spring has really come."

"I noticed that too, Cove, there's been a real change. Can feel it in the air."

"The Almanac says we are in for a stormy spring."

"That so?"

"Yup."

"Well, I guess we can get through a few storms."

"Hope so."

"Me, too."

A Note on the Type

This book was set on the Linotype in Janson, a recutting made direct from type cast from matrices long thought to have been made by the Dutchman Anton Janson, who was a practicing type founder in Leipzig during the years 1668–87. However, it has been conclusively demonstrated that these types are actually the work of Nicholas Kis (1650–1702), a Hungarian, who most probably learned his trade from the master Dutch type founder Dirk Voskens. The type is an excellent example of the influential and sturdy Dutch types that prevailed in England up to the time William Caslon developed his own incomparable designs from them.

Composed by The Fuller Organization, Lancaster, Pennsylvania.
Printed and bound by The Haddon Craftsmen, Scranton, Pennsylvania.
Typography and binding design by Virginia Tan.